PREFACES TO SHAKESPEARE

PREFACES TO SHAKESPEARE

VOLUME – 4

LOVE'S LABOUR'S LOST
ROMEO AND JULIET
THE MERCHANT OF VENICE
OTHELLO

Harley Granville-Barker

Foreword by
Mohit K. Ray

ATLANTIC
PUBLISHERS & DISTRIBUTORS (P) LTD

Published by

ATLANTIC

PUBLISHERS & DISTRIBUTORS (P) LTD

B-2, Vishal Enclave, Opp. Rajouri Garden,
New Delhi-110027
Phones : 25413460, 25429987, 25466842

Sales Office
7/22, Ansari Road, Darya Ganj,
New Delhi-110002
Phones: 23273880, 23275880, 23280451
Fax: 91-11-23285873
web: www.atlanticbooks.com
e-mail: info@atlanticbooks.com

ISBN 81-269-0716-9 (Vol. I)
ISBN 81-269-0717-7 (Vol. II)
ISBN 81-269-0718-5 (Vol. III)
ISBN 81-269-0719-3 (Vol. IV)
ISBN 81-269-0720-7 (Set)

Printed in India
at Nice Printing Press, Delhi

Foreword

Son of a mother, who was a teacher of elocution Harley Granville-Barker (1877–1946) who hyphenated his name after the first World War, became an actor when he was just fourteen years old. During the period from 1904–1907 he directed several productions at the Royal Court Theatre with remarkable success. But it was during the period from 1910 to 1913 when he was at the Savoy that he revolutionized Shakespearean productions with his highly imaginative approach from the practical perspective of the producer. He saw Shakespeare as a man of the theatre, and thus gave a life to Lamb's contention—a view held by the Romantic critics in general—that the plays of Shakespeare 'are less calculated for performance on a stage, than those of any dramatist whatsoever'. Lamb had emphasized on the richness of Shakespeare's poetry, the magic of which he thought is lost on the stage. He believed that the stage-representation, however skilful and creative, cripples our imagination. He remarked : "The Lear of Shakespeare cannot be acted...to see an old man tottering about the stage with a walking-stick, turned out of doors by his daughters in a rainy night, has nothing in it but what is painful and disgusting. We want to take him into shelter and relieve him". He further clarifies: "The greatness of Lear is not in corporal dimensions, but in intellectual: the explosions of his passion are terrible as a volcano: they are storms turning up and disclosing to the bottom that sea, his mind, with all its vast riches .... On the stage we see nothing but corporal infirmities and weakness, the impotence of rage; while we read it, we see not Lear, but we are Lear,—we are in his mind, we are sustained by a grandeur which baffles the malice of daughters and storms; in the aberrations of his reason, we discover a mighty irregular power of reasoning, immethodized from the ordinary purposes of life, but exacting its powers, as the wind blows where it listeth, at will upon the corruptions and abuses of mankind".

But Granville-Barker, as an actor, producer, a Shakespearean scholar, and above all a dramatist had the necessary experience and expertise to arrive at the conviction that a drama is meant for the stage. For Granville-Barker the play is the thing. Only one must be, as he supremely was, steeped in Elizabethan lore, and know, as he knew so thoroughly well, the circumstances leading to the production of the plays and the conditions under which they were produced in Shakespeare's time. If *King Lear* had been produced successfully on the Elizabethan stage, it could be produced with equal success on a twentieth century stage provided one was able to produce it according to the Elizabethan theatrical conventions, adapting it simultaneously to the demands of a modern theatre. Halliday writes: "His productions at the Savoy theatre of *The Winter s Tale* and *Twelfth Night* in 1912 and of *A Midsummer Night s Dream* in 1914 were revolutionary; with the aid of a false proscenium, proscenium doors, and built-out apron stage without footlights, he converted the picture-frame theatre into something like the Elizabethan; then, to make time for the unabridged texts, scenery was formalized, here was only one interval, the pace of acting and speaking was quickened, and traditional 'business' cut out...their influence on later productions has been incalculable".

Granville-Barker's historical scholarship, his profound knowledge of Shakespeare's stagecraft and his personal experience as a successful man of theatre went a long way in making his Shakespearean productions so eminently successful that no less a severe critic than G.B. Harrison who was the general editor of the Penguin Shakespeare (1937-59) based on the Folio text and had edited with Granville-Barker, *A Companion to Shakespeare Studies* (1934) conceded that they were "the most important productions for a hundred years not only because they were beautiful in themselves, but because for the first time since the seventeenth century Shakespeare's plays were played just as they were written, and not cut and re-arranged to suit the scene-shifter". He further added: "Without unduly horrifying his audiences, Granville-Barker evolved settings which allowed him to give the whole play entirely and quickly. For *Twelfth Night* the main setting was a formal conventional garden with Noah's ark, trees and a central staircase branching out right and left, which needed little rearrangement. For the smaller scenes, the drinking scene, for instance—he inserted a little tapcstried room and not the usual baronial hall, which made the whole affair cosy and hearty. He suppressed all the traditional foolery, the candles-to-bed business of Toby and Andrew, and he produced the play as whole, as a symphony. The result, astonishing at the time, was that *Twelfth Night* instead of being just a romp, became exquisitely beautiful and hauntingly sad". So it is not surprising that *Twelfth Night* had a run of 137 performances. For Granville-Barker, as Clare Byrne has rightly pointed out, the "staging of any scene was determined not by principles or by a rigid stagecraft, but by knowledge of how, in practice, to get the best theatrical effect out of it, to convey the dramatist's intention".

The Prefaces originally published in five series between 1927 and 1947 covering ten plays are now collected in four volumes. The Shakespearean criticism that we find in the prefaces may be described as what Eliot called "workshop criticism"— a craftsman talking about his craft. In other words, the prefaces are elaborate explications of what shaped the productions, and how and why. And, for Harrison whom we have already quoted at length the prefaces are the "finest examples of Shakespearean criticism which have been written since Samuel Johnson. An hour in his company taught one more of Shakespeare than a year's reading". John Gielgud, the noted Shakespearean actor who played the role of King Lear is reported to have remarked in an interview with *The Times*. "In 1940 I rehearsed the part with Granville-Barker for an hour and a half, day after day. Everything he said seared into my brain and I follow that interpretation still". When Granville-Barker says that the "text of a play is a score waiting performance, and the performance and its preparation are, almost from the beginning a work of collaboration" he is anticipating the postmodern stance that a text is an empty container waiting to be filled with meaning and that the reader (and in this case the actor) is the co-author. Granville-Barker's fine perception of the rich and complex dramatic quality of Shakespeare's poetry is evident in the following comments:

"The speaking of his verse must be studied, of course, in relation to the verse's own development. The actor must not attack its complexities in *Antony and Cleopatra* and *Cymbeline,* the mysterious dynamics of *Macbeth,* the nobilities of *Othello,* its final pastoral simplicities in *A Winter s Tale* and *The Tempest* without preliminary training in the lyricism, the swift brilliance and the masculine clarity of the earlier plays". About *Antony and Cleopatra* Granville-Barker points out that it is "a tragedy of sex without one single scene of sexual appeal" and hints at the challenge it throws to the actors to make the play theatrically effective. About soliloquy, his fine insightful comments are: "With the soliloquy upon the platform stage it is a case —as is often where convention is concerned—of extremes meeting. There is no illusion, so there is every illusion .... We now accept the convention frigidly, the actor manœuvres with it timidly. Banished behind footlights into that other world of illusion, the solitary self-communing figure rouses our curiosity at best". So he feels: "There is no more important task for the producer of Shakespeare than to restore to the soliloquy its rightful place in a play's economy, and in particular to regain for it full emotional effect".

Granville-Barker shows practical wisdom when he says that "Shakespeare was not a perfect playwright"; and hastens to add, "there can be no such thing. Nor did he aim at a mechanical perfection, but at *vitality,* and this he achieved" (emphasis added). For Granville-Barker drama has a life of its own. It is an organic whole pulsating with life, and no observation of mechanical rules can ensure its theatrical success. The success of a play must be judged not by examining whether it has religiously observed a body of rules but by its success at the performance and by its reception of the audience. No production can be hammered into a mathematical formula. The unpredictable complexity of human nature simply defies it.

As Granville-Barker discusses the nature of the action in *Hamlet* he evinces a keen awareness of what is called "whirligig of time" in Shakespeare as he remarks; "... there in Shakespeare's freedom in time, which is the natural product of his stage's freedom is space and which—coupled with this—permits him a panoramic display of his entire story, if need be, and uninterrupted action". His fine critical insight into the development of Shakespeare's dramatic art is evident in comments like, "We have in Claudius the makings of the central figure of a tragedy. Something of him will be found very highly developed in Macbeth". Equally penetrating are his comments on the verse of *Cymbeline* : "The verse throughout is very rich in texture; and if sometimes it seems over-rich, this suits it to the frank artifice of the play, and the actors may allow themselves a certain slight sophistication of style for its delivery. Shakespeare in fact—the wheel come full circle—seems almost to be cultivating a new Euphuism. It has no close likeness to the old; by the difference, indeed, we may measure something of the distance he has travelled in twenty years of playwriting. It is Euphuism of imagination rather than expression." That Granville-Barker is not a blind supporter of Shakespeare and would not indulge in any uncritical admiration of him is evident in the observations he makes about Brutus in *Julius Cæsar.* He writes: "Shakespeare's own artistic disposition is not sufficiently attuned to this tragedy of intellectual integrity, of principles too firmly held. He can appreciate the nature of the man, but not, in the end, assimilate it imaginatively to his own". The comments remind one of Eliot's criticism of *Hamlet* as a failure in 'objective correlative'. About *Antony and Cleopatra* Granville-Barker's observations not only bear eloquent testimony to the profundity of his Shakespearean scholarship but also his remarkable capacity to see a play in a broad comparative perspective. He writes: "Here is the most spacious of the plays. It may lack the spiritual intimacy of Hamlet, the mysterious power of Macbeth, the nobilities of Othello, may reach neither to the heights nor depths of King Lear; but it has a magnificence and a magic all its own, and Shakespeare's eyes swept no wider horizon". Similarly about *Coriolanus* he writes : '*Coriolanus* cannot be ranked with the greatest of the tragedies. It lacks their transcendent vitality and metaphysical power. But while neither story nor characters evoke such qualities, those they do evoke are here in full measure. The play is notable for its craftsmanship. It is the work of a man who knows what the effect of each stroke will be, and wastes no one of them'. About *Love s Labour s Lost* his witty but profound comment is that it is 'a fashionable play; now by three hundred years, out of fashion'. While discussing the producer's problems in presenting *Love s Labour s*

Lost he reaffirms that for "the full appreciation of anything in Shakespeare some knowledge is asked of its why and wherefore" and that "Drama, as Shakespeare will come to write it, is, first and last, the projection of character in action; and devices for doing this, simple and complex, must make up three-quarters of its artistry. All the elements of a drama must contribute to the development of a character in action. If the character does not come to life, then all these elements are "like paper and sticks in a fireplace, the flaring and cracking counting for nothing if the fire itself won't light..." Granville-Barker interprets *Romeo and Juliet* with a masterly analysis as a "lyric tragedy" as he examines *The Merchant of Venice* as a "fairy tale". He discusses *Othello* in great detail—more than half the volume is devoted to this play—and shows how Shakespeare "converts the anonymous Moor into Othello" and how "the whole brutal story is raised to the heights of tragedy". There is no point in multiplying examples. Granville-Barker's alert attention to the minutiae of a text and threadbare discussion of various aspects of the play—action, characters, construction, setting, versification, costumes, soliloquy etc.—reveal in every line the dramatic wealth of a Shakespearean play. The prefaces with their focus on the integrity of a play and its vitality have become a landmark of Shakespearean criticism. As a Shakespearean critic he may be regarded as one of the leading exponents of the modern historical approach to Shakespeare. T.S.Eliot has rightly remarked : "Perhaps more than any other single writer H. Granville-Barker by his prefaces, illuminating the plays with the understanding of the producer, has suggested the need for a synthesis of the several points of view from which Shakespeare can be studied".

I am grateful to Dr K.R.Gupta, Chairman, Atlantic Publishers and Distributors for requesting me to write the Foreword, and also for making the invaluable Prefaces available to the teachers and the students of English literature and all those who are fond of the Bard of Avon.

—Mohit K. Ray

Contents

Love's Labour's Lost

Here is a fashionable play; now, by three hundred years, out of fashion. Nor did it ever, one supposes, make a very wide appeal. It abounds in jokes for the elect. Were you not numbered among them you laughed, for safety, in the likeliest places. A year or two later the elect themselves might be hard put to it to remember what the joke was.

The Producer's Problem

Were this all one could say of *Love's Labour's Lost*, the question of its staging today—with which we are first and last concerned—would be quickly answered, and Lose No Labour here be the soundest advice. For spontaneous enjoyment is the life of the theatre. If a performance must be accompanied by a lecture, if, for instance, when Holofernes is at the point of

Bone, bone for bene: Priscian a little scratched. 'Twill serve

we need his modern exemplar in cap and gown, standing on one side of the proscenium, to interrupt with 'One moment, please! The allusion here, if you wish to appreciate its humour, is to..."; or if he must warn us, "In the next scene, ladies and gentlemen, you will notice a reference to the charge-house on the top of the mountain. This is thought by the best authorities to denote..." not much fun will servive. For a glossary in the programme something might be said, even for a preliminary lecture. No; this last, one fears, would leave the actors with too hard a task turning classroom back to theatre. Half-digested information lies a little heavily on one's sense of humour.

It is true that with no play three hundred years old can

we press our "spontaneous" too hard. For the full appreciation of anything in Shakespeare some knowledge is asked of its why and wherefore. Hamlet and Falstaff however, Rosalin and Imogen, are compact of qualities which fashion cannot change; the barriers of dramatic convention, strange habits, tricks of speech are of small enough account with them. But what is back of these word-gymnastics of Rosaline and Berowne, Holofernes' jargon, Armado's antics? The play is a satire, a comedy of affectations. The gymnastics, the jargon and the antics are the fun. Yet a play hardly lives by such brilliancies alone. While the humour of them is fresh and holds our attention, actors may lend it a semblance of life; for there at least *they* are, alive in their kind! No play, certainly, can count on survival if it strikes no deeper root nor bears more perennial flowers. If its topical brilliance were all, Shakespeare's name tagged to this one would keep it a place on the scholar's dissecting table; in the theatre *Love's Labour's Lost* would be dead, past all question. But there is life in it. The satire beside, Shakespeare the poet had his fling. It abounds in beauties of fancy and phrase, as beautiful today as ever. We find in it Shakespeare the dramatist learning his art. To students the most interesting thing about the play is the evidence of this; of the trial and error, his discovery of fruitful soil and fruitless. The producer, pledged to present an audience with a complete something, cannot, of course, be content with promise and experiment. Measuring this early Shakespeare by the later, we may as well own there is not much more. But the root of the matter is already in him; he is the dramatist born, and all, or nearly all, is at least instinct with dramatic life. It is oftenest his calculations and his cleverness that betray him.

For satire and no more is too apt to prove dramatically fruitless. A play's values are human values, and a playwright's first task is to give his creatures being. Imaginative love for them may help him to; even hate may; but a mocking detachment cannot. If he is to shoot at their follies he must yet build up the target first; and if it is not a convincing one there will be little credit in the shooting. He cannot, of course, in a play, take direct aim himself, unless he use the method of the Moralities or its like. There is the less direct method of twisting a set of familiar heroic figures awry. Shakespeare made this experiment, not too successfully, in *Troilus and Cressida*. But his obvious plan will be to turn one or more of his creatures satirists themselves, and under their cover plant his own shafts. Even so, he must give the victims their chance, or the play will be lopsided and come tumbling down.

The Shakespeare who sets out to write *Love's Labour's Lost* is a very clever young man, a wit, a sonneteer. He is "in the movement". He flatters his admirers by excelling in the things they admire; he will flatter his rivals hardly less by this attention he means to pay them. But your clever young man is usually more than a little impressed by the things he mocks at; he mocks at them in self-defence, it may be, lest they impress him too much. Mockery is apt, indeed, to capitulate to the thing mocked, to be absorbed by it. And these academic follies of Navarre, the fantastic folly of Armado, the pedantic folly of schoolmaster and parson—sometimes the satire is so fine that the folly seems the clever young man's own. Yet this weakness of the would-be satirist is the budding dramatist's strength. Shakespeare cannot resist his creatures; he never quite learned to. He cannot make mere targets of them. He cannot resist his own genius, poetic or dramatic; all through the play we find the leaven of it working.

He has not written ten lines before the poet in him breaks bounds. In this the voice of the frigid wiseacre Navarre; does this suggest the "little academe"?

> Therefore, brave conquerors—for so you are,
> That war against your own affections
> And the huge army of the world's desires.

But the clever young man recollects himself; and here, soon enough, is the sort of thing he has set out to write.

> KING: How well he's read, to reason against reading!
> DUMAIN: Proceeded well, to stop all good proceeding!
> LONGAVILLE: He weeds the corn, and still lets grow the weeding.

BEROWNE: The spring is near, when green geese are abreeding.
DUMAIN: How follows that?
BEROWNE: Fit in his place and time.
DUMAIN: In reason nothing.
BEROWNE: Something then in rhyme.

Pretty tricksy stuff! Well enough done to show that he quite enjoyed doing it, but the sort of thing that almost anyone could learn to do. No signpost on the road to *Hamlet*, certainly.

But mark the dramatist in his provision at the outset of the conflict and balance that every play needs, in the setting of Berowne against his companions, one man's common sense against the crowding affectations (a sporting conflict), an ounce of reality for counterweight to a ton of shams (an instructive balance). Here also, for the moralist-critic, is the play's moral issue defined at the outset; but let us not suppose Shakespeare to have been oppressed by this. Despite his present-day idolaters he was probably not high-purposed from his cradle; moreover, he is likely to have gained most of his knowledge of life by writing plays about it. That is not a provocative paradox, but a key to the mind and method of the artist. Time and again Shakespeare tells us that he sees the world as a stage. He would not think that a belittling comparison; he takes his art too seriously. Not pretentously, but as simply seriously as any man will take his purpose in life when he is lucky enough to be sure of it. We all need some centre of experience to argue from, if the world beyond our experience is to have any meaning for us. The artist transforms and multiplies experience by imagination, and may even come to think that what is true of his art will be true of the world it mirrors. This sounds absurd. But life does seem to be governed by surprisingly simple laws; and human beings, wherever and whatever they may be, do not greatly differ in essentials. That is the working hypothesis upon which art and religion, with imaginative genius to vitalize them, proceed. And let it be said of the theatre that a very short time in it will teach one how little fine clothes and fine manners may amount to. The theatre was for Shakespeare a laboratory where he worked—if but in a mimic sense—with human material. His method, his means to enlightenment, was to take a story and put the worth of it, its truth to nature, to the test of personal expression. The story might suffer; if it was not true to nature, it generally would. But Shakespeare was, on the whole, a most unconscientious story-teller, except when history bound him. Sometimes he would make a sacrifice to symmetry, as when, in *Measure for Measure*, he marries Isabella to the Duke; but he may have felt this to be poetic justice upon such a morally consistent lady. The story may be burked, neglected or finished off anyhow, as in *Much Ado About Nothing, Twelfth Night* and *As You Like It*. It may hang at the heels of the chief character, as in *Hamlet*. What men are, in fact, comes to concern him far more than what they do. Already in this pretty play of *Love's Labour's Lost* it instinctively concerns him, though not even doing but mere clever talk is his ostensible concern. And when he passes to the giant theme of *King Lear*, to the sweep of historic vision that is in *Antony and Cleopatra*, stretching his medium of expression till it seems to crack and break, he concerns himself, even then, with little which cannot be rendered into human passion, human pity—which cannot, in fact, be put to this laboratory test. He—literally—has no use for theories and abstract ideas. He is neither philosopher nor moralist, except as he must seem to be making his creatures one or the other. He is a playwright; he projects character in action, and with the truth of the one to the other his power and responsibility end. If this is the playwright's limitation, it is also his strength; for to this test of human response—not mimic, truly, but real; yet the mimic but reflects the real—all philosophy and morality must finally be put.

In this earliest essay, then, we may divine the dramatist to be; and we find dramatist putting wit and poet to the proof, Shakespeare will have set out to do his best by his creatures one and all; but while Berowne grows under his hand into a figure, finally, of some dramatic stature, while the Princess, simple, straightforward, shrewd, is made flesh and blood, in the speaking of seven lines, Navarre, though a natural focus of attention and discussing himself unsparingly, remains a bundle of phrases, and Dumain and Longaville have about the substance of echoes. Of the humbler folk; Costard for three-quarters of the play is the stage Fool, but suddenly, when he comes to the acting of his Worthy, we have:

COSTARD: I Pompey am, Pompey surnam'd the Big—
DUMAIN: The Great.
COSTARD: It is "Great", sir; Pompey surnam'd the Great; That oft in field, with targe and shield, did make my foe to sweat;
And travelling along this coast, I here am come by chance,
And lay my arms before the legs of this sweet lass of France.
If your ladyship would say, "Thanks, Pompey," I had done.
PRINCES: Great thanks, great Pompey.
COSTARD: 'Tis not so much worth; but I hope I was perfect: I made a little fault in "Great".

And these two last lines have, mysteriously and unexpectedly, given us the man beneath the jester. Then, with another thirty words or so, Costard (and Costard's creator) settles Sir Nathaniel the Curuate, till now little but a figure of fun, snugly in our affections.

> There, an't shall please you; a foolish mild man; an honest man, look you, and soon dashed! He is a marvellous good neighbour, in sooth; and a very good bowler: but, for Alisander,—alas, you see how 'tis;—a little o'erparted.

And settles himself there yet more snugly in the doing it! Throughout the play, but especially towards the end, we find such outcroppings of pure dramatic gold.

Drama, as Shakespeare will come to write it, is, first and last, the projection of character in action; and devices for doing this, simple and complex, must make up three-quarters of its artistry. We can watch his early discovery that dialogue is waste matter unless it works to this end; that wit, epigram, sentiment are like paper and sticks in a fireplace, the flaring and crackling counting for nothing if the fire itself won't light, if these creatures in whose mouths the wit is sounded won't "come alive". To the last he kept his youthful delight in a pun; and he would write and occasional passage of word-music with a minimum of meaning to it (but of maximum emotional value, it will be found, to the character that has to speak it). His development of verse to dramatic use is a study in itself. He never ceased to develop it, but for a while the dramatist had a hard time with the lyric poet. The early plays abound, besides, in elaborate embroidery of language done for its own sake. This was a fashionable literary exercise and Shakespeare was an adept at it. To many young poets of the time their language was a new-found wonder; its very handling gave them pleasure. The amazing things it could be made to do! He had to discover that they were not much to his purpose; but it is not easy to stop doing what you do so well. Yet even in this play we may note the difference between the Berowne of

> Light seeking light doth light of light beguile;
> So ere you find where light in darkness lies
> Your light grows dark by losing of your eyes!

and of the soliloquy beginning

> And I forsooth in love...[1]

Turn also from one of the many sets of wit to Katharine's haunting answer when Rosaline twits her with rebellion against Cupid:

> ROSALINE: You'll ne'er be friends with him: he kill'd your sister.
> KATHERINE: He made her melancholy, sad, and heavy;
> And so she died: had she been light, like you,
> Of such a merry, nimble, stirring spirit,
> She might have been a grandam ere she died;
> And so may you, for a light heart lives long.

Compare it with the set of wit that follows:

> ROSALINE: What's your dark meaning, mouse, of this light Word?
> KATHERINE: A light condition in a beauty dark.
> ROSALINE: We need more light to find your meaning out.
> KATHERINE: You'll mar the light, by taking it in snuff;
> Therefore I'll darkly end the argument.

---

1. Which, says Dr. Dover Wilson, belongs to the play's revising. But this does not invalidate my point; rather the contrary.

But Rosaline won't let her, and they manage to get five more rather spicier exchanges. It is all very charming; the mere sound is charming, and a "set of wit" describes it well. Get a knowledge of the game and it may be as attractive to watch for a little as are a few sets of tennis. But pages on pages of such smart repartee will not tell us as much of the speakers as those few simple lines of Katherine's tell us—of herself and her love of her sister, and of Rosaline too.

The play sets out, as we said, to be flattering satire upon such humours, and the playwright must set up before he pulls down, break before he satirizes; and the two processes do, doubtless, get mixed. Can we detect a Shakespeare impatient, for a moment, with his pleasant task? He has punned and joked his best.

BEROWNE: White-handed mistress, one sweet word with thee.
PRINCESS: Honey, and milk and sugar; there is three.
BEROWNE: Nay then, two treys, an if you grow so nice,
Metheglin, worth and malmsey:-well run, dice!

Nor will he neglect the ever-satisfying humours of cuckoldry.

KATHERINE: Veal, quoth the Dutchman:—is not veal a calf?
LONGVAILLE: A calf, fair lady?
KATHERINE: No, a fair lord calf.
LONGAVILLE: Let's part the word.
KATHERINE: No, I'll not be your half;
Take all and wean it; it may prove an ox.
LONGAVILLE: Look, how you butt yourself in these sharp mocks!
Will you give horns, chaste lady? do not so.
KATHERINE: Then die a calf, before your horns do grow.

It amused him, no doubt, as it amused his audience; it is just too well done to have been done mechanically. But when, of a sudden, the Princess breaks out with

Are these the breed of wits so wondered at?

may we not hear for the moment his voice sounding through hers? For it is a barren. business finally, and his fecund spirit could not long be subdued to it. With but little violence we could twist the play into a parable of his own dramatic progress. Even as Berowne at its end forswears

> Taffeta phrases, silken terms precise,
> Three-piled hyperboles, spruce affectation,
> Figures pedantical...

so might Shakespeare be swearing to pass from them himself on towards the prose of *As You Like It* and the strong verse of *Julius Cæsar.* A notion not to be taken too seriously, perhaps. But a few years hence he is to let Hamlet record a taste for plays set down with as much modesty as cunning, with

> no sallets in the lines to make the matter savoury, nor no matter in the phrase that might indict the author of affectation; but...an honest method, as wholesome as sweet and by very much more handsome than fine.

And certainly there are signs that, whether he knew it or not, the leaven was already working benetath this bright wit, this delight in words and their rhythm and melody, that was soon to turn a pretty speechifying Mercutio into the stark man of

> A plague of both your houses!
> They have made worms' meat of me: I have it,
> And soundly too...

and the word-spinning Romeo into that doomed figure of

> It is even so? Then I defy you, stars!

The dramatist was in the making who was to fashion a Falstaff out of the old pickpurse of Gadshill, who was to pitch on the preposterous tale of *The Merchant of Venice*, and charge it (triumphantly, yet all but disastrously) with the passion of Shylock.[2]

But the producer must consider carefully just what the carrying-power of this embryonic drama is, and how he can effectively interpret to a modern audience the larger rest of the

2. He pitched, we may say, upon two preposterous tales, and redeemed the second by the romantic beauty of Portia.

play. What life can his actors give to this fribble of talk and nice fantasy of behaviour? As satire it means nothing to us now. Where, then, are the prototypes of these cavaliers and ladies—of Armado and Holofernes, Moth and Nathaniel the Curate? We can at best cultivate an historical sense of them. There remains the verse, and the pretty moving picture of the action. Our spontaneous enjoyment will hang upon pleasant sounds and sights alone, sense and purpose apart. Really, it almost amounts to this! Better face the difficulty at its worst. Is there any surmounting it?

The Method of the Acting

If only the last act were in question we should not need, I think, to qualify our Yes; for this is throughout as much Masque as play, it is meant to charm us as much by sight and sound as by story and character. To take one passage:

ROSALINE: What would these strangers? Know their minds, Boyet.
If they do speak our language, 'tis our will
That some plain man recount their purposes:
Know what they would.
BOYET: What would you with the princess?
BIRON: Nothing but peace and gentle visitation.
ROSALINE: What would they, say they?
BOYET: Nothing but peace and gentle visitation.
ROSALINE: Why, that they have, and bid them so be gone.
BOYET: She says, you have it, and you may be gone.
KING: Say to her we have measured many miles
To tread a measure with you on the grass.
BOYET: They say that they have measured many a mile
To tread a measure with you on this grass.
ROSALINE: It is not so. Ask them how many inches
Is in one mile: if they have measured many,
The measure then of one is easily told.
BOYET: If to come hither you have measured miles,
And many miles, the princess bids you tell
How many inches do fill up one mile.
BEROWNE: Tell her we measure them by weary steps.
BOYET: She hears herself.

The action is implicit. Boyet must move, to the rhythm of the verse, between one group and the other. He bids fair to tread out a mile himself if the game last much longer. But the two groups draw together after this, and then break into couples. In a moment the music starts. Instead of dancing, however, we have a dance of dialogue. The couples circle the stage to the sound of the music, speaking their lines as they pass through the arc the audience commands. Finally, Boyet, who can have held his place in the centre, steps forward as chorus; and for comment, full to the audience:

> The tongues of mocking wenches are as keen
> As is the razor's edge invisible,
> Cutting a smaller hair than may be seen;
> Above the sense of sense; so sensible
> Seemeth their conference; their conceits having wings
> Fleeter than arrow, wind, thought, swifter things.

The music stops. Four lines more, and the scene is over.

Now this has no dramatic value, properly so-called. It hardly furthers such plot as the play has; unless to make a tangle to be disentangled a scene later without more consequence can be called the furthering of a plot. It does not develop character. The dialogue is mere mischief. There is, of course, the satire; its edge is blunted by time. But if the music is clear and fine, as Elizabethan music was, if the costumes strike their note of fantastic beauty, if, above all, the speech and movements of the actors are fine and rhythmical too, then this quaint medley of Masque and play can still be made delightful. But it asks for style in the acting. The whole play, first and last, demands style. A vexingly indefinable things, a hackneyed abracadabra of a word! One should apologize for bringing it into such a practical discussion as this pretends to be. Nor will the play as a whole, perhaps, be so entirely susceptible to its magic. But the theatre must deal in magic sometimes.

The conjecture that *Love's Labour's Lost* was first written for the delectation of a coterie of magnificent young men has been capped by the conjecture that some of them may have acted in it at the time. As custodians of the culture of the age, sponsors to this reborn mirroring art of the drama, they might well have recognized that they, in their own persons, apparel and conversation, mirrored and witnessed to that culture supremely. And they might, just for once, have condescended! They would have been cast, of course, for Navarre, Berowne, Dumain and Longaville. Some senior junior might have been found to fit Boyet, and someone who would modestly prefer himself to Monsieur Marcade. Whether there is much historical likelihood in the suggestion I do not know. If so, the other parts would be played, we may suppose, by professionals. There are the Masque and the antic (the anti-Masque) in the last act; and we know that in the great Court shows the lords and ladies did the graceful dancing and left the grotesque to trained tumblers and dancers. One would like to complete the picture by imagining the Princess and her ladies played by some of those Maids of Honour, who used on occasions to "friske and hey about". Would not that Mistress Fitton who—most historically— tucked up her skirts and, cloaked like a man, marched out of Whitehall to meet her lover, have been ready for once to play the boy and act the woman? It could further be argued that the dialogue for Navarre and his lords is of just such stuff as those young bloods of culture delighted to try their wits and tongues at; and that there is not much more in it, nothing emotional (except for Berowne; and his most emotional outburst is counted a later addition, when the play was perhaps being revised for the public stage), no impersonation, nothing that demands the professional actor with his greater comic or rhetorical force. Navarre and his lords are, in modern stage slang, "walking gentlemen"; but they need to walk magnificently and to talk with a fine assurance. The historical question is not pertinent to our present discussion, but these implications of it are. Whoever acted the play, it must have been in these respects exquisitely done, or it could not have endured its two hours' traffic, though its every joke made a topical hit. Happy-go-lucky, with the hope of a few guffaws for punctuation, could never have been a method for this sort of thing. The audience, too, must have been attuned to its fantasies, to its exquisite passions. How passionate the Elizabethans were! They were capable—those that were articulate and responsive at all—of intellectual passion, as Englishmen have hardly been since. And when poetry and rhetoric display it in the charged atmosphere of the theatre, the effect—even the distant echo of it—is intense. Navarre and his

> little academe,
> Still and contemplative in living art

are oath-bound fanatics; Berowne's gibing is but at the futility and hyposcrisy of their professions.

> Warble, child: make passionate my sense of hearing

says Armado, who is their caricature. Holofernes, that passionate latinist, Sir Nathaniel ridiculously emulating him, little Moth, with his piping and strutting, an incarnate mockery of them all, Costard reflecting their features in grimaces, their fine phrases in nonsense, the most reverberate things sounding hollow under the thwack of his bauble—all these, then, in accent and motion must be keyed to a sort or ecstasy, to a strange surpassing of this modern workaday world, if the play is to be anything at all but a sonata thumped out on a dumb piano, a picture painted by the colour-blind. A hard task for the actor; doubly hard, in that he must key up his audience too. For by time and subject it is all three hundred years' strange to us. We need an interpretation of absolute value; and that comes near to being a contradiction in terms. We must have a beauty of speech that will leave us a little indifferent to the sense of the thing spoken. Navarre and his friends and their ladies must show such distinction and grace that we ask no more pleasure in their company than that. Armado and the rest must command us by the very skill with which they remake mankind. It must indeed all be (to quote Berowne), if it is to exist at all,

> as the style shall give us cause to climb in the merriness.

The Staging, Costume and Casting

The play will profit little by any departure from Shakespeare's own staging; nor is this, in its simplicity, hard to deduce. A designer may shift the period of costume fifty years or so back—or forward, for that matter—if his taste dictate, and no great harm done. A certain grace may be added to Navarre and his friends by dressing them French fashion, or Italian. The Englishman was not famous for his taste in dress; though, if

Portia may be trusted, he only made matters worse when he picked up notions abroad, his doublet in Italy, his round hose in France, his bonnet in Germany and his behaviour everywhere. But these scrupulous young men would be purists in tailoring too. And a comedy of affectations, of nice phrases, asks that its characters should be expressive to their boot-toes, significant in the very curl of a feather. None of the others are hard to picture. Shakespeare sets Armado before us clearly, the refined traveller from tawny Spain, dignified and mock-melancholy, carrying his rapier as might a conqueror of kingdoms, though for "remuneration" to his messengers he cannot exceed three farthings, and must go shirtless, woolward for penance; he is black-suited, of course. Figure of fun as he is, though, his pride is not pinchbeck, nor must he look merely ridiculous. He sponges on no one, and hides his poverty all he can. When Costard infamonizes him among potentates—and the potentates, we may be sure, die with laughing—Shakespeare gives him great dignity in humiliation. We can picture Moth, that well-educated infant. Navarre, we may suppose, has made him page to the tall angular Spaniard for the fun of the contrast in the looks of them. Moth knows this well enough, be sure; and just how to make the best of his own share in the composition. He should not dress like Armado, that would coarsen the joke. He might still be wearing the King's livery. So might Costard, who makes a third in this conjuction, and has a flavour of Sancho Panza about him, even as Armado every now and then sets one thinking of that greater Don, yet in the womb of imagination. To complete this group we have the harsh, drab aspect of Holofernes; Sir Nathaniel, sober-suited but well-liking; and Dull, who is dull of countenance and clothing too. These will stand in somber contrast to the choice-garmented Court and the rainbow beauty of the Princess and her ladies; till, for their show of the Nine Worthies, they too burst into flower, and into most wondrous and gaudy flowering.

The pictorial values in the pegeantry of this last scene have their dramatic value too. The Russian maskings have been laid aside, cumbrously fantastic things, convenient cloakings. Yesterday Navarre and his friends were recluse philosophers; splendid even so, no doubt, but with a pallid splendour. Today they are in love and glowingly apparelled, in which sysbolism their ladies can match them; and against this delicately blended colouring the village pageant tells crude and loud. Into the midst there suddenly steps Marcade, in black from head to foot. He hardly needs to speak.

The king your father—

Dead, for my life!

Even so, my tale is told.

Berowne takes order.

Worthies, away! The scene begins to cloud.

And it must seem to cloud; the gay colours fading out, the finery folding about its wearers like wings. But this is not the end, for the end must not be melancholy. The countryfolk have yet to sing and dance their antic; a crowd of them, dressed to match the

daisies pied and violets blue,
And lady-smocks all silver white,
And cuckoo-buds of yellow hue...

The comedy of affectations comes to its full close upon notes of pastoral freshness and simplicity.

As with costume, so with scene; we shall gain nothing, we shall indeed be the worse for surrendering the freedoms of Shakespeare's stage. If we insist on placing and picturing the play's action now definitely here, now exactly there, we shall only be making complex what he has left simple, and find ourselves set to answer riddles which he never asked. The convention of place involved is "about Navarre's Court"; outdoors, it seems to be, nothing more definite. The recluse King and his courtiers may walk there, the Princess may be met there, and no vows be broken; a pricket may be driven near for shooting, a pageant be shown there, a measure trod on the grass. Armado and his page walk there; so do the parson and the schoolmaster, unquestioned. Closer definition than this will be troublesome. The place, in fact, is not a place at all, withing the modern scenic meaning. If we needs must paint the picture, it will need to be generalized, atmospheric, symbolic; the problem for a designer is quite a pretty one. Shakespeare, we may notice, hardly makes full practical demand upon the resources of the public theatre of the time. No use is made of the inner stage, though this might have served well for the Princess' pavilion. But the line:

> Whip to our tents as roes run o'er the land

suggests a further flight. Except for one episode the play asks no more than a bare stage with a couple of openings to it, just such a provision as would be found in that great hall where we may suspect it was first acted. The scene of the philosophers' mutual discovery that they are, all four of them, forsworn and in love calls, however, for three hiding-places, of which one must be aloft; for Berowne says:

> Like a demi-god here sit I in the sky.

But no harder mechanical problem faces the producer.[3]

---

3. And at this point in the play, also at this particular point in the scene, Dr. Dover Wilson scents revision. It may well be that Berowne, like the King and Longaville, originally hid on the stage level. But the stagecraft as we have it is worth examination. When Berowne is aloft Dumain does not come into his view till some minutes after Longaville espies him. This suggests that, if and when the play was revised for a public theatre, the tree (of some editors) to be climbed was no more than the gallery at the back of the stage, though a property tree might have been set against it, so that he would appear to be in its branches. Isolated property trees that can be climbed must be very solid affairs indeed. Berowne knows of Longaville's approach, for the King names him. But Longaville's only warning of Dumain's is "Company! Stay!" Then he bolts to hiding, not having himself seen, perhaps, who the intruder is. This is likely, for Shakespeare was from the beginning too good a dramatist to duplicate an effect. It would seem as if the stage stayed apparently empty for a moment, while Berowne said:

> All hid, all hid; an old infant play.

Next that Dumain entered, walking slowly down to the accompaniment of

> Like a demi-god here sit I in the sky.
> And wretched fool's secrets heedfully o'er-eye.

At which point Berowne sees his back:

> More sacks to the mill!

Then identifies him:

> O heavens, I have my wish
> Dumain transform'd: four woodcocks in a dish!

With all the emphasis on *four*, a climax well worked up!

This convention of place, and a similar freedom with time, encourages a very different method of construction from that proper to the theatre we know today, in which place, and even time, are positive and definit things. The dramatist, so set free, thinks more of his characters and less of their surroundings; he can manoeuvre them, absolved from such conformity, in the varied world of their own humours and passions. Elizabethan dramatic form has greater flexibility than ours; this, with its vehicle of verse (a further, more potent enfranchisement), gives it an emotional range which the modern dramatist must seek to compass by quite other means, by thrift of expression and tension sustained, by many hard economies. The scenic articulation of Shakespeare's later plays is masterly. They may seem loose-jointed, they are really supple and strong, delicate occasionally, never to be hacked at with impunity. *Love's Labour's Lost* is put together very simply; a little clumsily here and there, but alongside simplicity a little clumsiness will pass muster. The main device—an obvious escape from monotony—is the alternating of one group of characters with the other, and of verse scenes with prose. The blending of the two groups at the last is as obvious a conclusion. But in the contriving of the changes we find him feeling his way—now missing it, now forcing it, truly—to incidental dramatic advantage. Elasticity of form was always to suit him best; it gave full play to his power of developing character.

We come quickly to a petty crudity of construction, of which a later Shakespeare might not have been guilty; it is amusing to note how conventional editing, covering the fault, makes it worse. Berowne, at the King's behest, departs, with Costard in charge, to seek Armado. But close upon his heels Armado appears. The editors mark a change of scene. Some shift the locality; some are for *Scene ii, the same*. The shift of locality supposes, of course, a regard for its realities which Shakespeare never had; but *Scene ii, the same* suggests an interval of time which is the last thing a swift-moving comedy requires at its outset. Let us see how Shakespeare himself gets over the difficulty he creates. He wants to divide two scenes of comedy by a scene of caricature. He does not think of localities, Berowne and Costard are to leave the stage in search of Armado. Armado is to appear a second later upon that same stage. This is clumsy, it will seem resourceless; it will affect his audience as a false note in music would, or a trip in a dance. Therefore he has Berowne leave the stage first, lets Costard lag behind for a little solitary funniment, and then bolt after Berowne. If the funniment raises a laugh, that breaks contact, as it were, and continuity. The bolting breaks the rhythm of movement: it also brisks up the end of the scene[4] and provides a contrast to the slow, stately entrance of Armado. All of which, together with the curiosity the newcomer to the play arouses, will make us forget the incongruity and will compensate for the clumsiness. Shakespeare, of course, did not need to reason this out. His dramatic instinct served him; so would anyone's. Act the little passage as it is set down and its effect will be automatic. A pity to comment upon it! But these innocencies of drama must be protected against reasoning men; the more innocent they are the more protection they seem to need.

The rest of the play's coming and goings, by which its action is spaced and divided, look likely enough, if we do not insist upon looking at them through distorting spectacles. They have not much other dramatic value. If we want to make main divisions the play can be made to fall well enough into three parts. The Quarto (as usual) runs it through at a stretch; the Folio (as usual) divides it into five acts. If four pauses are to mean four intervals of distraction, this is a large allowance for so slight a play. I should myself prefer the two, which would leave Act I and II of the Folio as a unit of exposition; Acts III and IV for the uninterrupted working-out of the simple plot; and Act V (which is longer than either of the other two put together) for pagenatry. This arrangement happens to exhibit some consistency in time. The first part will mark the occasion—to all intent the day—of the Princess' arrival; the second fills

4. One cannot be always defining the sense in which one is using this word; the context, one hopes, will make it plain. Here, of course, it implies a division of dialogues.

the following morning; the third—Holofernes and Sir Nathaniel having dined presumably at midday—the afternoon following this.[5] But a producer might do well to abide by the Quarto. It would at least compel him to keep the acting brisk. The whole play could be put through in less than two hours.

The Folio's Act IV does show, perhaps, a more complex significance of structure; there is what looks like a deliberate use of the hunting subject as a link between scene and scene. It is as if Shakespeare wanted to lead on—despite the variety and incongruity of the action here—without a marked break to the dominatingly important scene of the sonnet-reading and the four woodcocks in a dish. No disturbing climax, at any rate, intervenes between Berowne's soliloquy (which closes the third act) and this scene, which is the crisis properly evolved from it and the crisis of the play besides. How far this is deliberate, how far instinctive, may be profitless speculation; the producer should undoubtedly observe the effect.[6]

---

5. There are some signs of confusion in Act III, Scene i. Berowne (and possibly at the moment Shakespeare) seems to think the Princess is coming to hunt in the afternoon. As it happens, she comes in the morning, only a minute or two after Berowne himself has started for his ride.

6. Hence he should not tolerate an interval, even if he allow a pause, after the Folio's Act III.

The scene following the soliloquy, after recording Berowne's distracted spurring of his horse uphill (the audience can easily tell that it was he, if he has just been before them, booted and spurred, whip in hand), goes practically straight to the hunting subject. This is returned to for a finish by means of a shout within (which, I believe, should rather be "shoot" within) and Costard's running out with a halloo. The next scene begins,

Very reverend sport, truly...

and ends with

Away! the gentles are at their game;

while berowne begins the scene following with

The king he is hunting the deer.

Conventionalized time is used, of course, throughout the four scenes. This, moreover, is all we hear of the day's hunting. But it is enough for Shakespeare. A hunt is towards; and no more excuse is needed in an English countryside or an English theatre—nor would be in the most categorical of plays—for anyone and everyone to turn up incontinently.

But the best of the play's craft is lodged in the dialogue; in its twists and turns, in the shifts of time and key, which are stage directions of the clearest sort. We have the brisking of a scene's end by such a piece of cross-fire as

BOYET: Do you hear, my mad wenches?
MARGARET: No.
BOYET: What then, do you see?
ROSALINE: Ay, our way to be gone.
BOYET: You are too hard for me.

The author of *Twelfth Night* might have thought this a little crude; but it serves its purpose.

We find another hint to the actors to "work up an exit", as the cant phrase has it, at the end of the scene of preparation for the pageant of the Nine Worthies. Dull, having spoken not a word nor understood one either, yet offers to make one in a dance and to play the tabor. Holofernes—no dancer, we presume!—Turns down the offer with contempt. He departs. Armado has taken precedence of him and bidden him follow, so he departs pretty testily. But if Dull, leaft last, does not show us in a dozen steps what a chance they are missing—Shakespeare did not know the comedian's craft! And Shakespeare, both to his joy and sorrow, did!

Half the dramatic meaning of a passage may lie in the action it suggests.

ARMADO: Is not lead a metal heavy, dull and slow?
MOTH: Minime, honest master, or rather, master no.
ARMADO: I say lead is slow.
MOTH: You are too swift to say so:
Is that lead slow which is fired from a gun?
ARMADO: Sweet smoke of rhetoric!
He reputes me a cannon; and the bullet, that's he;
I shoot thee at the swain.
MOTH: Thump, then, and I flee.

We must picture the long black barrel of a man, slow-gaited even in talk, and the little page, daintily at fence with him, and then off the stage at a bound. The art of it is akin to the artifice of a ballet.

The actor, in fine, must think of the dialogue in terms of music; of the tune and rhythm of it as at one with the sense—sometimes outbidding the sense—in telling him what to do and how to do it, in telling him, indeed, what to *be*. By the sense and sound together of the very first words spoken. Shakespeare is apt to make a character clear to actor and audience both.

Boy, what sign is it when a man of great spirit grows melancholy?

Who, after the ample measure and high tone of that, could mistake Armado? See, again, his taciturn, self-conscious, amorous condescension and the wench Jaquenetta's mumchance allurement—the comic likeness and contrast of the two—hit out for us in a duet just forty-five words long.

Maid.
Man.
I will visit thee at the lodge.
That's hereby.
I know where it is situate.
Lord, how wise you are!
I will tell thee wonders.
With that face?
I love thee.
So I heard you say.
And so, farewell.
Fair weather after you

—though, alas, Jaquenetta's country phrases have lost half their flavour for us now.

Shakespeare seems in the main content with the obvious contrast which the two groups and the shifts from verse to prose and back to verse again afford him. Prose is first brought into the play naturally enough by Costard and Dull and the reading of Armado's letter. The constricted pedantry of Armado's soliloquy ending the first act is followed pat—if no interval is allowed—by the strongest, simplest blank verse we have had yet. This effect is definitely dramatic, as of a sudden breeze of common sense blowing in. Berowne, it is true, has been preaching to us from this pulpit, but all tangled up himself in pun and antithesis. Even with the Princess and the ladies, however, we are back thirty lines later at

> The only soil of his fair virtue's gloss,
> If virtue's gloss will stain with any soil,
> Is a sharp with match'd with too blunt a will...

at

> The young Dumain, a well-accomplish'd youth,
> Of all that virtue love for virtue lov'd...

and the like. Shakespeare's dramatic instinct has prompted the change; his art does not sustain it. He is still too occupied with the actual writing of the play, with himself, in fact, and his own achievements, to spare to his characters that superabundant strength which can let them seem to develop a life of their own. He relapses, therefore, to the thing he has learned how to do; as a man may find every new tune he whistles turning, despite him, into that one old tune he knows. He is still a little tangled—to make the point again—as his own Berowne is, in the affectations he is out to satirize.

But Berowne is the play's truly dynamic figure, and he and Shakespeare struggle out of the toils together. His

> And I forsooth in love...

lifts the play into living comedy. It is his comic ecstasy that gives life to the scene planned as the play's crisis, when all four men discover that they are all four in love. The rest of it is mere liveliness of wit and humour, and as arbitrary as a practical joke. The King, Longaville and Dumain are as much frigid phrase-makers in love as ever they were out of it. Shakespeare has still a last act to write, it may be argued. He must not anticipate the promise to woo

> In russet yeas and honest kersey noes.

But we shall not find him in the flush of his genius missing one chance because another must be waited for and hanging up a character's development. If characters are only to be moved by a series of jerks from one rigidity to the next, they will be more suitably played by marionettes than men. Man as marionette will be amusing for one scene, for a second less so; we shall find as much interest in a third look at him as in a look at any other stage furniture. And when we do reach the last act, Shakespeare it seems can make no more of his king, Longaville and Durmain in the end than he could at the beginning. There is no life in the fellows, and that's all about it. This lack of dramatic life, then, from which, let us own, the larger part of the play, and its more proposed part, suffers, its producer must face. It is, five-sixths of it, more decorative exercise than drama. It must therefore be given, as near as may be, what we have called an absolute value in sight and sound.

In yet one more respect the play may suffer by its transference from the Elizabethan stage. The acting of women by boys was in itself a contribution to these absolute values. Further, if we do not allow for the effect of this stringency upon Shakespeare's stage-craft even at its most mature, we shall be constantly at fault. Not that he seems to have felt it a drawback; among all his side-glances at actors and acting we find, I think, no hint that it irks him. It did not impoverish his imagination nor lead, on the whole to any undue suppression of the womanly side in his play.[7] It may influence his choice of subject; he does not trouble with domestic drama. Without doubt it determines what he will and will not ask woman characters and boy actors to do. Their love scenes are never embarrassing. They do not nurse babies. They seldom weep. He puts them, in fact, whenever he can, upon terms of equality with men; and women have been critically quick ever since to appreciate the compliment, not well aware, perhaps, how it comes to be paid them. For those conficts of character which are the very life of drama he appoints weapons that each sex can wield with equal address; insight and humour, a quick wit and a shrewd tongue—the woman's the shrewder, indeed; in compensation, is it, for the softer advantages, the appealing charm, that his celibate theatre denied them? Out of a loss he plucks a gain. Release from such reality drew him to set the relation of his men and women upon the plane of

---

7. Except in the actual fewness of women's parts, for which the fewness of the boy apprentices allowed my be accountable.

the imagination. It asked from the boy actors a skill, and a quite impersonal beauty of speech and conduct; those absolute qualities, in fact, of which we speak. The Elizabethan theatre lack many refinements, but at least its work was not clogged nor its artistry obscured by the crude appeal of sex, from which the theatre today is perhaps not wholly free. No one wants to banish women from the stage; and it might not be an easy thing to do. But actresses may well be asked to remember what their predecessors achieved, and by what means.

In *Love's Labour's Lost*, however, the Princess and the ladies are not, and cannot be made, much more than mouthpieces for wit and good sense. As to love-making, the princess gives us the cue with

> We have received your letters, full of love;
> Your favours, the ambassadors of love;
> And, in our maiden council, rated them
> At courtship, pleasant jest, and courtesy,
> As bombast, and as lining to the time:
> But more devout than this, in our respects,
> Have we not been; and therefore met your loves
> In their own fashion, like a merriment.

It is all to be gallant, open and aboveboard.

> Saint Cupid, then! And, soldiers, to the field.

They are to be leagued encounters; and no two of the lovers are ever alone. But how few of Shakespeare's love scenes now or later need it embarrass anyone to overhear! In more than one sense he habitually wrote for daylight effect upon an open stage. Passion and tragedy and high romance he has still to deal with; he has still to find out to write Juliet and Isabella, Desdemona, Cleopatra. But already the problem of Portia and Beatrice is solved, and Rosalind can be heard telling Orlando:

> You shall never take her without her answer unless you take her without her tongue.

The Text, and the Question of Cutting It

The text presents practical difficulties, and one is fortunate to have Dr. Dover Wilson's fresh work upon it in the new *Cambridge Shakespeare.* A flaw or so in method or result there may be; to set about correcting them with his own tools one would need uncommon skill. But it will be worth while to test his conclusions by their effect—as far as we can divine it—upon the play's staging, for good or ill. This is, in fact, the ultimate test to which many of these bibliographical subtleties must submit.

The pronouncement upon two imperfectly cancelled passages in Act IV, Scene iii, and Act V, Scene ii, answers to this test well. Some repetition in the first passage is patent; and, given a blue pencil and told to consider the dramatic up-building of the speech, who could make any other cut than that between lines 292 and 315? The textual muddle in the second is as obvious; and if Dr. Dover Wilson's solution of it (though here, certainly, he but follows other editors) needs a stage-manager's support, it can be had for the sake of Berowne's

Studies my lady? Mistress, look on me.

For the dramatic intention is unmistakable. The King and princess have made their exchanges, important and effective ones. If Berowne's and Rosaline's follow close, the importance of theirs must be lessened, unless some violent contrast is achieved, boisterous and quite out of key. But by the simple device of keeping these two chief characters still and silent while Dumain and Katharine, Margaret and Longaville, say their say—it must not be too long a say, nor important enough to demand our entire attention—we are put on the alert, held is suspense, brought to be wondering whatever will occur when the silence between them is broken. And an actual silence, a pause—no actor could help making one—must occur before

Studies my lady?...

Thereafter, without effort or undue emphasis, or any illiberal self-assertion, Rosalin and Berowne, as they are meant to, top the scene.

This passage surely shows redrafting, and evidence of Shakespeare's more practised hand. But do the alterations run quite on Dr. Dover Wilson's lines? Would Dumain begin, "*But* what to me..." unless a previous speech had begun, "*And* what to me, my love?" It is unlikely that Shakespeare would ever have let the love-affairs even of two less important couples lapse in silence. May not Berowne's

> A twelvemonth! Well, befall what will befall...

originally have followed upon Margaret's

> The liker you; few taller are so young.

And why, here and elsewhere, does Dr. Dover Wilson bring in evidence the possible size of Shakespeare's writing-paper and the number of lines he could write on it? It was a scarcer substance with him, no doubt, than it is with his commentators. To suppose, though, that having taken a piece on which to write a new passage he could not stop till he had filled it...! But Dr. Dover Wilson *cannot* suppose this.

Another point of consequence is the Rosaline-Katharine confusion in Act II, Scene i. The suggested elucidation is best studied in the new *Cambridge Shakespeare* itself. It is as good as a detective story. Really, Scotland yard should turn sometimes to our scientific bibliographers! Is one graceless to make any question of a verdict reached by such ingenuity? By the practical, dramatic test it stands, in the main. It is only that these nice investigations have the defects of their qualities; they tend to prove too much.

The case for this transference of the masks and the mistaken identity motive from Act II, Scene i, to Act V is, of course, strong upon several grounds. But to conclude from this, as Dr. Dover Wilson does, that Shakespeare, making the alteration, meant to leave the earlier scene practically naked of everything but a dialogue between the King and Princess, and a little questioning of Boyet by the young men and a little chaff for the young ladies, is to brand him as a very slack craftsman indeed. First, it is well-nigh inconceivable that he can let this scene pass, Rosaline and Berowne both present, and deny them an encounter. (Besides, without the first of the two passages between them, or something in its place, how is the king to read his letter?) The dialogue was originally written for Rosaline to play masked, no doubt. Later, Shakespeare did not care to change it; there was no compelling reason he should. She could just as well hold up her travelling-mask at Berowne's approach to tantalize him and fog him in his patronizing recognition of her. We must remember the space convention of the Elizabethan stage; the distance across it was anything in reason. Cannot we see him stalking the lady? And a mask in those days was a woman's accustomed protection in more senses than one.

The scene's second encounter between the two, however, is redundant in itself, and of no constructional use; it is, indeed, an impediment to the action. Berowne and his fellows would not hang long behind when the King had departed; the Elizabethans appreciated ceremony in the theatre and out of it. But the stage, with its doors at the back, allowed for a many-paced exit. The three courtiers could follow with due observance if the questions to Boyet began promptly; hardly otherwise. The redundancy, a certain clumsiness of construction, and, not least, the extreme artificiality of this "set of wit" suggest it as part of an earlier growth, which, for some reason, was not clearly cut away. In its continuance, too, the dialogue shows every sign of having been hacked about. For instance,

> Good sir, be not offended:
> She is an heir of Falconbridge

is halt, if not maimed.

So much, then, for the test of stage effect. But (before we pass on) among Dr. Dover Wilson's own tests, are speech-headings such a safe guide to revision as he makes out? These are not, for the dramatist, a part of his play. Shakespeare, let us say, has a character in his head called Ferdinand, King of Navarre. If he wrote the play containing it at a sitting he might-though it is by no means inevitable—begin with one speech-heading and go on using it till the end. But it is likely enough that having made it "Ferd:" on Monday and spent Tuesday at work upon Armado, on Wednesday he may be putting "King" and on Friday "Nav:" and even by the Monday following be using "King" "Nav:" "Ferd:", whichever comes first from his pen. He does not give a thought—why should he?—To such an entirely irrelevant matters. It will be the same with stage directions. While he is waiting for a scene to take fire in his mind, he may write with careful elaboration: *Enter the Princess of France with three attending ladies and three lords*, even as a schoolboy hopefully heads his paper with a copperplate "Composition". But when he sits down to it all-fire, *Enter the ladies* is good enough. Then he can get to work.

No doubt there are clues to be picked from these confusions that will not prove loose-ended. But when the critical editor begins, "A natural and reasonable way of explaining...," one's concurrence is apt to be checked, even unfairly, by the overriding thought that what is reasonable to a critic is not therefore natural to a playwright.

We now come to the question of the permissible cutting of the text for modern performance, and no play in the canon presents greater difficulties. The principle is plain. A producer must take his stand with the first Cambridge editors and Garrick (Garrick! He may well exclaim) and resolve to "lose no drop of the immortal man". Still, no one need let his principles befool him. We need hardly hold sacred all that the printer has left us. The redundant passages in Act IV, Scene iii, and Act V, Scene ii, may go; Shakespeare's final intention is plain as a pikestaff.[8] There are besides a few sentences that are hoplessly corrupt; these we need not make a fuss about. But there are far more than a few that are nowadays almost, if not quite incomprehensible, that require, at any rate, a professor and a blackboard as first aid. And over these principle and common sense come to loggerheads. For common sense does seem to urge: the average man in an audience will either understand these things or he won't; if he won't, cut them. The problem, however, is not quite so simple as this. If there is life in a play we cannot cut even ounces of flesh from it with impunity. If it is an articulated whole we cannot remove a joint and a sinew or two and not risk laming it. Thirty lines may be thirty line and no more; but they me be—and they should be—an organic part of a scene.

For instance: Moth and Costard enter to Armado.

MOTH. A wonder, master; here's a Costard broken in a shin.

ARMADO. Some enigma, some riddle: come,—thy *l'envoy*; begin.

---

[8] It is the present redundancy, of course, that we keep.

COSTARD: No egma, no riddle, no *l'envoy*; no salve in the mail, sir. O, sir, plantain, a plain plantain! no *l'envoy*, no *l'envoy*: no salve, sir, but a plantain!

ARMOD: By virtue, thou enforcest laughter; thy silly thought, my spleen; the heaving of my lungs provokes me to ridiculous smiling: O, pardon me, my stars! Doth the inconsiderate take salve for *l'envoy, and* the word *l'envoy* for a salve?

MOTH: Do the wise think other? Is not *l'envoy* a salve?

ARMADO: No, page: it is an epilogue or discourse, to make plain.
Some obscure precedence that hath tofore been sain.

I will example it:

The fox, the ape, and the humble-bee,
Were still at odds, being but three.

There's the moral: Now, the *l'envoy*.

MOTH: I will add the *l'envoy*; say the moral again.

ARMADO: The fox, the ape, and the humble-bee,
Were still ad odds, being but three.

MOTH: Until the goose came out of the door,
And stay'd the odds by adding four.

Now will I begin your moral, and do you follow with my *l'enovy*.
The fox, the ape, and the humble-bee,
Were still at odds, being but three:

ARMADO: Until the goose came out of door,
Staying the odds by adding four.

MOTH: A good *l'envoy*, ending in the goose; would you desire more?

COSTARD: The boy hath sold him a bargain, a goose, that's flat:—
Sir, your pennyworth is good, an your goose be fat.
To sell a bargain well is as cunning as fast and loose:
Let me see a fat *l'envoy*; ay, that's a fat goose.

ARMADO: Come hither, come hither: How did this argument begin?

MOTH: By saying that a costard was broken in a shin.
Then call'd you for the *l'envoy*.

COSTARD: True, and I for a plantain; thus came your argument in:
Then the boy's fat *l'envoy*, the goose that you bought.
And he ended the market.

ARMADO: But tell me: how was there a costard broken in a shin?

MOTH: I will tell you sensibly.

MOSTARD: Thou hast no feeling of it, Moth: I will speak that *l'envoy:*
I, Costard, running out, that was safely within,
Fell over the threshold, and broke my shin.

ARMADO: We will talk no more of this matter.

Which last line alone we might expect an audience to appreciate!

What is a producer to do? How much of the stuff can any modern audience be brought to understand—even to understand, enjoyment apart? A glossary in the programme could give us first aid towards Moth's not very brilliant joke about Costard and shin, remind us that talk of a plantain leaf made the Elizabethans merry, even as a cry for brown paper and vinegar could once raise a laugh in Victorian farce—and a glossary will be needed for this very soon. But what can be done to recover such foundered word-play as

No egma, no riddle, no *l'envoy*, no salve in the mail, sir.

or to give life and sense to Moth's

Is not *l'envoy* a salve?

When we come to

The fox, the ape, and the humble-bee...

we can, grown desperate, find Folio authority for a cut. The new *Cambridge* editors insist that it is an obviously topical joke, its application long lost; we might get rid of it upon that ground.[9] But—worse and worse!—We next come to elaborate jesting about a goose and a market.

Should a producer expunge the whole thing and bring Costard on to hear at once of his enfranchisement? This may well be the lesser evil. But one cannot thus eviscerate a scene and expect to see no wound. Here is an effect gained by the resolving of the long Armado-Moth duet into a trio, by rounding off the sententious folly and nimble mockery with the crude humour of the clown. The dialogue passes from prose to rhymed couplets; then becomes gay with jingle, which Costard jollily burlesques in that long looping metre. We must think of it all in terms of music, of constrasts in tone and tune, rhythm and breaking of rhythm. There is the value of the picture too, set before us and held for its minute or two; of the egregious dignity of Armado, Moth delicately poised, and Costard square-toed and cunning, not such a fool as he looks. All this has histrionic value, the sheer sense of the dialogue apart. All plays exist, plots and character-schemes beside, as schemes of sound as shifting pictures, in decoration of thought and phrase, and the less their dependence on plot or conflict of character the more must they depend upon such means to beauty and charm. These "set pieces" may be loosely and easily contrived, so that they still give an illusion of life; and we must never be made overconscious of them, or the charm may vanish, even though the beauty remain. But in this play, as we have seen, much depends on them. We are, indeed, never very far from the formalities of song and dance. The long last act is half Masque and half play; and in song and dance the play ends.

Therefore, it being understood that pretty picture and pleasant sound alone will never suffice, before sentence is passed on a difficult passage it might well be put upon probation. Let the

---

9. But is this so? I can imagine an American editor three hundred years hence testing the verse which begins,

I never saw a purple cow...

for an allusion to President Wilson. Was not Roosevelt called a bullmoose? But the mere truth is that sixty million people or so once thought that funny in itself.

actors see what they can make of it by adroit movement and the nice turning of a phrase. There is danger here. Released from that troublesome obligation to make current sense of his goings-on, the actor too readily turns acrobat; and the audience, come to do their duty by Shakespeare, hardly expect to make much sense of the stuff anyhow. Better cut half the play than act any of it on these terms; but better, then, not act it a all. There are passages, however (though the one we have just quoted is not in its entirety one of them), which do yield something to such treatment. Who, with an ear for the music and rhythm of fine prose, will not take pleasure, for instance, in the very sound of

ARMADO: Go, tenderness of years! take this key, give enlargement to the swain, bring him festinately hither; I must employ him in a letter to my love.

MOTH: Will you win your love with a French brawl?

ARMADO: How meanest thou? Brawling in French?

MOTH: No, my complete master; but to jig off a tune at the tongue's end, canary to it with your feet, humour it with turning up your eyes; and sigh a note and sing a note as if you swallowed love with singing love, sometimes through the nose, as if you snuffed up love by smelling love; with your hat penthouse-like over the shop of your eyes; with your arms crossed on your thin belly-doublet like a rabbit on a spit: or your hands in your pockets, like a man after the old painting; and keep not too long in one tune, but a snip and away. These are complements, these are humours, these betray nice wenches that would be betrayed without these, and make them men of note—do you note me?—that are most affected to these.

ARMADO: How hast thou purchased this experience?

MOTH: By my penny of observation,

ARMADO: But O—but O,—

MOTH: The hobby-horse is forgot.

ARMADO: Call'st thou my love hobby-horse?

MOTH:	No, master; the hobby-horse is but a colt—and your love perhaps a hackney. But have jou forgot your love?
ARMADO:	Almost I had.
MOTH:	Negligent student! Learn her by heart.
ARMADO:	By heart, and in heart, boy.
MOTH:	And out of heart, master: all those three I will prove.
ARMADO:	What wilt thou prove?
MOTH:	A man, if I live: and this—by, in, and without, upon the instant. By heart you love her, because your heart cannot come by her; in heart you love her, because your heart is in love with her; and out of heart you love her, being out of heart that you cannot enjoy her.

It is pure *bravura*; it hangs up the action, it hardly develops character; Shakespeare the full-fledged dramatist would not have written it. We may indeed compare it to an *aria* in an opera. It calls for a comparable execution, an audience should get the same sort of pleasure from it. And if the musical value is not quite as great—well, we mostly miss the words of the *aria* as a rule.

To make a tentative list of the passages with which nothing can be done, of the bits of dead wood, one may call them:

ARMADO:	I love not crossed.
MOTH:	He speaks the mere contrary, crosses love not him.

Moth's line at least might come out. The joke can't be conveyed, nor is it worth the conveying.

The dancing horse is dead past resurrection. If a ruthless pencil does away with the lines that lead up to the point and the two that drop away from it, can the most fervid Shakespearian—more royalist than his kind—complain?

The reference to the ballad of the King and the Beggar might go too. On the other hand, anyone who would mangle the discourse upon the four complexions, if it were only that he might so deprive us of Armado's

Define, define, well-educated infant

is a butcher and botcher of texts.

The whole passage between Boyet, the ladies and Costard in Act IV, Scene, i, which begins with the now cryptogrammatic pun,

Who is the suitor? who is the suitor?

—if one pronounces it sewtor the joke is lost, so it to a modern audience if one calls it shooter—ask at first sight for drastic treatment. Say we surmount this first obstacle, eke out the everlasting jokes about cuckoldry that follow with a wink or two and a nod, we shall still be utterly lost in the tangle of talk—yet more equivocal in every sense—about archery and bowling. Nevertheless, if one is not to truncate the whole scene and end it with the Princess' departure—and this is structural alternation and inadmissible—it may be better to go through with the gibberish, to let it seem so if it must. For again, consider the action, the lively picture; Boyet surrounded by the teasing girls, Costard ecstatic at the encounter! And are we to miss the little singing dance with which Rosaline takes leave? Apart from the charm of it—the girl and the gay old courtier answering and counter-stepping each other—and apart from the value of this little turmoil of rhythmic gaiety before we drop to our first experience of Holofernes and his pedantry, Shakespeare is bringing Rosaline by degrees to her due place of importance in the play, and no item of the process should be omitted.

As to Holofernes and Sir Nathaniel, it is a good part of the fun of them that neither the innocent Dull, nor we, can make out half the time what they are talking about. No need then, after all, to be troubled by

Priscian a little scratched

or even by the mystery of the charge-house on the top of the mountain. But what can—what ever *can!*—Be made of Moth's pleasantries about the five vowels and the horn-book (yet once again a cuckold's horn-book!) in the first scene of the last act? If ever a passage could serve in a competition with a prize given to the set of actors that extracted some legitimate effect from it, this could! Nor is it of any constructive consequence, nor does it add one stroke of character. Why not pass boldly then, from Costard's achievement of

> honorificabilitudinitatibus: thou are easier swallowed than a flap-dragon

to

> Arts-man, perambulate

and so the play's business?

But really there is nothing more, save a line or two of obvious indecency easily left out, that the producer need wish to conjure away. There remains but to question one apparent corruption of text, which does obscure the action at an important point, then to point out one or two possible pitfalls in the casting of the parts, and this prefacing, grown longer than the play itself, may end.

The King, that noble gentlemen and Armados' very good friend, having set on his butt to provide the entertainment of the nine Worthies, encourages his guests in the doubtless far better entertainment of making outrageous fun of him. By the standards of the time this may not have seemed to be such very caddish behaviour. We recall the practical jokes played by the Duke and Duchess on Don Quixotic. Cervantes could have commented, as Shakespeare cannot; but he let the business speak for itself. Still, it is possible that Shakespeare, though flattered, no doubt, by the approval of his own play's very select audience, has his private opinion upon this aspect of their gentility. Certainly, when the final trick is played on Armado, it is he, fantastic fool as he is, who shines out as the best gentleman amongst them, even as Don Quixote shon. The manner of the trick itself, however, is all confused in the text as we have it, and its matter is somewhat obscure. Berowne incites Costard to bring Armado's play-acting to utter grief by rushing on distraught with the sudden news that the wench Jaquenetta is cast away, is two months gone, Armado the culprit. The stage directions that make this clear Dr. Dover Wilson has most justly restored. And as justly he restores to Armado the line that he must speak to give point to the interruption:

> The party is gone.
> Fellow Hector, she *is* gone...

exclaims Costard. But the effect is still incomplete. The first line must surely be a part of Hector the Worthy's speech (this Dr. Dover Wilson does not hold). Where is the comic incongruity of Costard's twist of the phrase otherwise? It is such an obvious trick; neither, Costard, nor Shakespeare at this moment, could neglect it. One suspects a pun in "party". It can mean an antagonist, Achilles against Hector. An intermediate line may be missing; it cannot be restored unless someone should discover a colourable original of the pageant. But at least the incident and its business can be rightly outlined in action.

Further, it is surely clear—though to many editors it does not seem to be—that in the accusation poor Armado *is* most scandalously "infamonized". Where would be the joke else? The King and Princess, the courtiers and ladies, must, most of them, know by this time of his ridiculous adoration of this country wench; and we have seen how she treats him. Armado a hypocrite! The whole character is destroyed at a blow. If there were a guilty party, we might rather suspect Costard, who did "confess the wench". But it may all be a joke. Armado, at least, is convinced so, for back he comes before the play's end, quite his magnificently absurd self again. Again he, faithful among the faithless, will be a votary still; but to philosophy no longer, to the plough, to rusticity. We can imagine him, though hardly a great success in the furrows behind a team, sitting like Don Quixote beneath a tree—again the comparison is irresistible—and piping to the virginal Jaquenetta. Though, if Moth's estimate of the young lady's character should, after all, be the right one Shakespeare is a finished ironist already.

As to the casting of the comic parts; only with Costard is it not plain sailing. Holofernes is pedant incarnate, and Sir Nathaniel simple parson. Jaquenetta is a country wench and Dull is the village constable. But Costard, swain though he is,[10] smacks both of Court-jester and stage clown. Shakespeare had often to make use of these chartered comedians. Sometimes, as in *Twelfth Night, As You Like It* and *King Lear*, he can fit them to the play. Sometimes, as there is evidence, they were a sore trial to its integrity. Costard is the conventional figure thinly disguised,

10. And this need imply nothing rustic about him. He is Armado's body-servant merely.

and he may quite rightly be played so. In his very first scene, though he is Armado's man brought by the constable for correction, he takes all the jester's liberties with the King.

> KING: Peace!
> COSTARD: Be to me and every man that dares not fight.
> KING: No words!
> COSTARD: Of other men's secrets, I beseech you.

His attitude towards the Princess is the same. The actor, then, is given a character to assume for the play's consistency's sake; he must keep within it about as much as a low comedian did in Victorian farce or in Edwardian musical comedy. But no more. The play does not need another slow-spoken countryman. For that we have Dull, sparse of words, and heavy of gait. Costard's is a nimble wit; we must feel that for diversion he makes himself out to be more of a fool than he is. And the actor himself must be skilful of speech and light of touch, as good jesters and stage clowns were.

The Music

The indications of music and of the one dance are plain enough. Moth's "Concolinel" of Act III, Scene, i, stands for a song, which no research has yet tracked. How anyone can doubt this it is hard to see. In the earlier scene Moth is asked to sing. There is no point whatever in his here disappointing Armado and the audience too with a comic catch-phrase. And why should Armado's comment upon it be

Sweet air!

Moreover, the stage direction in the Folio definitely says, *A song*. If what Shakespeare wrote of chose cannot be found, the producer must do the next best thing and make such a choice for himself as Shakespeare might have made. Many of the sources from which he picked ballads when he wanted them are open to us. A pity to have to do it, but obviously better than to leave a gap in the scene. The recurrent lightening of the play with lyrics sung or said is a part of its artistic economy.

The dance the blackamoors play, that Rosaline and the ladies will not respond to, may well be a "French brawl". A pity to miss the canarying with the feet; but the music probably lasts, as we have noted—the players in the background—till the finish of Boyet's apostrophe to the ladies' jigging tongues.

For the end we have song and dance both. *Enter all*, say Quarto and Folio too. The play finishes, as a play of merry-making should, with everyone ranged for our last look at them. The simplest sort of a thing will serve best. Pedantry, cleverness, set, poses, nice speaking, are all dropped. Armado, the incorrigible, the votary still, will have it, of course, that we are to hear a dialogue by the two learned men. The two learned men are to be found but a moment later dancing a hay with the best. Moth may sing the Spring song and Jaquenetta Winter's Dull, it turns, out, can do marvels on the pipe and tabor. Costard too, no doubt.

In fact, as there is no curtain to descend, no other-word of illusion to hide, the actors are already putting off the characters so lightly worn, and telling us that, after all, it is only a play. No, Armado does not dance. It is as if, the revels over, he stalked forward to speak an epilogue:

> The words of Mercury are harsh after the songs of Apollo...

and could get no further. Are they ready to mock him again? Then he bows to the quality:

> You, that way; we, this way

shepherds his motley flock and stalks after them.

Romeo and Juliet

Romeo and Juliet is lyric tragedy, and this must be the key to its interpreting. It seems to have been Shakespeare's first unquestionable success, proof positive of his unique quality. If marred by one or two clumsy turns, its stagecraft is simple and sufficient; and the command of dramatic effect is masterly already. It is immature work still, but it is not crude. The writing shows us a Shakespeare skilled in devices that he is soon to reject or adapt to new purpose. This, which to the critic is one of the most interesting things about the play, is a stumbling block to its acting. But the passion and poignant beauty of it all, when we surrender ourselves to them, make such reservations of small enough account.

Whether we have the play as Shakespeare first wrote it may be doubted; we probably have it in the second Quarto as it last left his hands. But signs, as they may seem to be, of re-writing and re-touching at one time or another, must always, in this or any of his plays, be warily viewed. They may, of course, be so obvious as to ask no proof; but when they depend on nice calculation one must remember that the critical foot-rule is poor measure for genius—and the very poorest for genius in its springtime.

The Mercutio of the Queen Mab speech is not, it can be argued, the Mercutio of

> No, 'tis not so deep as a well, nor so wide as a church-door; but 'tis enugh, 'twill serve.

Did the Juliet, one asks, of

> Hath Romeo slain himself? Say thou but "I",
> And that bare vowel "I" shall poison more
> Than the death-darting eye of cockatrice:

I am not I, if there be such an "I"...

and the rest of the fantasia, turn within a sitting or so into the Juliet of

Ancient damnation! O most wicked fiend!
Is it more sin to wish me thus forsworn,
Or to dispraise my lord with that same tongue
Which she hath praised him with above compare
So many thousand times?

and the Rameo of

more courtship lives
In carrion flies than Romeo: they may seize
On the white wonder of dear Juliet's hand...
This may flies do, when I from this must fly...

into the stark figure of the scene in Mantua, meeting the news of her death with

Is it even so? Then I defy you, stars!

—into the Romeo who pays the apothecary with

There is thy gold; worse poison to men's souls,
Doing more murder in this loathsome world
Than these poor compounds that thou mayst not sell:
I sell thee poison, thou hast sold me none.

By all the rules, no doubt, there should be two Shakespeares at work here. But in such a ferment as we now find him (himself, in some sort, a young Romeo on the turn from a Rosaline of phrase-making to a deeper-welling love) he may well have been capable of working on Tuesday in one fashion, on Wednesday in another, capable of couplet, sonnet, word-juggling, straight sober verse, or hard-bitten prose, often as the popular story he was turning to account and the need of the actor for the thing they and he were so apt at seemed to demand, at times out of the new strength breeding in him. Our present concern, however, is with the play as we have it, and its, and its interpreting in the theatre.

The Conduct of the Action

The dominating merit of this is that Shakespeare takes Brooke's tale, and at once doubles its dramatic value by turning its months to days.

> These violent delights have violent ends....

and a sense of swiftness belongs to them, too. A Hamlet may wait and wait for his revenge; but it accords with this love and its tragedy that four days should see its birth, consummation and end. Incidentally we can here see the "Double Time"—which has so exercised the ingenuity of commentators, who will credit him with their own—slipping naturally and easily into existence.[1] He makes dramatic use of time when he needs to.

> CAPULET: But soft, what day is this?
> PARIS: Monday, my lord.
> CAPULET: Monday! Ha! ha! Well, Wednesday is too soon;
> O' Thursday let it be:—o' Thursday, tell her,
> She shall be married to this noble earl...

This sense of the marriage looming but three days ahead is dramatically important; later to intensify it, he even lessens the interval by a day. But (his mind reverting now and then to Brooke's story as he read it, possibly before he saw that he must weave it closer) he will carelessly drop in phrases that are quite contradictory when we examine them. But what audience will examine them as they flash by?

> I anger her sometimes [says the Nurse to Romeo], and tell her that Paris is the properer man...

(when neither Paris nor Romeo has been in the field for four and twenty hours).

> Is it more sin to wish me thus forsworn,
> Or to dispraise my lord with that same tongue
> Which she hath praised him with above compare
> So many thousand times?

(when, all allowance made for Juliet's exaggeration, the Nurse has not had twice twenty-four hours in which to praise or

[1] In the Preface to *The Merchant of Venice* this discussion is raised again, and, of course, pursued at length in *Othello*.

dispraise). But notice that this suggestion of the casual slackness of normal life conveniently loosens the tension of the tragedy a little. There is, indeed, less of carelessness than a sort of instinctive artistry about it; and the method is a natural by-product of the freedom of Shakespeare's theatre.

But he marshals his main action to very definite purpose. He begins it, not with the star-crossed lovers (though a prologue warns us to them), but with a clash of two houses; and there is far more significance in this than lies in the fighting. The servants, not the masters, start the quarrel. If Tybalt is a firebrand, Benvolio is a peacemaker; and though Montague and Capulet themselves are drawn in, they have the grace to be little ashamed after. The hate is cankered; it is an ancient quarrel set new abroach; and even the tetchy Capulet owns that it should not be so hard for men of their age to keep the peace. If it were not for the servants, then, who fight because they always have fought, and the Tybalts, who will quarrel about nothing sooner than not quarrel at all, it is a feud ripe for settling; everyone is weary of it; and no one more weary, more impatient with it than Romeo;

O me! What fray was here?
Yet tell me not—for I have heard it all...

We are not launching, then, into a tragedy of fated disaster, but—for a more poignant if less highly heroic theme—of opportunity muddled away and marred by ill-luck. As a man of affairs, poor Friar Laurence proved deplorable; but he had imagination. Nothing was likelier than that the Montagues and Capulets, waking one morning to find Romeo and Juliet married, would have been only too thankful for the excuse to stop killing each other.

And the continuance of their parents' rage,
Which, but their children's end, nought would remove...

says the prologue. Nought in such a world as this, surmises the young Shakespeare; in a world where

I thought all for the best

avails a hero little; for on the heels of it comes

O, I am fortune's fool!

Having stated this theme, he develops it, as his habit already is (and was to remain; the method so obviously suits the continuities of the Elizabethan stage), by episodes of immediate contrast in character and treatment. Thus, after the bracing rattle of the fight and the clarion of the Prince's judgment, we have our first sight of Romeo, fantastic, rueful, self-absorbed. His coming is preluded by a long passage of word-music; and, that its relevance may bee plain, the verse slips into the tune of it at the first mention of his name. Benvolio's brisk story of the quarrel, dashed with irony, is finishing—

> While we were interchanging thrusts and blows,
> Came more and more, and fought on part and part,
> Till the Prince came, who parted either part

—when Lady Montague interposes with

> O, where is Romeo? Saw you him to-day?
> Right glad am I he was not at this fray

and promptly, like a change from wood-wind, brass and tympani to an andante on the strings, comes Benvolio's

> Madam, an hour before the worshipped sun
> Peered forth the golden window of the east...

Montague echoes him; and to the wooing smoothness of

> But he, his own affections' counsellor,
> Is to himself—I will not say how true—
> But to himself so secret and so close,
> So far from sounding and discovery,
> As is the bud bit with an envious worm,
> Ere he can spread his sweet leaves to the air,
> Or dedicate his beauty to the sun.
> Could we but learn from whence his sorrows grow,
> We would as willingly give cure as know

Romeo appears; moody, oblivious of them all three. It is a piece of technique that belongs both to Shakespeare's stage in its simplicity and to the play's down lyrical cast.

Then (for contrasts of character and subject), close upon Romeo's mordant thought-play and word-play with Benvolio come Capulet and Paris, the sugary old tyrant and the man of wax, matchmaking—and such a good match for Juliet as it is to be! Close upon this comes Benvolio's wager that he'll show Romeo at the feast beauties to put Rosaline in the shade; and upon that, our first sight of Juliet, when she is bid take a liking to Paris at the feast if she can.

The scene of the procession of the Maskers to Capulet's house (with Romeo a spoil-sport as befits his mood) is unduly lengthened by the bravura of the Queen Mab speech, which is as much and as little to be dramatically justified as a song in an opera is.[2] But Shakespeare makes it serve to quicken the temper of the action to a pitch against which—as against the dance, too, and Tybalt's rage—Romeo's first encounter with Juliet will show with a quiet beauty all its own. Did he wonder for a moment how to make this stand out from everything else in the play? They share the speaking of a sonnet between them, and it is a charming device.

One must picture them there. The dance is over, the guests and the Maskers are in a little chattering, receding crowd, and the two find themselves alone.[3] Juliet would be for joining the other; but Romeo, his mask doffed, moves towards her, as a pilgrim towards a shrine.

If I profane with my unworthiest hand...

It is hard to see what better first encounter could have been devised. To have lit mutual passion in them at once would have been commonplace; the cheapest of love tragedies might begin

2. The young gentlemen are gate-crashers, we perceive; there are few novelties in the social world! But Capulet its delighted; he even, when the unlooked-for fun is over and the recalcitrant regular guests have been coaxed to dance, presses a "trifling foolish banquet" upon the strangers; cake and wine upon the sideboard, that is to say, and not, as the word now implies, a substantial sit-down affair. But etiquette, it seems, is against this. Having measured them a measure and so wound up the occasion very merrily, the "strangers" do begone. Seriously, the conduct, of this scene, when it is staged, needs attention. It is generally quite misunderstood and misinterpreted.

3. The company, that is to say, drift up towards the inner stage, from which as from the withdrawing rooms beyond the great hall, Capulet and the guests had come to welcome the masked invasion, ad as they all move away the guessing at who the strangers are dies down.

like that. But there is something sacramental in this ceremony, something shy and grave and sweet; it is a marriage made already. And she is such a child; touched to earnestness by his trembling earnestness, but breaking into fun at last (her defence when the granted kiss lights passion in him) as the last quatrain's metre breaks for its ending into.

You kiss by the book.

The tragedy to come will be deepened when we remember the innocence of its beginning. The encounter's ending has significance too. They are not left to live in a fool's paradise for long. Romeo hears who she is and faces his fate. An hour ago he was affecting melancholy while Mercutio and his fellow laughed round him. Now, with the sport at its best, he braces to desperate reality. Then, as the guests and Maskers depart and the laughter dies, Juliet grows fearful. She hears her fate and must face it, too.

> My only love sprung from my only hate!
> Too early seen unknown, and known too late!
> Prodigious birth of love it is to me
> That I must love a loathed enemy.

The child is no more a child.

A chorus follows. This may have some further function than to fill up time while furniture is shifted or stage fittings are adjusted; it is of no dramatic use.[4] Then Romeo appears alone.

And now, with his finest stroke yet, all prepared and pending (the love duet that is to be spoken from balcony to garden), Shakespeare pauses to do still better by it; and at the same time fits Mercutio to his true place in the character scheme.[5] To appreciate the device we must first forget the obliging editors with their *Scene i, A lane by the wall of Capulet's orchard. Enter Romeo.*

---

4. But for more argument about the question of act-division that is involved, see p. 63.
5. The Bodleian has recently recovered its original First Folio, and the pages of the balacony-scene are the best thumbed of all.

...He climbs the wall and leaps down within it. ...Scene ii, Capulet's orchard. Enter Romeo—for all this has simply obliterated the effect.[6] The *Enter Romeo alone* of the Quartos and Folio is the only authentic stage direction concerning him. What happens when Mercutio and Benvolio arrive in pursuit? He hides somewhere about the stage. He has, they say, "leapt this orchard wall"; but no wall is there, and—more importantly there is no break in the continuity of the scene, now or later; it should be proof enough that to make one we must cut a rhymed couplet in two. The confusion of whereabouts, such as it is, that is involved, would not trouble the Elizabethans in the least; would certainly not trouble an audience that later on was to see Juliet play half a scene on the upper stage and half on the lower, with no particular change of place implied. The effect, so carefully contrived, lies in Romeo's being well within hearing of all the bawdry now to follow, which has no other dramatic point; and that the chaff is about the chaste Rosaline makes it doubly effective.

Dominating the stage with his lusty presence, vomiting his jolly indecencies, we see the sensual man, Mercutio; while in the background lurks Romeo, a-quiver at them, youth marked for tragedy.[7] His heart's agonizing after Rosaline had been real enough. He has forgotten that! But what awaits him now, with-another heart, passionate as his own, to encounter? This is the eloquence of the picture, which is summed up in Romeo's rhyming end of the picture, which is summed up in Romeo's rhyming end to the whole dithyramb as he steals out, looking after the two of them:

> He jests at scars that never felt a wound.

---

6. Rowe is responsible for this. A few of the later editors scented something wrong, but only half-heartedly tried to put it right. Grant White was an honourable exception; but the places Mercutio and Benvolio in the orchard too. Juliet's line

> The orchard walls are high and hard to climb...

discounts that.

7. The effect will, of course, be intensified if he never leaves our sight, but the mere continuity of the scene, and our sense of him there, produces it.

The discord thus struck is perfect preparation for the harmony to come; and Mercutio's ribaldry has hardly died from our ears before Juliet is at her window.

Throughout the famous scene Shakespeare varies and strengthens its harmony and sustains its drama by one small device after another. We must return to more careful study of it. At its finish, the brisk couplet,

> Hence will I to my ghostly father's cell,
> His help to crave, and my dear hap to tell

brings us to earth again; and the action speeds on, to find a new helmsman in Friar Laurence. His importance to the play is made manifest by the length of this first soliloquy, and Shakespeare is looking forward already, we find, to the potion for Juliet. All goes smoothly and happily; the Friar is sententious, the lovers are ecstatic. Mercutio, Benvolio and the Nurse make a merry work-à-day chorus. Only that one note or warning is struck, lightly casually:

> Tybalt, the kinsman of old Capulet,
> Hath sent a letter to his father's house.

The marriage-scene brings this "movement" to its close.

> FRIAR: So smile the heavens upon this holy act,
> That after-hours with sorrow chide us not!
> ROMEO: Amen, amen! But come what sorrow can,
> It cannot countervail the exchange of joy
> That one short miniute gives me in her sight.
> Do thou but close our hands with holy words,
> Then love-devouring death do what he dare,
> It is enough I may but call her mine.
> FRIAR: These violent delights have violent ends,
> And in their triumph die...

Youth triumphant and defiant, age sadly wise; a scene of quiet consummation, stillness before the storm. We are just halfway through the play.

> Come, come with me, and we will make short work;
> For, by your leaves, you shall not stay alone
> Till holy church incorporate two in one.

But upon this, in immediate, most significant contrast, there stride along Mercuitio and Benvolio, swords on hip, armed servants following them, Mercutio with mischief enough a-bubble in him for the prudent Benvolio to be begging:

> I pray thee, good Mercuito, let's retire;
> The day is hot, the Capulets abroad,
> And if we meet we shall not scape a brawl,
> For now, these hot days, is the mad blood stirring

—and (with one turn of the dramatist's wrist) tragedy is in train.[8]

The scene that follows is the most strikingly effective thing in the play. It comes quickly to its crisis when Romeo eneters to encounter Tybalt face to face. For this moment the whole action has been preparing. Consider the constituents of the situation. Tybalt has seen Romeo eying his cousin Juliet from behind a mask and its privilege, and to no good purpose, be sure. But in Benvolio's and Mercutio's eyes he is still the lackadaisical adorer of Rosaline, a scoffer at the famous family quarrel suddenly put to the proof of manhood by a Capulet's insult. We know—we only—that he has even now come from his marriage to Juliet, from the marriage which is to turn these

> households' rancour to pure love.

The moment is made eloquent by a silence. For what is Romeo's answer to be to an insult so complete in its sarcastic courtesy?

> Romeo, the love I bear thee can afford
> No better therm than this: Thou art a villain.

Benvolio and Mercutio, Tybalt himself, have no doubt of it; but to us the silence that follows—its lengthening by one pulse-beat mere amazement to them—is all suspense. We know what is in the balance. The moment is, for Romeo, so packed with emotions that the actor may interpret it in half a dozen ways, each legitimate (and by such an endowment we may value a dramatic situation). Does he come from his "one short miniute"

---

8. one cannot too strongly insist upon the effect Shakespeare gains by this vivid contrast between scene and scene, swiftly succeeding each other. It is his chief technical resource.

with Juliet so rapt in happiness that the sting of the insult cannot pierce him, that he finds himself contemplating this Tybalt and his inconsequent folly unmoved? Does he flash into passion and check it, and count the cost to his pride and the scorn of his friends, and count them as nothing, all in an instant? Whatever the effect on him, we, as we watch, can interpret it, no one else guessing. And when he does answer:

> Tybalt, the reason that I have to love thee
> Does much excuse the appertaining rage
> To such a greeting: villain am I none;
> Therefore, farewell; I see thou know'st me not

the riddle of it is plain only to us. Note that it is the old riddling Romeo that answers, but how changed! We can enjoy, too, the perplexity of those other onlookers and wonder if no one of them will jump to the meaning of the

> good Capulet, which name I tender
> As dearly as my own...

But they stand stupent and Romeo passes on.

Upon each character concerned the situation tells differently; yet another test of its dramatic quality. Benvolio stands mute. He is all for peace, but such forbearance who can defend?[9] For Tybalt it is an all but comic let down. The turning of the cheek makes the smiter look not brave, but ridiculous; and this "courageous captain of compliments" takes ridicule very ill, is the readier, therefore, to recover his fire-eating dignity when Mercutio gives him the chance. And mercuitio, so doing, adds that most important ingredient to the situation, the unforeseen.

> Why the devil came you between us? [he gasps out to Romeo a short miniute later] I was hurt under your arm.

---

9. He had been forced to a bout himself with Tybalt the day before; and his description a little later of Romeo,

> With gentle breath, calm look, knees humbly bowed...

has exasperation, as well, perhaps, as some politic exaggeration in it.

But what the devil had he to do with a Capulet-Montague quarrel? The fact is (if one looks back) that he has been itching to read fashion-monger Tybalt a lesson; to show him that "*alla stoccata*" could not carry it away. But "*alla stoccata*" does; and, before we well know where we are, this arbitrary catastrophe gives the sharpest turn yet to the play's action, the liveliest of its figures crumples to impotence before us, the charming rhetoric of the Queen Mab speech and petered out in a savage growl.

The unexpected has its place in drama as well as the plotted and prepared. But observe that Shakespeare uses Mercutio's death to precipitate an essential change in Romeo; and it is this change, not anything extrinsic, that determines the main tragedy. After a parenthesis of scuffle and harsh prose he is left alone on the stage, and a simpler, graver, sterner emotion than any we have known in him yet begins to throb through measured verse.

> This gentleman, the Prince's near ally,
> My very friend, hath got this mortal hurt
> In my behalf; my reputation stained
> With Tybalt's slander—Tybalt, that an hour
> Hath been my cousin. O sweet Juliet,
> Thy beauty hath made me effeminate,
> And in my temper softened volour's steel!

Then he hears that his friend is dead, accepts his destiny—

> This day's black fate on more days doth depend;
> This but begins the woe others must end

—and so to astonish the blood-intoxicated Tybalt! With a hundred words, but with expression and action transcending them, Shakespeare has tied the central knot of his play and brought his hero from height to depth.

We are sped on with little relaxation; returning, though, after these close-woven excitements, to declamation with Benvolio's diplomatic apologies (to the play's normal method, that is to say), while a second massed confronting of Montagues and Capulets marks, for reminder, this apex of the action.

We are sped on; and Juliet's ecstasy of expectation, the—

> Gallop apace, you fiery-footed steeds...

—makes the best of contrasts, in matter and manner, to the sternness of Romeo's banishing. A yet sharper contrast follows quickly with the Nurse's coming, carrying the ladder of cords (the highway to the marriage bed, for emphasis of irony), standing mute a minute while Juliet stares, then breaking incontinently into her

he's dead, he's dead, he's dead.

From now—with hardly a lapse to quiet—one scene will compete with the next in distraction till Friar Laurence comes to still the outcry of mourning over the drugged Juliet on her bed. The lovers compete in despair and desperate hope; Capulet precipitates confusion; the Friar himself turns foolhardy. All the action is shot through with haste and violence, and with one streak at least of gratuitous savagery besides. For if the plot demands Capulet's capricious tyrannies it does not need Lady Capulet's impulse to send a man after Romeo to poison him. But the freshly kindled virus of hatred (does Shakespeare feel?) must now spend itself even to exhaustion. From this point to the play's end, indeed, the one reposeful moment is when Romeo's

dreams presage some joyful news at hand.

But the next is only the more shattering; and from then to the last tragic accidents it is a tale of yet worse violence, yet more reckless haste.[10]

It is, of course, in the end a tragedy of mischance. Shakespeare was bound by his story, was doubtless content to be; and how make it otherwise? Nevertheless, we discern his deeper dramatic sense, which was to shape the maturer tragedies, already in revolt.

---

10. The slaughtering of Paris is wanton and serves little dramatic purpose. Lady Montague is dead also by the end of the play (through no one gives much heed to that) and Q1 even informs us that

...young Benvolio is deceased too.

Here, however, the slaughter is probably less arbitrary—from one point of view. The actors had other parts to play. By the time Q2 has come into being Shakespeare knows better than to call attention to Benvolio's absence. Who notices it? But his audiences—a proportion of them—no doubt loved a holocaust for its own sake, and he was not above indulging them now and then.

Accidents make good incidents, but tragedy determined by them has no significance. So he sets out, we see, in the shaping of his characters, to give all likelihood to the outcome. It is by pure -ill-luck that Friar John's speed to Mantua is stayed while Balthasar reaches Romeo with the news of Juliet's death; but it is Romeo's headlong recklessness that leaves Friar Laurence no time to retrieve the mistake. It is, by more subtle turn, Juliet's overacted reprentance of her "disobedient opposition", which prompts the delighted Capulet to

> have this knot up to-morrow morning.

And this difference of a day proves also to be the difference between life and death.

Before ever the play begins, the chorus foretells its ending. The star-crossed lovers must, we are warned,

> with their death bury their parents' strife.

But Shakespeare is not content with the plain theme of an innocent happiness foredoomed. He makes good dramatic use of it. Our memory of the Prologue, echoing through the first scenes of happy encounter, lends them a poignancy which makes their beauties doubly beautiful. The sacrament of the marriage, with Romeo's invocation—

> Do thou but close our hands with holy words,
> Then love-devouring death do what he dare,
> It is enough I may but call her mine

— read into it, stands as symbol of the sacrifice that all love and happiness must make to death. But character also is fate; it is, at any rate, the more dramatic part of it, and the life of Shakespeare's art is to lie in the manifesting of this. These two lovers, then must in themselves be prone to disaster. They are never so freed from the accidents of their story as his later touch would probably have made them. But by the time he has brought them to their full dramatic stature we cannot—accidents or no—imagine a happy ending, or a Romeo and Juliet married and settled as anything but a burlesque.

So, the turning point of Mercutio's death and Tybalt's and Romeo's banishing being past, Shakespeare brings all his powers to bear upon the moulding of the two figures to inevitable tragedy; and the producer of the play must note with care how the thing is done. To begin with, over a succession of scenes—in all but one of which either Romeo or Juliet is concerned—there is no relaxing of tension, vehemence or speed; for every flagging moment in them there is some fresh spur, they reinforce each other too, the common practice of contrast between scene and scene is more or less foregone.[11] And the play's declamatory method is heightened, now into rhapsody, now into a veritable dervish-whirling of words.

Shakespeare's practical ability—while he still hesitates to discard it—to turn verbal conventions to lively account is shown to the full in the scene between Juliet and the Nurse, with which this stretch of the action begins—his success, also his failure. The passage in which Juliet's bewildered dread finds expression in a cascade of puns is almost invariably cut on the modern stage, and one may sympathize with the actress who shirks it. But it is, in fact, word-play perfectly adapted to dramatic use; and to the Elizabethans puns were not necessarily comic things.

> Hath Romeo slain himself? Say thou but "I",
> And that bare vowel "I" shall poison more
> Than the death-dealing eye of cockatrice:
> I am not I, if there be such an "I",
> Or those eyes shut that make thee answer "I".
> If he be slain, say "I"; or if not, no:
> Brief sounds determine of my weal or woe.

Shut our minds to its present absurdity (but it is no more absurd than any other bygone fashion), allow for the rhetorical method, and consider the emotional effect of the word-music alone—what a vivid expression of the girl's agonized mind it makes, this intoxicated confusion of words and meanings! The whole scene is written in terms of conventional rhetoric. We pass from play upon words to play upon phrase, paradox, antithesis.

> O serpent heart, hid with a flowering face!
> Did ever dragon keep so fair a cave?
> Beautiful tyrant; fiend angelical!

---

11. I say deliberately "in all but one", not two, for the reason I give later.

Dove-feathered raven! wolfish ravening lamb!
Despised substance of divinest show!
Just opposite to what thou justly seem'st;
A damned saint, an honourable villain!...

The boy-Juliet was here evidently expected to give a display of virtuosity comparable to the singing of a *scena* in mid-nineteenth-century opera. That there was no danger of the audience finding it ridiculous we may judge by Shakespeare's letting the Nurse burlesque the outcry with her

There's no trust,
No faith, no honesty in men; all perjured,
All forsworn, all naught, all dissemblers!

For it is always a daring thing to sandwich farce with tragedy; and though Shakespeare was fond of doing it, obviously he would not if the tragedy itself were trembling on the edge of farce.

The weakness of the expedient shows later, when, after bringing us from rhetoric to pure drama with the Nurse's

Will you speak well of him that killed your cousin?

and Juliet's flashing answer,

Shall I speak ill of him that is my husband?

—one of those master touches that clarify and consummate a whole situation—Shakespeare must needs take us back to another screed of the sort which now shows meretricious by comparison. For a finish, though, we have the fine simplicity, set in formality, of

JULIET: Where is my father and my mother, Nurse?
NURSE: Weeping and wailing over Tybalt's corse:
Will you go to them? I will bring you thither.
JULIET: Wash they his wounds with tears! Mine shall be spent,
When their are dry, for Romeo's banishment.
Take up those cords. Poor rops, you are beguiled,
Both you and I, for Romeo is exiled.

He made you for a highway to my bed,
But I, a maid, die maiden-widowed.

By one means and another, he has now given us a new and a passionate and desperate Juliet, more fitted to her tragic end.

In the scene that follows, we have desperate Romeo in place of desperate Juliet, with the Friar to lift it to dignity at the finish and to push the story a short step forward. The maturer Shakespeare would not, perhaps, have coupled such similar scenes so closely; but both likeness and repetition serve his present purpose.

To appraise the value of the next effect he makes we must again visualize the Elizabethan stage.[12] Below

Enter Capulet, Lady Capulet and Paris.

With Tybalt hardly buried, Juliet weeping for him, it has been no time for urging Paris' suit.

'Tis very late [says Capulet], she'll not come down to-night:
I promise you, but for your company,
I should have been a-bed an hour ago.

Paris takes his leave, asks Lady Capulet to commend him to her daughter. She answers him:

I will, and know her mind early to-morrow;
To-night she's mewed up to her heaviness.

But *we* know that, at this very moment, Romeo and Juliet, bride and bridegroom, are in each other's arms.

Paris is actually at the door, when, with a sudden impulse, Capulet recalls him.[13]

Sir Paris, I will make desperate tender
Of my child's love. I think she will be ruled

12. But we must do this throughout.

13. And we may rely on this as one of the very few authenticated pieces of Shakespearean "business". For Q1 says

Paris offers to goes in and Capolet calls him againe.

If the presumed reporter watching the performance thought it important and had the time to note this down, it must have been markedly done.

In all respects by me; nay, more, I doubt it not.
Wife, go you to her ere you go to bed;
Acquaint her here of my son Paris' love,
And bid her, mark you me, on Wednesday next...

And by that sudden impulse, so lightly obeyed, the tragedy is precipitated. Capulet, bitten by an idea, is in a ferment.

Well, Wednesday is too soon;
O' Thursday let it be:—o' Thursday, tell her,
She shall be married to this noble earl.

Will you be ready? Do you like this haste?...

(In a trice he has shaken off the mourning uncle and turned jovial, roguish father-in-law.)

Well, get you gone! O' Thursday be it then.—
Go you to Juliet ere you go to bed,
Prepare her, wife, against this wedding day...

(What, we are asking, will Lady Capulet find if she does go?)

Farewell, my lord.—Light to my chamber, ho!
Afore me, it's so very late
That we may call it early by and by:—
Good-night.

Now comes the well-prepared effect. Hardly have the three vanished below, bustling and happy; when with

Wilt thou begone? It is not yet near day...

Juliet and Romeo appear at the window above, clinging together, agonized in the very joy of their union, but all ignorant of this new and deadly blow which (again) *we* know is to fall on them.

Only the unlocalized stage is capable of just such an effect as this. Delay in the shifting of scenery may be overcome by the simple lifting of a front scene to discover Romeo and Juliet in her chamber behind it; but Shakespeare's audience had not even to shift their imaginations from one place to another. The lower stage was anywhere downstairs in Capulet's house. The upper stage was associated with Juliet; it had served for her balcony and had been put to no other use.[14] So while Capulet is planning the marriage with Paris not only will our thoughts have been travelling to her, but our eyes may have rested speculatively, too, on those closed curtains above.

Shakespeare speeds his action all he can. Capulet, itching with his new idea, gives invaluable help. Romeo has hardly dropped from the balcony before Lady Capulet is in her daughter's room.[15] Capulet himself comes on her heels. It is barely day-break and he has not been to bed. (The night is given just that confused chronology such feverish nights seem to have.) With morning Juliet flies to the Friar, to find Paris already with him, the news already agitating him; she herself is the more agitated by the unlooked-for meeting with Paris. The encounter between them, with its equivoque, oddly echoes her first encounter with Romeo; but it is another Juliet that now plays a suitor with words. It is a more deeply passionate Juliet, too, that turn from Paris' formal kiss with

> Oh, shut the door, and when thou hast done so,
> Come weep with me; past hope, past cure, past help!

than so passionately greeted the news of Tybalt's death and Romeo's banishment. Child she may still be, but she is now a wife.

We should count the Friar's long speech with which he gives her the potion, in which he tells her his plan, as a sort of strong pillar of rhetoric, from which the play's action is to be swung to the next strong pillar, the speech (in some ways its counterpart) in which Juliet nerves herself to the drinking it. For, with Romeo removed for the moment, the alternating scene falls to Capulet and his bustlings; these are admirable as contrast, but of no dramatic power, and the action at this juncture must be well braced and sustained.

We come now to another and still more important effect, that is (yet again) only to realized in the theatre for which it

---

14. The musicians at Capulet's supper would probably have sat in it; but this is hardly a dramatic use. Nor does the mere association with Juliet *localize* it. There is no such scientific precision in the matter.

15. For the stage business involved here, see p. 67.

was designed. The curtains of the inner stage are drawn back to show us Juliet's bed. Her nurse and her mother leave her; she drinks the potion, and—says that note-taker at the performance, whose business it was, presumably, to let his employers know exactly how all the doubtful bits were done—

She falls upon the bed within the curtains.

There has been argument upona argument whether this means the curtains of the bed or of the inner stage—which would then close on her. The difference in dramatic effect will be of degree and not kind. What Shakespeare aims at in the episodes that follow is to keep us conscious of the bed and its burden; while in front of it, Capulet and the servants, Lady Capulet and the Nurse pass hither and thither, laughing and joking over the preparation for the wedding, till the bridal music is playing, till, to the very sound of this, the Nurse bustles up to draw back the curtains and disclose the girl there stark and still.[16]

This is one of the chief dramatic effect of the play; and it can only be gained by preserving the continuity of the action, with its agonies and absurdities check by jowl, with that bridal music sharpening the irony at the last. It is a comprehensive effect, extending from the drinking of the potion to the Nurse's parrot scream when she finds Juliet stiff and cold; and even beyond, to the coming of the bridegroom and his train, through the longspoken threnody, to the farce of the ending—which helps to remind us that, after all, Juliet is not dead. It is one scene, one integral stretch of action; and its common mutilation by *Scene iv. Hall in Capulet's house...Scene v. Juliet's chamber. Enter Nurse...*, with the consequences involved, is sheer editorial murder.

Modern producers, as a rule do even worse by it than the

---

16. To Shakespeare's audience it would make little matter which sort of curtains they were. A closed bed standing shadowed on the inner stage is at once to be ignored and recognized. We also, with a little practice, can ignore it, with Capulet; though to our more privileged gaze there it significantly is, in suspended animation, as it were, till the Nurse, fingering its curtains, brings it back to dramatic life, as we have known she must, as we have been waiting breathlessly for her to do. Whether they should be bed curtains or stage curtains is a matter of convention, a question of more imagination or less.

editors. They bring down a curtain upon a display of virtuosity in a "potion-scene", long drawn out, worried to bits, and leave us to recover till they are ready with Romeo in Mantua and the apothecary. And even faithful Shakespearians have little good to say of that competition in mourning between Paris and Capulet, Lady Capulet and the Nurse. It has been branded as deliberate burlesque. It is assuredly no more so than was Juliet's outbreak against Romeo upon Tybalt's death; to each, we notice, the Nurse provides a comic, characteristic echo, which would have little point if it did not contrast, rather absurdly, with the rest. Burlesque, of a sort, comes later with Peter and the musicians; Shakespeare would not anticipate this effect, and so equivocally! The passage does jar a little; but we must remember that he is working here in a convention that has gone somewhat stale with him and constrainedly; and that he can call now on no such youthful, extravagant passion as Juliet's or Romeo's to make the set phrases live. The situation is dramatically awkward, besides; in itself it mocks at the mourners, and Friar Laurence's reproof of them, which comes unhappily near to cant, hardly clarifies it. Shakespeare comes lamely out; but he went sincerely in. Nor does the farce of Peter and the musicians, conventional as it is, stray wholly beyond likelihood. Peter is comic in his grief; but many people are. Will Kempe, it may be, had to have his fling; but this part of the scene has its dramatic value, too. It develops and broadensvulgarizes, if you will—the irony of the bridal music brought to the deathbed; and, the traditional riddle-me-ree business done with (and Will Kempe having "brought off an exit" amid cheers), there is true sting in the tail of it:

> FIRST MUSICIAN: What a pestilent knave is this same!
> SECOND MUSICIAN: Hang him, Jack! Come, we'll in here; tarry for the mourners, and stay dinner.

And, of course, it eases the strain before tragedy gets its final grip of us.

We find Romeo in Mantua poised upon happiness before his last sudden plunge to despair and death. Shakespeare has now achieved simplicity in his treatment of him, brought the character to maturity and his own present method to something like perfection. What can be simpler, more obvious yet more effective than the dream with its flattering presage of good news—

I dreamt my lady came and found me dead—
Strange dream, that gives a dead man leave to think! –
And breathed such life with kisses in my lips,
That I revived, and was an emperor...

—followed incontinently by Balthasar's

Her body sleeps in Capels' monument,
And her immortal part with angels lives...

So much for dreams! So much for life and its flatteries! And the buying of the poison shows us a Romeo grown out of all knowledge away from the sentimental, phrase-making adorer of Rosaline.

There is thy gold; worse poison for men's souls
Doing more murder in this loathsome world
Than these poor compounds that thou mayst note sell:
I sell thee poison, thou hast sold me none.

This aging of Romeo is marked by more than one touch. To the contemptuous Tybalt he was a boy; now Paris to him, when they meet, is to be "good gentle youth".

Then, after one more needed link in the story has been riveted, we reach the play's last scene. Producers are accustomed to eliminate most of this, keeping the slaughtering of Paris as a prelude, concentrating upon Romeo's death and Juliet's, possibly providing a sort of symbolic picture of Montagues and Capulets reconciled at the end. This is all very well, and saves us the sweet kernel of the nut, no doubt; but it happens not to be the scene that Shakespeare devised. To appreciate that we must once more visualize the stage for which it was devised. The authorities are in dispute upon several points here, but only of detail. Juliet lies entombed in the inner stage; that is clear. The outer stage stands for the churchyard; as elastically as it stood before for the street or the courtyard of Capulet's house in which the Maskers marched about, while the serving-men coming forth with their napkins converted it, as vaguely, into the hall. Now it is as near to the tomb or as far from it as need be, and the action on it (it is the larger part of this that is usually cut) will be prominent and important. The tomb itself is the inner stage, closed in, presumably, by gates which Romeo breaks open, through the bars of which Paris casts his flowers. Juliet herself lies like a recumbent effigy upon a rectangular block of stone, which must be low enough and wide enough for Romeo to lie more or less beside her; and other such monuments, uneffigied, Tybalt's among them, may surround her.[17]

Once more Shakespeare hurries us through a whole night of confusion; from the coming of Paris, the cheated bridegroom, and Romeo the robbed husband, to this ghastly bridebed, through one tragic miscarrying after another; to the Prince's summing-up:

> A glooming peace this morning with it brings...

All is confusion; only the regularity of the verse keeps it from running away. Paris is fearful of disturbance,[18] and Romeo, when he comes is strained beyond endurance or control. It is not till he has fleshed the edge of his desperation upon poor Paris, till he is sobered by seeing what he has done, that, armed securely with his poisons, he can take his clam farewell. Once he is dead, confusion is let loose. The Friar approaches with

> Saint Francis be may speed! How oft to-night
> Have my old feet stumbled at graves!...

Balthasar and he whisper and tremble. Then Juliet wakes; but before he can speak to her, the watch are heard coming. He

---

17. We need not comb the text for objections to this arrangement, which is practicable, while no other is. For an explanation of

    Why I *descend* into this bed of death...

    for instance, we have only to turn to Brooke's poem (lines 2620-2630). The frontispiece to Rowe's edition of the play is (incidentally) worth observing. It does not show a stage-setting, even a Restoration stage-setting, but the tomb itself may well be the sort of thing that was used. Paris and Romeo, it can be seen, wear semi-Roman costume. Is this, by any hazardous chance, explicable by the fact that Otway's perversion of the play, *Caius Marius*, was then current in the theatres (*Romeo and Juliet* itself was not, it seems, revived till 1744; and then much altered)? Did Du Guernier begin his drawing with the Roman lovers in his mind?

18. For no compelling reason; but Shakespeare felt the need of striking this note at nonce, since a first note will tend to be the dominant one.

flies; and she has but time to find the empty phial in Romeo's hand, bare time to find his dagger and stab herself before they appear, and the hunt is up:

> PARIS' PAGE: This is the place; there, where the torch doth burn.
>
> CAPTAIN OF: THE WATCH: The ground is bloody; search about the churchyard:
> Go, some of you, whoe'er you find, attach.
> Pitiful sight! here lies the country slain,
> And Juliet, bleeding, warm and newly dead,
> Who here hath lain this two days buried.[19]
> Go, tell the Princes; run to the Capulets;
> Raise up the Montagues; some others search...

Cries, confusion, bustle; some of the watch bring back Balthasar, some others the Friar; the Prince arrives with his train, the Capulets surge in, the Montagues; the whole front stage is filled with the coming the going, while, in dreadful contrast, plain to our sight within the tomb, the torchlight flickering on them, Romeo and Juliet lie still.[20]

The play is not over, another hundred lines go to its finishing; and, to appease our modern impatience of talk when no more is to be done, here, if nowhere else, the producer will wield the blue pencil doughtily. Why should the Friar recount at length—after saying he'll be brief, moreover!—What we already know, with Balthasar to follow suit, and Paris' page to follow him? There are half a dozen good reasons. Shakespeare neither could nor would, of course, bring a play to a merely catastrophic end; the tradition of his stage no less than its conditions forbade this. Therefore the Prince's authoritative

> Seal up the mouth of outrage for a while,
> Till we can clear these ambiguities,
> And know their spring, their, head, their true descent;
> And then I will be general of your woes,
> And lead you even to death: meantime forbear...

---

19. Another instance of Shakespeare's use of time for momentary effect—or of his carelessness. Or will someone find a subtle stroke of character in the Watchman's inaccuracy?

20. It is of some interest to note that *Antony and Cleopatra* ends with a similar stage effect.

with which he stills a tumult that thretens otherwise to end the play, as it began, in bloody rough-and-tumble—this is the obvious first note of a formal full-close. But the Friar's story must be told, because the play's true end is less in the death of the star-crossed lovers than in the burying of their parents' strife; and as it has been primarily a play of tangled mischances, the unravelling of these, the bringing home of their meaning to the sufferers by them, is a natural part of its process. How else lead up to the Prince's

> Where be these enemies? Capulet—Montague!
> See what a scourge is laid upon your hate...

and to the solution with Capulet's

> O brother Montague, give me thy hand...

For us also—despite our privileged vision—it has been a play of confused, passion-distorted happenings, and the Friar's plain tale makes the simple pity of them clear, and sends us away with this foremost in our minds. Again, declamation is the norm of the play's method, and it is natural to return to that for a finish. Finally, as it is a tragedy less of character than of circumstance, upon circumstance its last emphasis naturally falls. Yet, all this admitted, one must own that the penultimate stretch of the writing, at least, is poor in quality. Shakespeare has done well by his story and peopled it with passionate life. But, his impulse flagging, his artistry is still found immature. Compare the poverty of this ending with the resourceful breadth of the effect made in the rounding of the story of *Cymbeline* to a close.

The Question of Act-Division

Neither Quartos nor Folio mark act-division; Rowe first supplies it, and his arrangement has commonly been accepted since. There are several questions involved. Did Shakespeare plan out the play as an indivisible whole? If he did, was it so acted; and, if not, were the pauses made mere formal pauses, or intervals, in which the emotional tension would not only relax, but lapse altogether? And, pauses or intervals, is Rowe's placing of them authentic? With the historical aspect of all this I am incompetent to deal. But Rowe's dividing-up of the action is, clearly, neither here nor there; and even if it is not his, but a somehow inherited tradition, that still will not make it Shakespeare's. A play, as we know, soon passed beyond its author's control, and Elizabethan practice may have differed from play to play, and as between the public theatre and the private. How did Shakespeare *plan* his play? That is what we have to divine if we can; and from that we may pass directly to the question of our own convenience in the acting of it.

The one internal piece of evidence of a lost scheme of act-division is the second chorus. This, incidentally, does not appear in the first Quarto. Is it capable of any other explanation? It has little dramatic point, as to this Johnson's robust verdict suffices; "...it conduces nothing to the progress of the play, but relates what is already known, or what the next scene will show; and relates it without adding the improvement of any moral sentiment". It has been held very doubtfully Shakespearian. There is one thing to note about it and the scene which precedes it. This requires stools to be set on the outer stage for the use of Capulet and his cousin. They are presumably the joint-stools of the text, and the text makes provision for their setting. But we find none for their taking-away, no dialogue to help out the business, and they could not well be moved during the latter half of the scene, when Romeo and Juliet are love-making. In an act-pause they could presumably have been moved; but if there were none—was the chorus by chance written in to cover this technical clumsiness? It is possible; but the remedy seems as clumsy as the fault.[21]

Later, Shakespeare lands himself in a more serious technical difficulty, from which, though at some sacrifice of dramatic effect, an act-pause would have extricated him,. He wants to show us Romeo and Juliet parting on their wedding night, Romeo descending from the very balcony which had seen their wooing and their brief happiness, and to follow this quickly by the bringing of the news to Juliet that she is to marry Paris. The double blow, no respite given, was the important thing to

---

21. It looks as if another stool were needed on the outer stage when the Nurse returns to Juliet with her news of Romeo. But in this case no special provision is made either for its placing or removing.

him dramatically, without doubt. But would he not have saved himself, if he well could, from the present ensuing clumsiness that brings Juliet from upper stage to lower in the middle of a scene, her bedroom on her back, as it were? Though an Elizabethan audience might make light of a lapse of this sort, it is none the less clumsy, and from the beginning he was an apt if a daring craftsman[22]

Lastly, was the scene between Peter and the musicians written for its own sake, or to please Will Kempe, or (possibly) to make more time than the two scenes which carry on the plot allow for the moving of the bed and the setting of the tomb upon the inner stage?[23] If Rowe's act-pause had intervened there would have been time enough. These are trivial matters, but not wholly negligible.

If five acts there must be, Rowe's five may serve. But one could vary the division as legitimately in half a dozen different ways; and this in itself argue against any division at all. Nor is there any scene-division in the play, where an act-division might fall, over which some immediate bridge does not seem to be thrown. Either a strong contrast is devised between the end of one scene and the beginning of the next that a pause

---

22. The scene could have been staged in no other way. *Enter Romeo and Juliet at the window*, says Q1; *Enter Romeo and Juliet aloft, says* Q.2. Late Q1 tells us, *He goeth down*; and later still we have

Enter Nurse hastily

Nurse. Madame, beware, take heed the day is broke,
Your Mother's comming to your Chamber. Make
all sure.

She goeth down from the window.

Whether Juliet or the nurse, does not matter. In fact they both must go down; for there follows immediately:

Enter Juliet, Mother, Nurse

And a second later, after her

How now, who calls?

Juliet is on the stage. By Q2 the scene has been much rewritten. The Nurse is given more time for her descent. The later stage directions are less explicit. But that the business was approximately the same is certain, if for no other reason than that the last part of the scene, containing Capulet's outburst, could have been effectively played nowhere but on the lower stage.

23. "Or/and", as the lawyers sometimes have it, with regard to the last possibility.

would nullify, or the quick succession of event to event is an integral part of the dramatic effect Shakespeare is seeking. (But it is, of course, in the very nature of the play, of its precipitate passion, to forge ahead without pause.) What value is there in an act-pause after Capulet's supper, between Romeo's first meeting with Juliet and the balcony-scene? There is no interval of time to account for, nor has the action reached any juncture that asks for the emphasis of a pause. An act-pause after the marriage falls with a certain effect, but it nullifies the far better effect by which Tybalt is shown striding the streets in search of Romeo at the very moment when the Friar is marrying him to Juliet; and that Romeo should seem to come straight from the marriage to face Tybalt's challenge is a vital dramatic point. The whole action surges to a crisis with the deaths of Tybalt and Mercutio and Romeo's banishing; and here, one could argue, a pause while we asked, "What next?" Might have its value. But Rowe marks no act-pause here; and if he did, the fine effect by which Juliet's ecstatic

> Gallop apace, you fiery-footed steeds...

follows pat upon the Prince's

> let Romeo hence in haste,
> Else, when he's found, that hour is his last

would be destroyed. The break made between Juliet's departure to the Friar's cell for counsel how to escape the marriage with Paris and her arrival there and the encounter with him relates to no pause, nor check, nor turn in the action. Rowe's Act IV, we may say, then begins with the new interest of the giving of the potion, as it ends upon an echo of its taking. And a pause—a breathing-space before the great plunge into tragedy—before we find Romeo in Mantua waiting for news (before Rowe's Act V, that is to say) may have dramatic value. But the comic scene with the musicians provides just such a breathing-space. And if we remove it (and there may have been, as I suggest, merely incidental reasons for putting it in) a continuity of action is restored which gives us a most dramatic contrast between the mouring over Juliet and Romeo's buoyant hopes.

What we should look for, surely, in act-division, is some

definite advantage to the play's acting. Where, in this play, do we find that? But the gains are patent if we act it without check or pause. Whatever the Elizabethan practice may have been, and whatever concessions are to be made to pure convenience, everything seems to point to Shakespeare having *planned* the play as a thing indivisible. It can be so acted without much outrunning the two hours' traffic.[24] If this will overtax the weakness of the flesh—the audience's; for actors will profit by the unchecked flow of action and emotion—some sacrifice of effect must be made. The less then, the better. A single pause after the banishing of Romeo would be my own solution.

Staging, Costume, Music, Text

The producer wishing to enscene the play must devise such scenery as will not deform, obscure or prejudice its crafts-manship or its art. That is all. But it is not easy to do.

There are no signs in the text that Shakespeare saw Italian touches added to the players' normal costumes. Italian costumes will serve, as long as rapier and dagger go with them, and may add something to the effect of the play upon us; but Elizabethan doublet and hose will take next to nothing of it away.

The text tells us pretty plainly what music is needed. It is a consort of recorders that Paris brings with him to the wedding; and the musicians either enter with him, playing, to be stopped incontinently by the sight of the tragic group round the bed; or (this is, I think, more likely) they stay playing the bridal music without, a tragically ironical accompaniment to the lamenting over Juliet, till they are stopped and come clustering—scared, incongruous figures—into the doorway.[25]

---

24. A casual phrase, surely, which means nearer two hours than either one or three.

25. According to Q1 they were fiddlers, *i.e.* a consort of viols, so they could not enter playing. Also, viols would not be well heard through dialogue except from the musicians' gallery, so their entrance was perhaps delayed by the time it took them to finish there and descend. Q2 has the first reference to "pipes". (Had the Globe acquired another quarter in the meantime?) These could easily be heard playing "off". Q2, however, marks no entrance for them. They are there when the mourners departs; that is all. The entrance with Paris and the Friar belongs to the undated Quarto, which is of doubtful authority.

Faith, we may put up our pipes and be gone

says the leader, when the mourners depart (all but the Nurse, who needs a line or two to speak while she draws the inner-stage curtains), leaving them alone.

The recorders could play for the dance at Capulet's too. But a consort of viols is perhaps likelier here, for there is dialogue throughout the music, and one does not speak through wood-wind with impunity. The musicians probably sat in their gallery.

The text itself raises many minor questions that need to be dealt with here. But no one should omit to read the first Quarto. For all its corruptions, it gives us now and then a vivid picture of a performance Shakespeare himself must presumably have supervised. It may not be much to know that Juliet entered *somewhat fast* and embraced Romeo;[26] that when Romeo offers to stab himself the Nurse snatches *the dagger away*; that (but this point we have remarked as important) at one juncture *Paris offers to goe in and Capolet calls him againe*; that they cast rosemary on the Juliet they think dead; and that Paris comes with his page to the tomb bringing flowers and *sweete water* with him too. But Shakespeare's stage directions are rareties indeed; and these and other such small touches give life to the rudimentary text, and an actuality to the play that scrupulous editing seems, somehow, to reform altogether.

Not but that the text has needed editing enough; and there are puzzles, such as the notorious "runaway's eyes" (twenty-eight pages devoted to it in the Furness Variorum!), yet unsolved. But few, if any, of them are of dramatic moment; and there is amply varied authority to bow to. The producer has his own few problems to face. There is the minor one of indecency. One or two of Mercutio's jokes are too outrageous for modern public usage; they will create discomfort among a mixed audience instead of laughter. But this full-blooded sensuality is (as we have seen) set very purposefully against Romeo's romantic idealism, and the balance and contrast must not be destroyed. A Mercutio

---

26. But this scene was badly muddled, either by the reporter of these performances, or the actors, or by somebody. For further discussion of the point, see p. 88, note 37.

who lets his mouth be stopped by a prim Benvolio each time he launches on a smutty joke will be a cowed, a "calm, dishonourable, vile" Mercutio indeed.

But a producer is tempted to far more cutting than this, and most producers fall. The play as commonly presented to us starts fairly true to Shakespeare, a troublesome passage suppressed here and there; but, as it advances, more and more of the text disappears, till the going becomes hopskip-and-jump, and "Selections from the tragedy of Romeo and Juliet" would be a truer title for it. This will not do. The construction, very naturally, does not show the skill of Shakespeare's maturity, nor does every character stand consistent and foursquare; the writing runs to extravagant rhetoric and often to redundancy. But his chosen method of close consecutive narrative will be lamed by mutilation; and rhetoric and redundancy, the violence, the absurdities even, are the medium in which the characters are quite intentionally painted. To omit the final scurry of Montagues and Capulets and citizens of Verona to the tomb and the Friar's redundant story for the sake of finishing upon the more poignant note of Juliet's death is, as we have seen, to falsify Shakespeare's whole intention; and to omit the sequel to the drinking of the potion is as bad and worse! Restoring the play to its own sort of stage will serve to curb these follies, at least.

The verbiage and its eccentricities—as they sound to our modern incurious ears—seem, at first blush, harder to compass. No producer need be pedantic; it is his business to gain an effect, not to prejudice it. But much that strikes one as strange in print, that may jar under the repetition and cold-blooded analysis of rehearsals, will pass and make its own effect in the rush of performance. The cutting of a speech or two from a scene is like the removal of a few bricks from a wall; it may be a harmless operation and it may not. The structure may stand up as strongly with the hole in it, or it may sag, or come tumbling altogether. The antiphonal mourning over Juliet is crude, doubtless, and one is tempted to get rid of it, or at least to modify it. Do so, and what becomes of the calming effect of Friar Laurence's long speeches? There will be nothing for him to calm. Cut this too, and Capulet will have to turn without rhyme or reason from distracted grief to dignified resignation, while the others the Friar included, stand like foolish lay figures.

To protest against the omission of the—to us—incongruous pun which bisects Romeo's passionate outburst, his

> This may flies do, when I from this must fly...

would be pedantry. The play will not be the worse for its loss; the only question is whether it is worth omitting. But to shirk Juliet's delirium of puns upon "Ay" and "I" and "eye" is to lower the scene's temperature and flatten it out when Shakespeare has planned to lift it, by these very means, to a sudden height of intoxicated excitement, giving us a first and memorable taste of the Juliet of quick despair, who later, in a flash of resolution, will sheath Romeo's dagger in her heart.

There is no more dangerous weapon than the blue pencil.

The Characters

This is a tragedy of youth, as youth sees it, and age is not let play a very distinguished part. Friar Laurence is sympathetic, but he is compact of maxims, of pedagogic kindness; he is just such a picture of an old man as a young man draws, all unavailing wisdom. There is no more life in the character than the story asks and gives; but Shakespeare palliates this dramatic weakness by keeping him shadowed in his cell, a ghostly confessor, a refuge for Romeo, Paris and Juliet alike, existing—as in their youthful egoism we may be sure they thought—in their interests alone.

It is noteworthy what an arbitrary line is drawn between youth and age; arbitrary, but at times uncertain. Capulet and Montague are conventionally "old", though their children are young enough for them not to have passed forty. Capulet gives some excuse for this by saying of Juliet that

> The earth hath swallowed all my hopes but she...

So we may surmise, if we will, a cluster of sons killed in the vendetta, or that sad little Elizabethan procession of infant effigies to be carved in time on his tomb. But Lady Capulet passes from saying that she was but fourteen herself at Juliet's birth fourteen years ago to telling us in the end that

> This sight of death is as a bell
> That warns my old age to a sepulchre.[27]

And the Nurse is old, though not fourteen years ago she had a child of her own and was suckling Juliet. It is futile trying to resolve these anomalies. Shakespeare wants a sharp conflict set between youth and age; he emphasizes every aspect of it, and treat time of life much as he treat time of day-for effect.

THE NURSE

The Nurse, whatever her age, is a triumphant and complete achievement. She stands foursquare, and lives and breathes in her own right from the moment she appears, from that very first

> Now, by my maidenhead at twelve year old,
> I bade her come.

Shakespeare has had her pent up in his imagination; and out she gushes. He will give us nothing completer till he gives us Falstaff. We mark his confident, delighted knowledge of her by the prompt digression into which he lets her launch; the story may wait. It is not a set piece of firework such as Mercutio will touch off in honour of Queen Mab. The matter of it flows spontaneously into verse, the phrases are hers and hers alone, character unfolds with each phrase. You may, indeed, take any sentence the Nurse speaks throughout the play, and only she could speak it. Moreover, it will have no trace of the convention to which Shakespeare himself is still tied (into which he forces, to some extent, every other character), unless we find her burlesquing it. But the good Angelica—which we at last discover to be her perfect name—needs no critical expanding, she expounds herself on all occasions; nor explanation, for she is plain as day-light; nor analysis, lest it lead to excuse; and she stays blissfully unregenerate. No one can fail to act her well that can speak her lines. Yet they are so supercharged with life that they will accommodate the larger acting—which is the revelation of a personality in terms of a part—and to the full; and it may be

---

27. In her speech to Juliet "a" mother has been read for "your" mother; but without any warrant.

as rich a personality as can be found. She is in everhting inevitable: from her

My fan, Peter

when she means to play the discreet lady with those gay young sparks, to that all unexpected

Faith, here 'tis; Romeo
Is banished; and all the world to nothing,
That he dares ne'er come back to challenge you;
Or if he do, it needs must be by stealth.
Then, since the case so stands as now it doth,
I think it best you married with the country

—horrifyingly unexpected to Juliet; but to us, the moment she has said it, the inevitable thing for her to say.

This last turn, that seems to casually made, is the stroke that completes the character. Till now we have taken her—the "good, sweet Nurse"—just as casually, amused by each comicality as it came; for so we do take the folk that amuse us. But with this everything about her falls into perspective, her funniments, her endearments, her grossness, her good nature; upon the instant, they all find their places in the finished picture. And for a last enrichment, candidly welling from the lewd soul of her, comes

O, he's a lovely gentleman;
Romeo's dishclout to him; an eagle, Madam,
Hath not so green, so quick, so fair an eye
As Paris hath. Beshrew my very heart,
I think you are happy in this second match,
For it excels your first; or if it did not,
Your first is dead, or 'twere as good he were
As living hence and you no use of him.

Weigh the effect made upon Juliet, fresh from the sacrament of love and the bitterness of parting, by the last fifteen words of that.

Speak'st thou from thy heart?
And from my soul too,
Or else beshrew them both.
Amen!

It is gathered into the full-fraught "Amen". But best of all, perhaps, is the old bawd's utter unconsiousness of having said anything out of the way. And when she finds her lamb, her ladybird, returning from shrift with merry look—too merry!—how should she suppose she has not given her the wholesomest advice in the world?

We see her obliviously bustling through the night's preparations for this new wedding. We hear her—incredibly!—start to stir Juliet from her sleep with the same coarse wit that had served to deepen the girl's blushes for Romeo's coming near. We leave her blubbering grotesquely over the body she had been happy to deliver to a baser martyrdom. Shakespeare lets her pass from the play without comment. Is any needed?[28]

CAPULET

Capulet, again, is a young man's old man. But he is more opulently done than the Friar, if he has not the flesh, blood, bones and all of the good Angelica. He suffers more than any other character in the play by its customary multilations; for these leave him a mere domestic tyrant, and Shakespeare does not. With his benevolent airs, self-conscious hilarity, childish ill-temper, he is that yet commoner type, the petted and spoiled husband and father and head of the house; and the study of him might be more effective if it were not strung out through the play, and so intermittently touched in. But he is planned consistently-with all his inconsistencies—from the beginning.

The flavour of gratified vanity in

> But Montagu is bound as well as I
> In penalty alike...

puts us at once upon easy terms with him. And Shakespeare hardly wrote,

> But woo her, gentle Paris, get her heart,
> My will to her consent is but a part...

---

28. Unless it be for Juliet's youthful, ruthless
Ancient damnation! O most wicked fiend!...

without having

> An you be mine, I'll give you to my friend;
> An you be not, hang, beg, starve, die in the streets...

in his mind already. Our next sight of him gives us the breeze with Tybalt, the chop and change of

> Well said, my hearts! You are a princox; go:
> Be quiet, or—More light, more light!—For shame!
> I'll make you quiet.—What, cheerly, my hearts!

This is Capulet at home, a familiar figure in many a home; the complete gentleman, the genial host, the kindliest of men—as long as no one crosses him.

Old as he is, he was ready enough to take part in the earlier brawl; but we note that he stands silent before Tybalt's body, and Lady Capulet is left to cry out for revenge. He did not the less love Tybalt dearly because he can turn promptly from the thought of him to Juliet's marriage to Paris, and change his decorous resolve to

> keep no great ado; a friend or two;
> For, hark you, Tybalt being slain so late,
> It may be thought we held him carelessly,
> Being our kinsman, if we revel much

into

> Sirrah, go hire me twenty cunning cooks.

He is incorrigibly hospitable, that is one thing. For another, it is obviously a wise move, Capulets and Montagues both being now in worse odour than ever in Verona, to marry Juliet as soon as may be to this kinsman of the Prince. And except for the haste of it (nor would even that greatly astonish them) his

> Sir Paris, I will make a despearate tender
> Of my child's love. I think she will be ruled
> In all respects by me; nay, more, I doubt it not

would not seem to an Elizabethan audience very unusual. His vituperative raging aginst the obstinate girl does bring his wife and the Nurse to her rescue.

> Out, you green-sickness carrion! out, you baggage!
> You tallow face!

—moves even Lady Capulet to protest. But he is merely raging; and parents of the day, finding their fingers itch to chastise young ladies of riper years than Juliet, did not always let them itch in vain. For a thrashing then and there ample precedent could be cited. And an hour or two later he is quite good-tempered again.

> How now, my headstrong! where have you been gadding? he hails her.

He is not insincere, as he is not undignified, in his heart-broken outcry at her supposed death, if we may divine Shakespeare's intention through a crudely written scene. And he stands, dignified and magnanimous in his sorrow, at the last. It is a partial picture of man, no doubt, ill-emphasized at times, and at times crippled by convention; but of a most recognizable man, and never untrue. Note lastly that it is the portrait of a very English old gentleman.[29] When did the phlegmatic Englishman—or the legend of him—come into fashion as the type of his kind?

THE MINOR CHARACTERS; AND MERCUTIO

The play has its full share of merely conventional figures, from the Prince to Peter, Abram and his fellows, to Balthasar and Paris' page; and they must be treated for what they are. Lady Capulet is sketchily uncertain. Benvolio is negative enough, confidant to Romeo, foil to Mercuito . But there are such men; and Shakespeare endows him with a kindly patience, sharpens his wit every now a again to a mild irony, gives him a steady consitency that rounds him to something more than a shadow.

Tybalt we must see somewhat through Mercutio's eyes. Pretty obviously we are meant to; and the actor must take the hint, nor make him a mere blusterer, but something at least of a

---

29. But *not* (to compare his position to Capulet's in Verona) of an English nobleman; of a prosperous English merchant, rather. See Miss St. Clare Byrne's chapter on "The Social Background" in *A Companion to Shakespearian Studies.*

> courageous captain of compliments...the very butcher of a silk button, a duellist, a duellist; a gentleman of the very first house, of the first and second cause.

He need not, however, place him irretrievably among the

> antic, lisping, affecting fantasticoes, these new tuners of accents...these fashion-mongers, these *pardonnezmois*...

He may reasonably discount a little Mercutio's John Bull prejudices.

For Mercutio, when Shakespeare finally makes up his mind about him, is in temperament very much the young John Bull of his time; and as different from the stocky, stolid John Bull of our later picturing as Capulet from the conventional heavy father. There can be, a course, no epitomizing of a race in any one figure. But the dominant qualities of an age are apt to set in a pattern, which will last in literature, though outmoded, till another replaces it.

We learn little about Mercutio as he goes racketing to Capulet's supper, except that John Bull is often a poetic sort of fellow, or as he returns, unless it be that a man may like smut and fairy tales too. But he is still in the toils of conventional versifying, and a victim besides, probably, to his author's uncertainty about him. The authentic Mercutio only springs into life with

> Where the devil should this Romeo be? Came he not home to-night?

when he springs to life indeed. From now on he abounds in his own sense, and we can put him to the test the Nurse abides by; not a thing that he says could anyone else say. He asks a little exposition, he is what he is with perfect clarity; the more so probably because he is wholly Shakespeare's creation, his namesake in Brooke's poem giving no hint of him. And (as with the Nurse) we could transport this authentic Mercutio into the maturest of the plays and he would fall into place there, nor would he be out of place on any stage, in any fiction.

A wholesome self-sufficiency is his cradinal quality; so he suitable finds place among neither Capulets nor Montagues.

Shakespeare endows him, we saw, with a jolly sensuality for a set off to Remeo's romancings; and, by a later, significant touch, adds to the contrast. When their battle of wits is ending—a breathless bandying of words that is like a sharp set at tennis—suddenly, it would seem, he throws an affectionate arm round the younger man's shoulder.[30]

> Why, is not this better now than groaning for love? Now art thou sociable now art thou Romeo, now art thou what thou art...

Mercutio's creed in a careless sentence! At all costs be the thing you are. The more his—and the more John Bullish—that we find it dropped casually amid a whirl of chaff and never touched on again! Here is the man. no wistful ideals for him; but life as it comes and death when it comes. A man of soundest common sense surely; the complete realist, the egoist justified. But by the day's end he has gone to his death in a cause not his own, upon pure impulse and something very like principle. There is no inconsistency in this; such vital natures must range between extremes.

> Rightly to be great
> Is not to stir without great argument,
> But greatly to find quarrel in a staw,
> When honour's at the stake.

That is a later voice, troublously questioning. Mercutio pretends neither to greatness nor philosophy. When the moment comes, it is not his own honour that is at stake; but such calm, dishonourable, vile submission is more than flesh and blood can bear. That the Mercutios of the world quarrel on principle they would hate to be told. Quarrel with a man for cracking nuts, having no other reason but because one has hazel eyes; quarrel, with your life in your hand, for quarrelling's sake, since quarrelling and fighting are a part of life, and the appetitie for them human nature. Mercutio fights Tybalt because he feels he must, because

30. We are not definitely told so, but certainly Mercutio seems a little the older of the two; and here again he is exempt from that other party-division into young and old.

he cannot stand the fellow's airs moment longer. He'll put him in his place, if no one else will. He fights without malice, not in anger even, and for no advantage. He fights because he is what he is, to testify to this simple unconscious faith, and goes in with good honest cut and thrust. But *alla stoccata* carries it away; and he, the perfect realist, the egoist complete, dies for an ideal. Extremes have met.

No regrets though; nor any hypocrisy of resignation for him! He has been beaten by the thing he despised, and is as roubustly angry about it as if he had years to live in which to get his own back.

> Zounds! a dog, a rat, a mouse, a cat, to scratch a man to death! A braggart, a rogue, a villain that fights by the book of arithmetic!

He is brutally downright with Romeo:

> Why the devil came you between us? I was hurt under your arm.[31]

and, after that, says no more to him, ignores the pitifully futile

> I thought all for the best

dies with his teeth set, impenitently himself to the last.

ROMEO

We have Romeo and Juliet themselves left to consider; the boy and girl—they are no more—caught with their love as in a vice between the hatreds of their houses, to be crushed to death there.

Romeo has been called an early study for Hamlet. It is true enough to be misleading. The many ideas that go to make up Hamlet will have seeded themselves from time to time in Shakespeare's imagination, sprouting a little, their full fruition delayed till the dominant idea ripened. We can find traits of Hamlet in Romeo, in Richard II, in Jaques, in less likely habitations. But Romeo is not a younger Hamlet in love, though

31. All the technical talk of swordplay must, of course, have been a dozen times livelier to the Elizabethans than it ever can be to us.

Hamlet in love may seem a disillusioned Romeo. The very likeness, moreover, is largely superficial, is a common likeness to many young men, who take life desperately seriously, some with reason, some without. The study of him is not plain sailing. If Hamlet's melancholy is of the soul, Romeo's was something of a pose; and there is Shakespeare's own present convention to account for, of word-spinning and thought-spinning, in which he cast much of the play, through which he broke more and more while he wrote it; there are besides, the abundant remains of Brooke's Romeus. Romeo is in the making till the end; and he is made by fits and starts. Significiant moments reveal him; but, looking back, one perceives screeds of the inessential, more heat than light in them. The actor's first task will be to distinguish between the significant and the passingly effective, and his last, as he plays the part, to adjust and reconcile the two.

Decorative method allowed for, the Romeo of

> Why then, O brawling love! O loving hate!
> O anything, of nothing first create!
> O heavy lightness! serious vanity!
> Misshapen chaos of well-seeming forms!
> Feather of lead, bright smoke, cold fire, sick health!
> Still-waking sleep, that is not what it is!...

pictures an actual Romeo truly enough; and, if it seems to over-colour him, why this Romeo was busy at the moment over-colouring himself. Yet amid all the phrase-mongering we may detect a phrase or two telling of a deeper misprision than the obduracy of Rosaline accounts for. The inconsequent

> Show me a mistress that is passing fair,
> What doth her beauty serve but as a note
> Where I may read who passed that passing fair?

is very boyish cynicism, but it marks the unhappy nature. And Rosaline herself was a Capulet, it seems (in that camp, at any rate); so, had she smiled on him, his stars would still have been crossed. He is posing to himself certainly, more in love with love than with Rosaline, posing to his family and friends, and not at all displeased by their concern. But beneath all this, the mind that, as he passes with the Maskers and their festive drum to Capulet's feast,

> misgives
> Some consequence, yet hanging in the stars...

shows the peculiar clarity which gives quality to a man, marks him off from the happy-go-lucky crowd, and will at a crisis compel him to face his fate. By a few touches, then, and in a melody of speech that is all his own, he is set before, us, a tragic figure from the first.

He sees Juliet. Shakespeare insists on the youth of the two, and more than once on their innocence, their purity—his as well as hers. It is not purposelessly that he is given the Dian-like Rosaline for a first love; nor that his first words to Juliet, as he touches her finger tips, are

> If I profane with my unworthiest hand
> This holy shrine...

nor that their first exchange is in the pretty formality of a sonnet, the kiss with which it ends half jest, half sacrament.[32] But their fate is sealed by it, there and then. They cannot speak again, for Lady Capulet calls Juliet away; and Benvolio, ever cautious, urges Romeo out of danger before there may be question of unmasking and discovery. Not before he has accepted his fate, though, and she hers—for better, for worse, without doubt, question, or hesitation! He (if we are to note niceties) accepts it even more unquestioningly than she. But her cry when she first hears his name gives us early promise of the rebellious Juliet, the more reckless and desperate of the two.

They look into the abyss and then give no more heed to it. Viriginal passion sweeps them alott and away, and to its natural goal. What should hinder? Nothing in themselves, none of the misgiving that experience brings; and for counsellors they have Nurse and Friar, the conscienceless, he as little wordly as they. Juliet in no questioner, and Romeo's self-scrutinies are over.

---

32. Elizabethan kisses were given and taken with greater freedom and publicity and less significance than Victorian kisses, at any rate, were. But was not the kiss of greeting (which Erasmus found so pleasant) oftenest a kiss on the cheek? Romeo kisses Juliet on the lips.

The balcony-scene is like the singing of two birds; and its technical achievement lies in the sustaining at such length—with no story to tell, no enlivening clash of character—of those simple antiphonies of joy.

Rosaline's adorer, aping disillusioned age, is hardly to be recognized in the boyishly, childishly happy Romeo that rushes to the Friar's cell. From there he goes to encounter Mercutio, still overflowing with spirits, apt for a bout of nonsense, victorious in it, too. From this and the meeting with the Nurse, back to the cell, to juliet and the joining of their hands!

Note that the marriage and its consummation are quite simply thought of as one, by them and by the Friar. And fate accepts Romeo' challenge betimes.

> Do thou but close our hands with holy words,
> Then love devouring death do what he dare,
> It is enough I may but call her mine.

It is of the essence of the tragedy that, for all their passionate, haste, the blow should fall upon their happiness before it is complete, that they must consummate their marriage in sorrow. And, in a sense, it is Romeo's ecstatic happiness that helps precipitate the blow. It lets him ignore Tybalt's insult:

> O sweet Juliet,
> Thy beauty hath made me effeminate,
> And in my temper softened valour's steel.

But, for all that, it has fired him to such manliness that he cannot endure the shame put upon him by Mercutio's death. Nothing is left now of the young Romeo, lovesick for Rosaline, and so disdainful of the family feud. His sudden hardihood is the complement to his chaffing high spirits of a few hours earlier; even as the girm

> This day's black fate on more days doth depends;
> This but begins the woe others must end

makes a counterpart to his confident challenge to fate to give him Juliet and do its worst after. He must seem of a higher stature as he stands over Tybalt's body, stern, fated and passive to the next Capulet sword that offers, did not Benvolio force him away.

The hysterics of the next scene with the Friar, when he hears of his banishment, may seem as retrograde in character as they certainly are in dramatic method; but Shakespeare has taken the episode almost intact—and at one point all but word for word—from Brooke. And it does attune us, as we noted, to the fortuitous disasters of the story. Then the tragic parting of the two echoes the happy wooing of the first balcony-scene; and later in Mantua we find Shakespeare's Romeo, come to his full height.

Euphuism has all but vanished from the writing now. We have instead the dynamic phrase that can convey so much more than its plain meaning, can sum up in simplicty a ferment of emotion and thought.

> Is it even so? Then I defy you, stars!

is his stark comment on the news of Juliet's death; but what could be more eloquent of the spirit struck dead by it? He knows in a flash what he means to do. We are not told; Balthasar is to hire horses, that is all. Then, when he is alone:

> Well, Juliet, I will lie with thee to-night.

And what better epitome of the love in death, which is all that is left them![33]

There follows the scene with the apothecary; its skeleton Brooke's, its clothing Shakespeare's, who employs it, not so much for the story's sake, as to give us, in repose, a picture of the Romeo his imagination has matured.

> How oft, when men are at the point of death,
> Have they been merry! which their keepers call
> A lightning before death...

he lets him say later. He does not make him merry; but he gives him here that strange sharp clarity of eye and mind which comes to a doomed man, a regard for little things when his own end

33. This whole passage is also notable in that it calls for sheer acting, for the expression of emotion without the aid of rhetoric. This demand was a comparatively new thing when the play was written. Its fulfilment will have been one of the factors in the great success won.

means little to him. He brings him to a view of life far removed from that first boyish, selfish petulance, to a scornful contemplation of what men come to, who will not dare to throw with fate for happiness, and be content to lose rather than be denied. As he watches the apothecary fumble for the forbidden poison:

> Art thou so bare, and full of wretchedness,
> And fearest to die?...

But for him it is:

> Come, cordial and not poison, go with me
> To Juliet's grave, for there must I use thee.

Life has broken him and he is turn breaks all compact with live. If Balthasar dares to spy into the tomb his blood be on his head. He knows that he sins in killing himself: very well, he will sin. He implores Paris not to provoke him; but, provoked, he slaughters him savagely. At last he is alone with his dead.

At this juncture we lose much by our illegitimate knowledge of the story's end, and the actor of Romeo, presuming on it, usually make matters worse. He apostrophizes Paris and Tybalt and Juliet at his leisure. But the dramatic effect here lies in the chance that at any minute, as we legitimately known, Juliet may wake or Friar Laurence come; and it is Romeo's haste—of a piece with the rest of his rashness—which precipitates the final tragedy. Shakespeare has provided, in the speech to the dead Juliet, just enough delay to stimulate suspense, but it must appear only as the last convulsive checking of a headlong purpose. He has added a last touch of bitter irony in letting Romeo guess at the truth that would have saved him, and her, and never guess that he guesses it.

> O my love! my wife!
> Death, that hath sucked the honey of thy breath,
> Hath had no power yet upon thy beauty:
> Thou art not conquered; beauty's enisgn yet
> Is crimson in thy lips and in thy cheeks,
> And death's pale flag is not advanced there...

After his glance at the dead Tybalt he turns to her again, obscurely marvelling:

Ah, dear Juliet,
Why art thou yet so fair?...

And it is upon a sardonic echo of the eloquence to which his love's first happiness lifted him that he ends. Then it was

I am no pilot, yet, wert thou as far
As that far shore washed by the farthest sea,
I would adventure for such merchandise.

Now, the phial in his hand, it is

Thou despearate pilot, now at once run on
The dashing rocks thy sea-sick weary bark!
Here's to my love!...

With that he drinks and dies.

From the beginning so clearly imagined, passionately realized in the writing, deeply felt at the end; this Romeo, when he had achieved him, must have stood to Shakespeare as an assurance that he could now mould a tragic figure strong enough to carry a whole play whenever he might want to.

JULIET

The first thing to mark about Juliet, for everything else depends on it, is that she is, to our thinking, a child. Whether she is Shakespeare's fourteen or Brooke's sixteen makes little difference; she is meant to be just about as young as she can be; and her actual age is trebly stressed.[34] Her tragedy is a child's tragedy; half its poignancy would be gone otherwise. Her bold innocence is a child's, her simple trust in her nurse; her passionate rage at the news of Tybalt's death is easily pardonable in a child, her terrors when she takes the potion are doubly dreadful as childish terrors. The cant saying that no actress can play Juliet

34. It has been held that Shakespeare may have taken her age from a later edition of Brooke's poem in which the XVI had perhaps been transformed by the printer into XIV; also that he may have reduced her age to suit the very youthful appearance of some boy-actress. This is at any rate unlikely; fourteen is not distinguishable from sixteen on the stage. Moreover, he has other almost as youthful heroines: Miranda is fifteen, Perdita sixteen.

till she is too old to look her should therefore go the way of all parroted nonsense. A Juliet must have both the look and the spirit of a girl of from fourteen to sixteen, and any further sophistication—or, worse, a mature assumption of innocence—will be the part's ruin. One must not compare her, either, to the modern girl approaching independence, knowing enough to think she knows more, ready to disbelieve half she is told. Life to Juliet, as she glimpsed it around her, was half jungle in its savagery, half fairy tale; and its rarer gifts were fever to the blood. A most precocious young woman from our point of view, no doubt; but the narrower and intenser life of her time ripened emotion early.

Not that there is anything of the budding sensualist in her;for to be sensual is to be sluggish, not fevered. Her passion for Romeo is ruled by imagination. And were this not the true reading of it, Shakespeare would have been all but compelled, one may say, to make it so; doubly compelled. Of what avail else would be his poetry, and through what other medium could a boy-actress realize the part? The beauty of the girl's story, and its agonies too, have imagination for their fount. The height of her joy (anticipated, never realized) is reached in the imaginative ecstasy of

> Gallop apace, you fiery-footed steeds...

And she suffers to the full, even in thinking of them, all the shame of the marriage to Paris and the terrors of the vault.

Her quick florescence into womanhood is the more vivid for its quiet prelude; for the obedient

> Madam, I am here.
> What is your will?

when she first appears, for the listening to the Nurse's chatter, the borrowed dignity with which she caps her mother's snub that ends it, the simple

> It is an honour that I dream not of

with which she responds to the hint of the great match awaiting her, the listening to her mother's talk of it and the

I'll look to like, if looking liking move;
But no more deep will I endart mine eye
Than your consent gives strength to make it fly

that seal our first impression of her. Where could one find a more biddable young lady?

What could one guess, either, from her first meeting with Romeo, from the demure game of equivoque she plays; though something shows, perhaps, in the little thrust of wit-

You kiss by the book

—by which she evades the confession of a kiss returned.[35] One moment later, though, there comes the first flash of the true Juliet; a revelation to herself, is it, as to us?

My only love sprung from my only hate!...

And she stands, lost in amazement at his miracle that has been worked in her (even As Romeo will stand later lost in the horror of Tybalt's slaying), till the puzzled Nurse coaxes her away.

We next see her at her window. Yet again Shakespeare holds her silent a little, but for that one "Ay me!" to tell us that now the still depths in her are brimming; when they brim over, again it is to herself she speaks.[36] The scene is conventionalized to a degree, with its overheard soliloquies, its conceits, its lyric flow. It turns every exigency of stage and acting to account, and its very setting, which keeps the lovers apart, stimulates passionate expression and helps sustain it. It left the boy-actress in imaginative freedom; nothing asked of him that his skill could not give. But the conceits come to life and blend insensibly with the simplicites. The fanciful

Thou know'st the mask of night is on my face,
Else would a maiden blush bepaint my cheek...

flows into the frank coquetry of

O gentle Romeo,

---

35. And how admirably suited to the effective resources of the boy-actress the pretty formality of this passage is!

36. Not a sigh, this! There is nothing sentimental about Juliet.

> If thou dost love, pronounce it faithfully;
> Or if thou think'st I am too quickly won,
> I'll frown and be perverse and say thee nay,
> So thou wilt woo; but else, not for the world

and

> My bountry is an boundless as the sea,
> My love as deep; the more I give to thee,
> The more I have, for both are infinite

comes from her as naturally as the very practical

> Three words, dear Romeo, and good-night indeed.
> If that thy bent of love be honourable,
> Thy purpose marriage, send me word to-morrow...

And the scene's finest moment comes with

> JULIET: Romeo!
> ROMEP: My dear?
> JULIET: At what o'clock to-morrow
> Shall I send to thee?
> ROMEO: By the hour of nine.
> JULIET: I will not fail. 'Tis twenty years till then.
> I have forgot why I did call thee back.
> ROMEO: Let me stand here till thou remember it.
> JULIET: I shall forget, to have thee still stand there,
> Remembering how I love thy company.
> ROMEO: And I'll still stay, to have thee still forget,
> Forgetting any other home but this.

This is the commonplace made marvellous. What is it, indeed, but the well-worn comic theme of the lovers that cannot once for all say good-by and part turned to pure beauty by the alchemy of the poet? Modesty, boldness, shyness, passion, chase their way through the girl's speech; and Romeo, himself all surrender, sings to her tune. Together, but still apart, this is their one hour of happiness, and she is enskied in it, even as he sees her there.

We find her next, two scenes later, impatient for the Nurse's return with news of him; and in reckless delight and quick imagery for its expression she rivals Romeo now—the Juliet that could stand so mute! Then comes the quiet moment of the marriage.

Making her reverence to the Friar, she may seem still to be the self-contained young lady we first saw; but even in the few lines of formal speech we hear a stronger pulse-beat and a deeper tone. She stands, not timidly at all, but just a little awed upon the threshold of her womanhood.[37]

After the tragic interval that sees Mercutio and Tybalt killed we find her alone again, and again her newly franchised self, expectant of happiness, the blow that is to kill it pending. To the modern Juliet, as we have noted, this scene probably presents more difficulties than any other in the play. Victorian Juliets customarily had their drastically eased by the eliminating of

Gallop apace, you fiery-footed steeds...

(some of the finest verse in the play) on the ground—God save the mark!—of its immodesty. One hopes that the last has been heard of such nonsense. But few performances since Shakespeare's time can have given the rest of the scene, with its elaborately embroidered rhetoric intact.[38] It will all of it, needless to say, be out of place upon a realistic stage; acted by a mature, ultra-feminie Juliet it will be introlerable. But we can hardly blame Shakespeare for that. He took here full advantage of his theatre's convention. The epithalamium has no more realism about it than a song or a sonnet would have; and the verbal embroideries which follow, meant to be taken at a high pitch of emotion and at a surpirising pace, owe their existence in great part to the bravura

---

37. I make no attempt to say how and why this scene as it is in Q1 is so completely changed in Q2. But it is worth while remarking that we have far more than a rewritng of the words.

Enter Juliet somewhat fast and embraceth Romeo

says Q1; and her first word is "Romeo". In Q2, on the contrary, it is

Good even to my ghostly confessor

and there is no sure sign that she embraces Romeo at all. I think myself that she does not, that the short scene was kept formal and dignified, the lovers standing on either side the Friar as if they were already before the altar.

38. For whatever reason, much of this is missing from Q1.

skill of the boy-actresses who could compass such things with credit. The actress of today need not lack the skill, though the audiences may (and no great harm done) less consciously admire it; they probably will not break into applause as audiences at an opera do, as do French audiences at the declaiming of a fine passage of verse. She must think of the scene largely in terms of virtuosity; but there is far more in it, of course. It brings us the first clash of Montague and Capulet in other and sharper terms than swordplay, in the heart agonies of this child, as she is torn, now one way, now the other:

> NURSE: Will you speak well of him that kill'd your cousin?
>
> JULIET: Shall I speak ill of him that is my husband?

The tragedy is summed up for the first time in that.

Till now, we have seen Juliet at intervals; but with Romeo's farewell to her and his passing to Mantua she becomes for a space the sole centre of the play, while misfortune batters at her. In her helpless courage is the pathos, in her resolve from the first to kill herself sooner than yield—she is fourteen!—is the high heroism of the struggle. She is a child in the world's ways still. But she faces her mother when the marriage to Paris is broached, dignified and determined—and takes that good lady very much aback. The next moment, though, she has broken into a storm of impotent tears, which puzzle her father, but move him not at all, except to match and outdo her in storming. Her mather repulses her, her nurse betrays her; the trap is closing on her. She flies to the Friar. There is Paris himself; and for appearance sake she must stop and parley with him while he claims her with calm assurance as his wife, must let him kiss her, even! Back she flies again from the shaken old man, armed with the only aid he can give her, one little less desperate than the dagger that never leaves her. The time is so short; and, in her distraction—playing the hypocrite as she must, and overplayingit—she even contrives to make it shorter. It escapes her quite that she will now—and fatally—not be following the

Friar's directions.[39] She easily hoodwinks her mother and her nurse; then, left alone, outfacing terror, she drinks the potion.

She wakes in the vault, hopefully, happily:

> O comfortable friar, where is my lord?
> I do remember well where I should be,
> And there I am, Where is my Romeo?

to have for all answer,

> Thy husband in thy bosom there lies dead

and to see Friar Laurence—even he!—turn and desert her. Should we wonder at the scorn sounded in that

> Go, get thee hence, for I will not away.

Romeo's dagger is all she has left.

The simplest reason for Juliet's leave-taking of life being short is that Romeo's has been long. But, theatrical effect apart, the sudden brutal blow by which her childish faith in the "comfortable Friar" is shattered, and her unquestioning choice of death, make a fitting end to the despearate confidence of her rush to escape from what is worse than death to her. In the unreflecting haste of it all lies her peculiar tragedy. One day a child, and the next a woman! But she has not grown older as Romeo has, nor risen to an impersonal dignity of sorrow. Shakespeare's women do not, for obvious reasons, so develop. They are vehicles of life, not of philosophy. Here is life cut short in its brightness; and it is cruel business, this slaughter of a child betrayed.

---

39. "Tomorrow night" she was to take the potion; but the wedding is suddenly put forward by a day. Juliet does not seem to notice what this may involve, and we may not either. Quite possibly Shakespeare didn't. At any rate he makes no use of the mistake, but brings in Friar John's mishap instead. The immediate effect of the extra haste was all be cared about.

The Merchant of Venice

The Mercahnt of Venice is a fairy tale. There is no more reality in Shylock's bond and the Lord of Belmont's will than in Jack and the Beanstalk.

Shakespeare, it is true, did not leave the fables as he found them. This would not have done; things that pass muster on the printed page may become quite incredible when acted by human being, and the unlikelier the story, the likelier must the mechanism of its acting be made. besides, when his own creative impuse was quickened, he could not help giving life to a character; he could no more help it than the sun can help shining. So Shylock s real, while his story remains fabulous; and Portia and Bassanio become human, though, truly, they never quite emerge from the enchanted thicket of fancy into the common light of day. Aesthetic logic may demand that a story and its characters should move consistently upon one plane or another, be it fantastic or real. But Shakespeare's practical business, once he had chosen these two stories for his play, was simply so to charge them with humanity that they did not betray belief in the human beings presenting them, yet not so uncompromisingly that the stories themselves became ridiculous.

What the producer of the play must first set himself to ascertain is the way in which he did this, the nice course that—by reason or instinct—he steered. Find it and follow it, and there need be no running on the rocks. But logic may land us anywhere. It can turn Bassanio into a heartless adventurer. Test the clock of the action by Greenwich time, it will either be going too fast or too slow. And as to Portia's disguise and Bellario's law, would the village policeman be taken in by either? But the actor will find that he simply cannot play Bassanio as a humbug, for Shakespeare does not mean him to. Portias and Nerissas have been eclipsed by wigs and spectacles. This is senseless tomfoolery; but how make a wiseacre producer see that if he does not already know? And if, while Shylock stands with his knife ready and Antonio with his bared breast, the wise young judge lifting a magical finger between them, we sit questioning Bellario's law—why, no one concenrned, actors or audience, is for this fairyland, that is clear.

The Merchant of Venice is the simplest of plays, so long as we do not bedevil it with sophistries. Further, it is—for what it is!—as smoothly and completely successful, its means being as well fitted to its end, as anything Shakespeare wrote. He was happy in his choice of the Portia story; his verse, which has lost glitter to gain a mellower beauty and an easier flow, is now well attuned to such romance. The story of Shylock's bond is good contrast and complement both; and he can now project character upon the stage, uncompromising and complete. Yet this Shylock does not overwhelm the play, as at a later birth he might well have done—it is a near thing, though! Lastly, Shakespeare is now enough of the skilled playwright to be able to adjust and blend the two themes with fruitful economy.

The Construction of the Play

THE PROBLEM OF "DOUBLE-TIME"

This blending of the themes would, to a modern playwright, have been the main difficulty. The two stories do not naturally march together. The forfeiture of the bond must be a matter of months; with time not only of the essence of the contract, but of the dramatic effect. But the tale of the caskets cannot be enlarged, its substance is too fragile; and a very moderate charge of emotion would explode its pretty hollowness altogether. Critics have credited Shakespeare with nice calculation and amazing subtlety in his compassing of the time-difficulty. Daniel gives us one analysis, Halpin another, Eccles a third, and Furness finds the play as good a peg for the famous Double Time theory as Wilson its inventor, found Othello. All very ingenious; but is the igenuity Shakespeare's or their own?[1] For him dramatic time was a naturally

1. If the effect is one and the same, one might think the question unimportant. But Daniel, making out his three months, is generous of "intervals", not only between acts, but between scenes; and even →

elastic affair. (It still is, though less so, for the modern playwright, whose half-hour act may commonly suggest the passing of an hour or two; this also is Double Time.) Shakespeare seems to think of it quite simply in terms of effect, as he thought of dramatic space, moving his characters hither and thither withut considering the compassing of yards or miles. The one freedom will imply and enhance the other. The dramatist working for the "realistic" stage must settle definitely where his characters are to be and keep them there till he chooses to change the scenery. Shakespeare need not; and, in fact, he never insists upon place at all, unless it suits him to; and then only to the extent that suits him.[2] In this play, for instance, where we find Shylock and Antonio will be Venice, but whereabouts in Venice is usually no matter; when it is—at Shylock's door or in court before the Duke—it will be made clear enough to us. And where Portia is, is Belmont. He treats time—and the more easily—with a like freedom, and a like aim. Three months suits for the bond; but once he has pouched the money Bassanio must be off to Belmont, and his calendar, attuned to his mood, at once starts to run by hours only. The wind serves, and he sails that very night, and there is no delay at Belmont. Portia would detain him some month or two before he ventures; and what could be more convenient for a Shakespeare bent on synchronizing the two stories? For that matter, he could have place Belmont a few hundred miles off, and let the coming and going eke out the time. Did the problem as a whole ever even occur to him? If it did, he dismissed it as of no consequence. What he does is to set each story going according to its nature; then he punctuates them, so to speak, for effect. By the clock they are not even consistent in themselves, far less with each other. But we should pay just the sort of attention to these months, days or hours that we do, in another connection, to the commas and semicolons elucidating a sentence. They give us, and are meant

→ Furness, on his subtler scent, can say, "One is always conscious that between the acts of a play a certain space of time elapses. To convey this impression is one of the purposes for which a drama is divided into acts". Therefore an important and a much-disputed question is involved—and begged. And, in practice, the pernicious hanging-up of performances by these pauses in encouraged, to which scenery and its shifting is already a sufficient temptation.

2. See also Preface to *Antony and Cleopatra*.

to, simply a sense of time and its exactions. It is the more easily done because our own sense of time in daily life is far from consistent. Time flies when we are happy, and drags in anxiety, as poets never tire of reminding us. Shakespeare's own reflections on the phenomenon run to half a column of the concordance, and he turns it quite naturally to dramatic account.

THE TRUE PROBLEM

How to blend two such disparate themes into a dramatically organic whole; that was his real problem. The stories, linked in the first scene, will, of themselves, soon part company. Shakespeare has to run them neck and neck till he is ready to join them again in the scene of the trial. But the difficulty is less that they will not match each other by the clock than that their whole gait so differs, their very nature. How is the flimsy theme of the caskets to be kept in countenance beside its grimly powerful rival? You cannot, as we said, elaborate the story, or charge it with emotion; that would invite disaster. Imagine a Portia seriously alarmed by the prospect of an Aragon or a Morocco for husband. What sort of barrier, on the other hand, would the caskets be to a flesh-and-blood hero and heroine fallen in love? Would a Romeo or Rosalind give a snap of the finger for them? As it is, the very sight of Bassanio prompts Portia to rebellion; and Shakespeare can only allow his lovers a few lines of talk together, and that in company, dare only colour the fairy tale with a rhetorically passionate phrase or so before the choice is made and the caskets can be forgotten—as they are!—altogether. Nor does anything in the play show the artist's supreme tact in knowing what *not* to do better than this?

But you cannot neglect the Portia story either, or our interest in her may cool. Besides, this antiphony of high romance and rasping hate enhances the effect of both. A contrasting of subjects, scene by scene, is a trick (in no depreciatory sense) of Shakespeare's earliest stagecraft and he never lost his liking for it.[3] Then if the casket-theme cannot be neglected, but cannot be elaborated, it must somehow be drawn out, it peculiar character sustained, its interest husbanded while its consummation is delayed.

---

3. It is, one may say, a commonplace of stagecraft, Elizabethan or other; but none, the less worthy for that.

Shakespeare goes straightforwardly enough to work. He puts just as little as may be into Portia's first scene; but for the one sounding of Bassanio's name there would be only the inevitable tale of the caskets told in tripping prose and the conventional joking upon the suitors. Portia and Nerissa, however, seen for the first time in the flesh, give it sufficient, life, and that "Bassanio" one vivid spark more. Later in due course, come Morocco's choice of the gold casket and Aragon's of the silver. We remark that Morocco is allotted two scenes instead of one. The reason is, probably, that Shakespeare has now enriched himself with the Lorenzo-Jessica story (not to mention the episode of the Gobbos, father and son), and, with this extra weight in the Venetian scale of the action, is put to it to maintain the balance. He could, of course, finish with both Morocco and Aragon earlier and give Bassanio two scenes instead of one.[4] and if a romantic hero could not well wait till after dinner to make his choice, as Morocco does, Solanio's arrival with the ill news of Antonio could easily have been kept for the later scene. But this will not do either—most characteristically will not do for Shakespeare. He has held his lovers apart, since the air of the Belmont of the caskets is too rarefied for flesh and blood to breathe. And Portia herself has been spellbound; we have only had jaunty little Nerissa to prophesy that love (by the pious previous of the late lord) would somehow find out the way.[5] But once he bring them together Bassanio must break

4. And such interest as there is in Aragon's scene is now lessened, perhaps, by our knowledge that Bassanio is on his way; even more, by the talk in the scene before of Antonio's misfortune. But Shakespeare, as his wont is, plucks some little advantage from the poverty of the business by capping Aragon's vapidity with the exitement of the news of Bassanio's arrival.

5. Though there are commentators who maintain that Nerissa—even Portia, perhaps—gives Bassanio the hint to choose lead, or has it sung to him:

> Tell me, where is fancy *bred*,
> In the heart, or in the *head*?
> How begot, how *nourished*?

And if he'll only listen carefully he will note that they all rhyme with *lead*.

Shakespeare was surely of a simpler mind than this—his audiences too. And he had some slight sense of the fitness of things. Would he—how *could* he?—wind up this innocent fairy tale with such →

the spell. It is the story of the sleeping beauty and the prince in another kind; a legitimate and traditional out-come. And once Shakespeare himself has broken free of the fairy tale and brought these two to life (for Bassanio as well has been till now a little bloodless) it is not in him to let them lapse from the scene unproved,and to the full. The long restraint has left him impatient, and he must, here and now, have his dramatic fling. We need not credit—or discredit him, if you like—with much calculation of the problem. It was common prudence both to keep Belmont as constantly in our view as Venice, and the emancipating Basanio clear of it for a long as possible. And he is now in the middle of his play, rather past it, ready to link his two stories together again. He worked forthrightly; that is written plain over most of his work. Though he might now find that he had here material for two scenes, he would not return in his tracks, telescope Aragon and Morocco—and take, in fact, all the sort of trouble we, who are his critics, must take to explain what a much more compact job he could have made of it! Besides, here is his chance to uplift the two as hero and heroine, and he will not dissipate its effectiveness.

For Bassanio, as we said, has been till now only litle less bound than Portia in the fetters of a fairy tale; and later, Shylock and the bond will condemn him to protesting helplessness, and the affair of the rings to be merrily befooled.[6] The wonder indeed, is, considering the rather poor figure—painfully poor by the gospel according to Samuel Smiles—the coercion of the story makes him cut, that throughout he measures up so well to the stature of sympathetic hero. Shakespeare contrives it in two ways.

→ a slim trick? Besides, how was it to be worked; how is an audience to be let into the secret? Are they likely to tag extra rhymes to the words of a song as they listen to it? Or is Nerissa—not Portia, surely!—at some point to tip Bassanio "the wink" while he smiles knowingly back to assure her that he has"cottoned on"? Where, oh, where indeed, are such dramatic fancies bred? Not in any head that will think out the effect of their realization.

6. Little to be found in him, upon analysis, to refute the frigid verdict lately passed upon him by that distinguished and enlightened—but in this instance, surely, most mistakenly whimsical—critic, Sir Arthur Quiller-Couch, for fortune-hunter, hypocrite and worse. Is anything more certain than that Shakespeare dd not *mean* to present us with such a hero? If Sir Arthur were producing the play, one pities the actor asked to give effect to his verdict.

He endows him with very noble verse; and, whenever he can, throws into strong relief the Bassanio of his own uncovenanted imagination. He does this here. The fantasy of the caskets brought to its due crisis, charged with an emotion which blows it for a finish into thin air, he shows us Bassanio, his heart's desire won, agonized with grief and remorse at the news of Antonio's danger. Such moments do test a man and show him for what he is; and this one, set in bright light and made the scene's turning point, counts for more in the effect the character makes on us than all the gentlemanly graces of his conventional equipment. Unless the actor is much at fault, we shall hear the keynote to the true Bassanio struck in the quiet simplicity—such contrast to his rhetoric over the caskets, even though this was less mere rhetoric than Morocco's and Aragon's—of the speech which begins

> O sweet Portia,
> Here are a few of the unpleasant'st words
> That ever blotted paper!...
> Rating myself at nothing, you shall see
> How much I was a braggart. When I told you
> My state was nothing, I should then have told you
> That I was worse than nothing; for indeed
> I have engaged myself to a dear friend,
> Engaged my friend to his mere enemy,
> To feed my means...

Here speaks Shakespeare's Bassonio; and it is by this, and all that will belong to it, that he is meant to live in our minds.

Producer and actors must look carefully into the way by which in this scene the method that has served for the casket story is resolved into something better fitted to the theme of he bond (dominant from the beginning of the play, and now to absorb and transform the dedicated Portia and her fortunes). It is a change—though we must not insist on the contrast more than Shakespeare does—from dramatic convention to dramatic life. From the beginning the pluse of the scene beats more strongly; and Portia's

> I Pray you, tarry: pause a day or two
> Before you hazard; for in choosing wrong,
> I lose your company; therefore forbear awhile...

is not only deeper in feeling (there has been little or nothing to rouse her till now; she has had to be the picture of a Portia, hardly more, with a spice of wit to help her through), but how much simpler in expression! When Bassanio turns to those obsessing caskets she must lapse again for a space into fancies of his swanlike end, her eye the watery deathbed for him, into talk about Hercules and Alcides (borrowed, one fears, from Morocco), about Dardanian wives and the like—even as he will be conventionally sententious over his choice. But note how, within the convention, preparing an escape from it, emotion is roused and sustained. With the rhetoric of Portia's

Go Hercules!
Like thou, I live: with much, much more dismay
I view the fight, than thou that mak'st the fray

for a springboard, the song and its music are to stir us.

whilst Bassanio comments on the caskets to himself.

So (let the actor remember) when he does at last speak, the emotional ascent will have been half climbed for him already. And while he pays his tribute of trope and maxim, Portia, Nerissa and the rest watch him in silence, at full strain of attention, and help to keep us, too, intent. The speech itself sweeps unhinderd to its height, and the pause while the casket is unlocked is filled and enriched by the intensity of Portia's

How all the other passions fleet to air...

most cunningly contrived in meaning and melody, with its emphasis on "despair" and "ecstasy" and "excess", to hold us upwrought. The fairy tale is finally incarnate in the fantastic word-painting of the portrait and the reading of the scroll. Then, with a most delicate declension to reality, Basanio comes to face her as in a more actual world, and the curtains can be drawn upon the caskets for the last time. Observe that not for a moment has Shskespeare played his fabulous story false. He takes his theatre too seriously to go spoiling an illusion he has created. He consummates it, and turns the figures of it to fresh purpose, and they seem to suffer no change.

Throughout the scene—throughout the play, and the larger part of all Elizabethan drama for that matter—effects must be valued very much in terms of music. And, with the far adventuring of his playwriting hardly begun, Shakespeare's verse is already fairly flawless, and its manoeuvring from mood to mood masterly, if still simple. We have the royal humility of the speech in which Portia yields herself (Bassanio slips back to his metaphors for a moment after this); then, for contrast, the little interlude of Gratiano and Nerissa, with the tripping monosyllables of Gratiano's

> I wish you all the joy that you can wish;
> For I am sure you can wish none from me...

to mark the pace and the tone of it. Then follows the arrival of Antonio's messenger with Lorenzo and Jessica; done in plain, easy-moving verse that will not discount the distressed silence in which he reads the letter, nor the quiet candour of his confusion to Portia. Now comes another crescendo—two voices added to strengthen it—leading up to her generous, wide-eyed

> What sum owes he the Jew?
> Bassanio: For me, three thousand ducats.
> Portia: What, no more!
> Pay him six thousand, and deface the bond;
> Double six thousand, and then treble that...

which itself drops to the gentleness of

> Since you are dear bought I will love you dear.

Then, to strengthen the scene's ending, we have the austere prose of Antonio's letter chilling us to misgiving. And since—in stage practice, and with the prevailing key of the play's writing to consider—this will not do for an actual finish, there is a last modulation into the brisk coda of

> Since I have your good leave to go away,
> I will make haste: but till I come again,
> No bed shall e'er be guilty of my stay,
> Nor rest be interposer 'twixt us twain.

Lorenzo and Jessica make another link (though their relation to Belmont is pretty arbitrary) between the two stories. This, however, is but the secondary use of them. There must be a sense of time passing in Venice while the bond matures, yet we must have continuous action there, too, while the ritual at Belmont goes its measured way; so, as there can be little for Shylock and Antonio to do but wait, this third, minor theme is interposed. It brings fresh impetus to the action as well as new matter; and it shows us—very usefully—another and more human side of Shylock. Shakespeare does not scheme it out overcarefully. The masking and the elopement and the coming and going they involve are rather inconveniently croweded together (the pleasant episode of the Gobbos may have stolen a little necessary space); and one chapter of the story—for were we perhaps to have seen Shylock at supper with Bassanio, Lorenzo and the rest while the disguised Jessica waited on them?—was possibly crowded out altogether.

Once the fugitives, with some disregard of likelihood, have been brought to Belmont, Gobbo in attendance, Shakespeare turns them to account quite shamelessly. They play a mighty poor scene to give Portia and Nerissa time to disguise themselves as doctor and clerk.[7] They will have to play another while doctor and clerk change to Portia and Nerissa again; but for that, as if in compensation, they are to be dowered with the loveliest lines in the play.[8] With the juction of the themes in the trial-scene the constructive problem is, of course, solved. Shylock disappearing, the rest is simple.

Shakespeare's Venice

If Lorenzo and Jessica and a little poetry and the consort of music, which no well-regulated great household of his time would be without, are Shakespeare's resources (he had no other; and what better should we ask?) for the painting of the starlit garden of Belmont at the play's end, for its beginning he must show us Venice. He troubles with no verbal scene-painting here; throughout the first scene the very word is but spoken twice, and quite casually. We might be anywhere in the city, or out of it, even. Thereafter we hear of the Rialto, of a gondola, of

7. Possible extra time was needed for the shifting of the caskets and ther furniture and the setting of the chairs of state for the Duke and the Magnificoes. But is that case these last must have been very elaborate.
8. For the bearing of this upon the question of act-division, see p. 132.

the common ferry and suchlike incidentals; but of the picturesque environemnt to which modern stagins has accustomed us there is no suggestion at all. Yet he does present a Venice that lived in the Elizabethan mind, it is the Venice of his dramatic needs; a city of royal merchants trading to the gorgeous East, of Jews in their gaberdines (as rare a sight, remember, as to us a Chinese mandarin is, walking the London streets today), and of splendid gentlement rustling in silks. To the lucky young Englishman who could hope to travel there Venice stood for culture and manners and the luxury of civilization; and this—without one word of description—is how Shakespeare pictures it.

We are used nowadays to see the play begun by the entry of a depressed, sober-suited, middle-aged man and two skipping youths, who make their way with a sort of desperate merriment through such lines as the producer's blue pencil has left them, vanish shamefacedly, reappear at intervals to speak the remnant of another speech or two, and slip at last unregarded into oblivion. These are Solanio and Salarino, cursed by actors as the two worst bores in the while Shakespearean canon; not excepting, even, those other twin brethren in nonentity, Rosencrantz and Guildenstern[9] As characters, Shakespeare has certainly not been at much pains with them; they could exchange speeches and no one would be the wiser; and they move about at everybody's convenience but their own. But they have their use, and it is an important one; realize it, and there may be some credit in fulfilling it. They are there to paint Venice for us, the Venice of the magnificent young man. Bassanio embodies it also; but there are other calls on him, and he will be off to Belmont soon. So do Gratiano and Lorenzo; but they will be gone too. Solanio and Salarino will not fail us; they hoist this flag at the play's beginning and keep it bravely flying for as long as need be. When Salarino, for a beginning, addresses Antonio with

> There, where your argosies with portly sail,
> Like signiors and rich burghers on the flood,
> Or, as it were, the pageants of the sea,
> Do overpeer the petty traffickers,

---

9. But Rosencrantz and Guildenstern, as Shakespeare wrote them, are not the mere puppets that the usual mangling of the text leaves them.

> That curt'sy to them, do them reverence
> As they fly by them with their woven wings

—there should be no skipping merriment in this.

They are argosies themselves, these magnificent young men, of high-flowing speech; pageants to overpeer the callow English ruffians, to whom they are here displayed. The talk passes from spices and silks into fine classical phrases; and with what elaborate, dignified dandyism it ends!

Enter Bassanio, Lorenzo and Gartiano

SOLANIO: Here comes Bassanio, your most noble kinsman,
Gratiano, and Lorenzo. Fare you well;
We leave you now with better company.
SALARINO: I would have stayed till I had made you merry,
If worthier friends had not prevented me.
ANTONIO: Your worth is very dear in my regard.
I take it, your own business calls on you,
And you embrace the occasion to depart.
SALARINO: Good-morrow, my good lords.
BASSANIO: Good signiors both, when shall we laugh? Say, when?
You grow exceeding strange: Must it be so?
SALARINO: We'll make our leisures to attend on yours.

No apologetic gabbling here: but such a polish, polish as might have satisfied Mr. Turveydrop. Solanio—if one could distinguish between them—might cut the finer figure of the two. When the Masque is in question:

> 'Tis vile [he says], unless it may be quaintly ordered,
> And better, in my mind, not undertook.

Salarino has a cultured young gentleman's turn for classical allusion. He ranges happily from two-headed Janus and Nestor to Venus' pigeons.

But it is, as we said, when Bassanio and Gratiano and Lorenzo with his Jessica have departed, that the use these two are to the play becomes plainest. They give us the first news of Antonio's losses, and hearsay, filtering through them, keeps the disaster conveniently vague. If we saw the blow fall on Antonio, the far more dramatic scene in which Shylock is thrown from depth to heights and from heights to depth as ill news and this good news strike upon him would be left at a discount. In this scene they are most useful (if they are not made mere targets for a star actor to shoot at). For here again is Venice, in the contrast between sordid Shylock and Tubal and our mgnificent young gentlemen, superfine still of speech and manner, but not above a little Jew-baiting. They sustain that theme—and it must be sustained—till it can be fully and finally orchestrated in the trial-scene. It is a simple stagecraft which thus employs them, and their vacuity as characters inclines us to forget this, their very real utility. Forgetting it, Shakespeare's histrionic Venice is too often forgotten also.

The Characters, and the Crisis of the Action

None of the minor characters does much more than illustrate the story; at best, they illuminate with a little lively detail their own passage through it. Not the Duke, nor Morocco, Aragon, Tubal, Lorenzo, Jessica, nor the Gobbos, nor Nerissa, had much being in Shakespeare's mind, we feel, apart from the scenes they played, and the use they were to him. It is a futile, that is to say, to discuss Jessica's excuses for gilding herself with ducats when she elopes as it is to work out her intinerary via Genoa to Belmont; we might as well start writing the life-story of Mistress Margery Gobbo.

PORTIA

Shakespeare can do little enough with Portia while she is still the slave of the caskets; incidentally, the actress must resist the temptation to try and do more. She has this picture of an enchanted princess to present, verse and prose to speak perfectly, and she had better be content with that. But we feel, nevertheless (and in this, very discreetly, she may at once encourage us), that here, pent up and primed for escape, is one of that eminent succession of candid and fearless souls: Rosaline, Helena, Beatrice, Rosalind—they embodied an ideal lodged for long in Shakespeare's imagination; he gave it expression whenever he could. Once he can set his Portia free to be herself, he quickly makes up for lost time. He has need to; for from the moment of that revealing

> You see me, Lord Bassanio, where I stand...

not half the play's life is left her, and during a good part of this she must pose as the young doctor of Rome whose name is Balthasar. He does not very deliberately develop her character; he seems by now to know too much about her to need to do that. He reveals it to us mainly in little things, and lets us feel its whole happy virtue in her melody of her speech. This it is that casts its spell upon the strict court of Venice. The

> Shed thou no blood...

is an effective trick. But

> The quality of mercy is not strained;
> It droppeth as the gentle rain from heaven
> Upon the place beneath...

with its continuing beauty, gives the true Portia. To there very end she expands in her fine freedom, growing in authority and dignity, fresh touches of humour enlightening her, new traits of graciousness showing. She is a great lady in her perfect simplicity, in her ready tact (see how she keeps her guest Antonio free from the mock quarrel about the rings), and in her quite unconscious self-sufficiency (she jokes without embarrassment about taking the mythical Balthasar to her bed, but she snubs Gratiano the next minute for talking of cuckoldry, even as she snubbed Nerrisa for a very mild indelicacy—she is fond of Nerissa, but no forward waiting-woman for her!). Yet she is no more than a girl.

Here is an effect that we are always apt to miss in the acting of Shakespeare today. it is not the actress's fault that she cannot be what her predecessor, the boy-Portia, was; and she brings us compensation for losses which should leave us—if she will mitigate the losses as far as she can—gainers on the whole. But the constant play made in the Comedies upon the contrast between womanly passion or wisdom and its very virginal enshiring gives a delicacy and humour to these figures of romance which the limited resources of the boy left vivid, which the ampler endowment of the woman too often obscures. This is no paradox, but the obvious result of a practical artistry making the most of its materials. Portia does not abide in this dichotomy as fully as, for instance, Rosalind and Viola do; but Shakespeare turns it to account with her in half a hundred little ways, and to blur the effect of them is to rob her of much distinction.

The very first line she speaks, the

> By my troth, Nerissa, my little body is aweary of this great world

is likely to come from the mature actress robbed of half its point. This will not matter so much. But couple that "little body" with her self-surrender to Bassanio as

> an unlessoned girl, unschooled, unpractised;
> Happy in this, she is not yet so old
> But she may learn...

and with the mischief that hides behind the formal courtesies of the welcome to Aragon and Morocco, with the innocence of the amazed

> What no more!
> Pay him six thousand and deface the bond...

with the pretty sententiousness of her talk of herself, her

> I never did repent of doing good,
> Nor shall not now...

followed by the artless

> This comes too near the praising of myself...

and the figure built up for us of the heiress and great lady of Belmont is seen to be a mere child, too, who lived remote in her enchanted world. Set beside this the Portia of resource and commond, who sends Bassanio post haste to his friend, and beside that the schoolgirl laughing with Nerissa over the trick they are to play their new lords and masters. Know them all for one Porta, a wise and gallant spirit so virginally enshrined;

and we see to what profit Shakespeare turned his disabilities. There is, in this play, a twofold artistry in the achievement. Unlikelihood of plot is redeemed by veracity of character; while the artifice of the medium, the verse and its convention, and the stylized acting of boy as woman, reconciles us to the fantasy of the plot.

But a boy-Portia's advantage was chiefly manifest, of course, in the scene of the trial; and here in particular the actress of today must see that she lessens it no more than she need. The curious process of what we may call the "double negative", by which an Elizabethan audience first admitted a boy as a girl and then enjoyed the pretence that the girl was a boy, is obsolete for us; make-believe being the game, there was probably some pleasure just in this complication of it. This beside, there was the direct dramatic effect, which the boy made supremely well in his own person, of the wise young judge, the Daniel come to judgment. Shylock (and Shakespeare) plucks the allusion from the popular story of Susanna; but there may be some happy confusion, perhaps, with that other Daniel who was among "...the children of Israel, of the king's seede and of the Prince's: Springaldes without any blemish, but well-favoured, studious in all wisdome, skillful for knowledge, able to utter knowledge, and such as have liveliness in them, that they might stand in the king's palace...". For this is the very figure we should see. Here is the strict court of Venice, like enough to any law court, from East to West, from Shakespeare's time to now, in that it will seem to the stranger there very dry and discouraging, airless, lifeless. Age and incredulity preside; and if passion and life do enter, they must play upon muted strings. The fiercely passionate Shylock is anomaly; enough is such surroundings. Then comes this youth, as brisk and business like as you please, and stands before the judges' bench, alert, athletic, modest, cofident. He is life incarnate and destined to victory; and such a victory is the fitting climax to a fairy tale. So the Portia that will—as most Portias do—lapse into feminine softness and pitch the whole scene in the key of the speech on mercy, and that in a key of sentiment, damns the scene and herself and the speech, all three. This amazing youth has the ear of the court at once; but he'll only hold it by strict attention to business. Then, suddenly, out of this, comes the famous appeal, and catches us and the court unaware, catches us by the throat, enkindles us. In this lies the effect. Prepare for it, or make the beauty of it overbeautiful (all the more now, because it is famous and hackneyed) and it becomes a dose of soothing syrup.

This, be it further remembered, is not the scene's top note; conflict and crisis are to come. They are brought about simply and directly; the mechanical trick of the "No jot of blood" that is to resolve them asks nothing else. Shakespeare keeps the medium of the verse as simple; it flows on with hardly a broken line. The conflict is between Portia and Shylock. Basanio's agony, Antonio's stoic resignation cannot be given great play; the artifice of the story will not even now sustain cross-currents of human passion. But the constraint of the business of a court accounts well enough for their quiescence (the actors need do nothing to discount it) and the few notes that are struck from them suffice. The action must sweep ahead and no chance be given us to question its likelihood. Even when all is over the Duke departs with not much more comment upon this amazing case than an invitation to the learned young doctor to come to dinner, and Antonio and his friends are as casual about it and almost as calm. There is tractful skill in this Shylock has gone, that fairy tale is done with; the less we look back upon it, the sooner we come to fresh comedy again the better.

Throughout the scene a Portia must, of course, by no smallest sign betray to us—as well betray it to Bassanio—that she is other than she now seems. No difficulty here, as we said, for Shakespeare's Portia, or his audience either. There was no wondering as he faced the judges why they never saw this was a woman (since very obviously he now wasn't) nor why Bassanio did not know his wife a yard off. The liquid sentences of the Mercy speech were no betrayal, nor did the brusque aside of a young lawyer, intent upon his brief

> Your wife would give you little thanks for that,
> If she were by to hear you make the offer

—lose its quite casual humour. All this straightforwardness the modern actress must, as far as she can, restore.

ANTONIO GRATIANO AND OTHERS

In these early plays character does not as a rule outrun the requirements of the plot. Shakespeare is content enough with the decorative, the sententious, the rhetorical, in his casual Venetians, in Aragon and Morocco; with the conventional in Launcelot, who is the stage clown—the juggler with words, neat agile, resourceful and occasionally familiar with the audience, as a clown and a juggler should be under a thin disguise of character; with old Gobbo for a minute or two's incidental fun; with the pure utility of Tubal.

Antonio is flesh and blood. He is the passive figure of the story's demand; but Shakespeare refines this in the selflessness that can send Bassanio to Belmont and be happy in a friend's happiness, in the indifference to life that lets him oppose patience to his enemy's fury; and he makes him more convincingly this sort of man by making him just a little self-conscious too.

> In sooth, I know not why I am so sad...

If he does not, it is not for want to thinking about it. He takes a sad pleasure in saying that he is

> a tainted wether of the flock,
> Meetest for death...

But there is a redeeming ironic humour in

> You cannot better be employed, Bassanio,
> Then to live still and write mine epitaph.

He is sufficiently set forth, and there is conveyed in him a better dignity than mere words give.[10]

Nerissa is echoing merriment; not much more.

Shakespeare may have had half a mind to make something a little out of the way of Gratiano. He starts him with a temperament and a witty speech; but by the play's end we have not had much more from him than the "infinite deal of nothing" if Bassanio's gibe, rattling stuff, bouncing the play along, but revealing no latent Gratanio. It all makes a good enough pattern

10. It is worth remarking that the word "sad", as Shakespeare uses it, may mean rather solemn and serious than definitely miserable.

of this sort of man, who will be a useful foil to Bassanio, and can be paired off for symmetry with Portia's foil, Nerissa; and the play needed no more. But there is enough of him, and enough talk about him, for one to feel that he missed by only a little the touch of magic that would have made something more of him and added him to the list of those that survive the lowering of the lights and the theatre's emptying. There is a moment while he waits to take his share in Jessica's abduction, and sits reflecting:

> All things that are,
> Are with more spirit chased than enjoyed.
> How like a yonker or a prodigal,
> The scarfed bark puts from her native bay,
> Hugg'd and embraced by the strumpet wind!
> How like a prodigal doth she return;
> With over-weather'd ribs, and ragged sails,
> Torn, rent and beggared by the strumpet wind!

Harsh enough similes for such an occasion! Is this another side to the agreeable rattle? Does the man who exclaims

> Let me play the fool!
> With mirth and laughter let old wrinkles come...

find life in fact rather bitter to his taste? But one must beware of reading subtleties into Shakespeare. If such a Gratiano was ever shadowed in his mind, he made no solid substance of him.

Bassanio we have spoken of; play the part straightfor-wardly and it will come right.

SHYLOCK

There remains Shylock. He steps into the play, actual and individual from his first word on, and well might in his strength (we come to feel) have broken the pinchbeck of his origin to bits, had a later Shakespeare had the handling of him. As it is, his actuality is not weakened by the fantasy of the bond, as is Portia's by her caskets. For one thing, our credulity is not strained till the time comes for its maturing, and by then—if ever—the play and its acting will have captured us. For another, the law and its ways are normally so uncanny to a layman that the strict court of an exotic Venice might give even stranger judgments than this and only cofirm us in our belief that once litigation begins almost anything may happen. Despite the borrowed story, this Shylock is essentially Shakespeare's own. But if he is not a puppet, neither is he a stalking-horse; he is no more a mere means to exemplifying the Semitic problem than is Othello to the raising of the colour question. "I am a Jew." "Haply, for I am black..." Here we have—and in Shylock's case far more acutely and completely—the *circumstancs* of the dramatic conflict; but at the heat of it are men; and we may surmise, indeed, that from a maturer Shakespeare we should have had, as with Othello, much more of the man, and so rather less of the alien and his griefs. However that may be, he steps now into the play, individual and imaginatively full-grown, and the scene of his talk with Bassanio and Antonio is masterly exposition.

The dry taciturnity of his

Three thousand ducats; well?

(the lure of the thrice-echoed "Well"!) and the cold disecting of the business in hand are made colder, drier yet by contrast with the happy sound of Portia's laughter dying in our ears as he begins to speak. And for what a helpless innocent Bassanio shows beside him; over-anxious, touchy, over-civil! Shylock takes his time; and suddenly we see him peering, myopic, beneath his brows. Who can the newcomer be? And the quick brain answers beneath the question's cover: They must need the money badly if Antonio himself comes seeking me. Off goes Bassanio to greet his friend; and Shylock in a long aside can discharge his obligations to the plot.[11] These elven lines are worth comment. In them is all the motive power for drama that the story, as Shakespeare found it, provides; and he throws this, with careless opulence, into a single aside. Then he returns to the upbuilding of *his* Shylock.

---

11. This is one of the ever-recurring small strokes of stagecraft that are hardly apreciable apart from an Elizabethan stage. Shylock and Bassanio are to the front of the platform. Antonio, near the door, is be convention any convenient distance off; by impression, too, with no realistic scenery to destroy the impression. Shylock is left isolated, so isolated that the long aside has all the importance and the force of a soliloquy.

Note the next turn the scene takes. From the snuffling depreciation of his present store, for his own wonted fawning on these Christian clients, Shylock unexpectedly rises to the dignities of

> When Jacob grazed his uncle Laban's sheep...

And with this the larger issue opens out between Gentile and Jew, united and divided by the scripture they revere, and held from their business by this tale from it—of flocks and herds and the ancient East. Here is another Shylock; and Antonio may well stare, and answer back with some respect—though he recovers contempt for the alien creature quickly enough. But with what added force the accusation comes:

> Signior Antonio, many a time and oft
> In the Rialto you have rated me...
> You called me misbeliever, cut-throat dog,
> And spit upon my Jewish gaberdine...

The two Venetians see the Ghetto denizen again, and only hear the bondman's whine. But to us there is now all Jewry couched and threatening there, an ageless force behind it. They may make light of the money bond, but we shall not.

Shakespeare keeps character within the bounds of story with great tact; but such a character as this that has surged in his imagination aks more than such a story to feed on. Hence, partly at least, the new theme of Jessica and her flight, which will give Shylock another and more instant grudge to satisfy. It is developed with strict economy. Twenty-one lines are allowed to Jessica and Launcelot, another twenty or so to her lover and their plans; then, in a scene not sixty long, Shylock and his household are enshrined. As an example of dramatic thrift alone this is worth remark. The parting with Launcelot: he has a niggard liking for the fellow, is even hurt a little by his leaving, touched in pride, too, and shows it childishly.

> Thou shalt not gormandize
> As thou hast done with me...

But he can at least pretend that he parts with him willingly and makes some profit by it. The parting with Jessica, which we of the audience know to be a parting indeed; that constant calling her by name, which tells us of the lonely man! He has looked to her for everything, has tasked her hard, no doubt; he is her jailer, yet he trust her, and loves her in his extortionate way. Uneasy stranger that he is within these Venetian gates; the puritan, who, in a wastrel world, will abide by law and prophets! So full a picture of the man does the short scene give that it seems hardly possible we see no more of him than this between the making of the bond and the climacteric outbreak of passion upon Jessica's loss and the news of Antonio's ruin.[12]

References to him abound; Shylock can never be long out of our minds. But how deliberate is the thrift of opportunity we may judge by our being shown the first effect of the loss on him only through the ever-useful eyes of Salarino and Solanio. This is politic, however, from other points of view. Look where the scene in question falls, betwen Morocco's choice of his casket and Aragon's. Here or here-abouts some such scene must come, for the progress of the Antonio and Shylock story cannot be neglected. But conceive the effect of such a tragic outcry as Shylock's own,

> So strange, outrageous, and so variable...

—of such strong dramatic meat sandwiched between pleasant conventional rhetoric. How much of the credibility of the casket story would survive the association, with how much patience should we return to it? But Salarino and Solanio tone down tragedy to a good piece of gossip, as it becomes young men of the world to do. We avoid an emotional danger zone; and, for the moment at least, that other danger of an inconvenient

12. And so strange has this seemed to many a producer of the play and actor of Shylock, that we have been given scenes of pantomime in which Shylock comes back from Bassanio's supper to find Jessica flown. The solitary figure with a lantern, the unanswered rapping at the door, has become all but traditional. Irving did it, Coghlan had already done something of the sort, and—I fancy—Booth. An ingenious variation upon a theme by Shakespeare, that yet merely enfeebles the theme. The lengthier elaboration of a Shylock seen distracted at the discovery of his loss is, of course, even more inadmissible, since Shakespeare has deliberately avoided the situation.

sympathy with "the dog Jew". When Shylock's outbreak of anguish does come, the play is nearer to its climax, Bassanio's choice is about to free Portia's story from its unreality, and his savage certainty of revenge upon Antonio will now depress the sympathetic balance against him.

But, considering the story's bounds, what a full-statured figure we already have! Compare the conventional aside, the statement of the theme, in the earlier scene, the blad

I hate him for he is a Christian...

with the deluge of molten passion which descends upon the devoted Solanion and Salarino, obliterating their tart humour; compare the theme, that is to say, with its development, mere story with character, and measure in the comparison Shakespeare's growing dramatic power.

In tone and temper and method as well this scene breaks away from all that has gone before. The very start in prose, the brisk

Now, what news on the Rialto?

even, perhaps, Solanio's apology for former

slips of prolixity or crossing the plain highway of talk

seem to tell us that Shakespeare is now asserting the rights of his own imagination, means, at any rate, to let this chief creature of it, his Shylock, off the leash. And verily he does.

The scene's method repays study. No whirling storm of fury is asked for; this is not the play's crisis, but preparation for it still. Shylock is wrapped in resentful sorrow, telling over his wrong for the thousandth time. Note the repetition for thought and phrase. And how much more sinister this sight of him with the wound festering than if we had seen the blow's instant fall! His mind turns to Antonio, and the thrice told

let him look to his bond

is a rope of salvation for him; it knots up the speech in a dreadful strength. Then, on a sudden, upon the good young Salarino's reasonable supposition that what a moneylender wants is his money back; who on earth would take flesh instead? –

What's that good for?

—there flashes out the savagery stripped naked of

> To bait fish withal: if it will feed nothing else, it will feed my revenge.

Now we have it; and one salutes such purity of hatred. There follows the famous speech—no need to quote it—mounting in passionate logic, from its

He hath disgraced me...and what's his reason? I am a Jew

to the height of

> If a Jew wrong a Christian, what is his humility? Revenge. If a Christian wrong a Jew, what should his sufferance be by Christian example? Why, revenge. The villainy you teach me I will execute, and it shall go hard but I will better the instruction.

This is a Shylock born of the old story, but transformed, and here a theme of high tragedy, of the one seemingly never-ending tragedy of the world. It is the theme for a greater play than Shakespeare was yet to write. But if this one connot be sustained on such a height, he has at least for the moment raised it there.

Solanio and Salarino are quite oblivious to the great moral issue opened out to them; though they depart a little sobered—this Jew seems a dangerous fellow. There follows the remarkable passage with Tubal; of gruesome comedy, the apocalyptic Shylock shrunk already to the man telling his ill-luck against his enemy's, weighing each in scales (love for his daughter, a memory of his dead wife thrown in!) as he is used to weigh the coin which is all these Christians have left him for his pride. It is technically a notable passage, in that it is without conflict or contrast, things generally necessary to dramatic dialogue; but the breaking of a rule will be an improvement, now and then, upon obedience to it. So Shakespeare, for a finish, lowers the scene from its crisis, from that confronting of Christian and Jew, of hate with hate, to this raucous assonance of these two of a kind and mind, standing cheek to cheek in common cause, the excellent Tubal fueling up revenge.

Such a finish, ousting all nobility, both shows us another facet of Shylock himself (solid figure enough now to be turnted any way his maker will) and is, as we saw, a shadow against which the high romance of Bassanio's wooing will in a moment shine the more brightly. Sharp upon the heels of this, he comes again; but once more apocalyptic, law incarnate now.

SHYLOCK: Gaoler, look to him; tell me not of mercy;
This is the fool that lent out money gratis:
Gaoler, look to him.
ANTONIO: Hear me yet, good Shylock.
SHYLOCK: I'll have my bond; speak not against my bond:
I have sworn an oath that I will have my bond.

Verse and its dignity are needed for this scene; and note the recurring knell of the phrases:

I'll have my bond; I will not hear thee speak:
I'll have my bond, and therefore speak no more.
I'll not be made a soft and dull-eyed fool,
To shake the head, relent, and sigh, and yield
To Christian intercessors. Follow not;
I'll have no speaking: I will have my bond.

Here is a Shylock primed for the play's great scene; and Shakespeare's Shylock wrought ready for a catastrophe, which is a deeper one by far than that the story yields. For not in the missing of his vengeance on Antonio will be this Shylock's tragedy, but in the betrayal of the faith on which he builds.

I've sworn an oath that I will have my bond...

How many times has the synagogue not heard it sworn?

An oath, an oath. I have an oath in Heaven...

He has made his covenant with an unshakable God:

What judgment shall I dread, doing no wrong?

—and he is to find himself betrayed.

It is the apocalyptic Shylock that comes slowly into court, solitary and silent, to face and to outface the Duke and all the moral power of Venice.[13] When he does speak he answers the Duke as an equal, setting a sterner sanction against easy magnanimity—at other people's expense! One could complain that this first appeal for mercy discounts Portia's. To some extent it does; but the more famous speech escapes comparison by coming when the spell of the young doctor is freshly cast on us, and by its finer content and larger scope. Structurally, the Duke's speech is the more important, for it sets the lists, defines the issue and provokes that

> I have possessed your grace of what I purpose;
> And by our holy Sabbath have I sworn
> To have the due and forfeit of my bond...

So confident is he that he is tempted to shift ground a little and let yet another Shylock peep—the least likable of all. He goes on

> You'll ask me, why I rather choose to have
> A weight of carrion flesh, than to receive
> Three thousand ducats: I'll not answer that,
> But say it is my humour...

Legality gives license to the hard heart. Mark the progression. While the sufferer cried

> The villainy you teach me I will execute, and it shall go hard but I will better the instruction.

with the law on his side it is

> What judgment shall I dread, doing no wrong?

from which he passes, by an easy turn, to the mere moral anarchy of

> The pound of flesh, which I demand of him,
> Is dearly bought; 'tis mine, and I will have it...

---

13. Upon the modern stage he usually has Tubal for a companion; one has even seen him second by a small crowd of sympathetic Jews. How any producer can bring himself so to discount the poignant sight of that drab, heroic figure, lonely amid the magnificence around, passes understanding!

and is satanic heroism stands defiant:

> If you deny me, fie upon your law!
> There is no force in the decrees of Venice.
> I stand for judgment. Answer: shall I have it?

There is a dreadful silence. For who, dwelling unquestioningly under covenant of law, shall gainsay him?

It says much for the mental hypnosis which the make-believe of the theatre can induce that this scene of the trial holds us so spell-bound. Its poetry adds to the enchantment—let anyone try re-writing it in prose—and the exotic atmosphere helps. But how much more is due to the embroidering of character upon story so richly that the quality of the fabric comes to matter little! Shakespeare, at any rate, has us now upon the elemental heights of drama. He cannot keep us there. Portia must perform her conjuring trick; perhaps this is why he gives Shylock full scope before she arrives. But he brings us down with great skill, manceuvring character to the needs of the story, and turning story to character's account.

The coming of the young judge's clerk does not impress Shylock. How should it? Little Nerissa! He has won, what doubt of it? He can indulge then—why not?—the lodged hate and loathing he bears Antonio. The Duke is busy with Belario's letter and the eyes of the court are off him. From avenger he degenerates to butcher. To be caught, lickerishlipped, by Bassanio; and Gratiano's rough tongue serves him as but another whetstone for savagery! He turn surly at first sight of the wise young judge—what need of such a fine fellow and more fine talk?—and surlier still when it is talk of mercy. He stands there, he tells them yet again, asking no favours, giving none.

> My deeds upon my head! I crave the law,
> The penalty and forfeit of my bond.

Why does Shakespeare now delay the catastrophe by a hundred lines, and let Portia play cat-and-mouse with her victim? From the story's standpoint, of course, to keep up the excitement a while longer. We guess there is a way out. We wonder what it can be; and yet, with that knife shining, Antonio's doom seems to come nearer and nearer. This is dramatic child's play, and excellent of its sort. But into it much finer stuff is woven. We are to have more than a trick broguht off; there must be a better victory; this faith in which Shylock abides must be broken. So first she leads him on. Infatuate, finding her all on his side, he finally and formally refuses the money—walks into the trap. Next she plays upon his fanatical trust in his bond, sets him searching in mean mockery for a charitable comma in it—had one escaped his cold eye—even as the Pharisees searched their code to convict Christ. Fold by fold, the prophetic dignity falls from him. While Antonio takes his selfless farewell of his friend, Shylock must stand clutching his bond and his knife, only contemptible in his triumph. She leads him on to a last slaveringly exultant cry: then the blow falls.

Note that the tables are very precisely turned on him.

> if thou tak'st more,
> Or less, than just a pound, be it so much
> As makes it light or heavy in the substance,
> Or the division of the twentieth part
> Of one poor scruple, nay, if the scale do turn
> But in the estimation of a hair...

is exact retaliation for Shylock's insistence upon the letter of his bond. Gratiano is there to mock him with his own words, and to sound, besides, a harsher note of retribution than Portia can; for the pendulum of sympathy now swings back a little—more than a little, we are apt to feel. But the true catastrophe is clear. Shylock stood for law and the letter of the law; and it seemed, in its kind, a noble thing to stand for, ennobling him. It betrays him, and in the man himself there is no virtue left.

> Is *that* the law?

he gasps helplessly. It is his only thought. The pride and power in which legality had wrapped him, by which he had outfaced them all, and held Venice herself to ransom, are gone. He stands stripped, once more the sordid Jew that they may spit upon, greedy for money, and hurriedly keen to profit by his shame.

> I take this offer then; pay the bond thrice,
> And let the Christian go.

Here is Shakespeare's Shylock's fall, and not in the trick the law plays him.

He is given just a chance—would the story let him take it!—to regain tragic dignity. What is passing in his mind that prompts Portia's

> Why doth the Jew pause? Take thy forfeiture.[14]

No, nothing, it would seem, but the thought that he will be well out of the mess with his three thousand ducats safe.

Shakespeare has still to bring theme full circle. He does it with doubled regard to character and story.

> Why, then the devil give him good of it!
> I'll stay no longer question.

If he were not made to stay, by every canon of theatrical justice Shylock would be let off too lightly; wherefore we find that the law has another hold on him. It is but a logical extending of retribution, which Gratiano is quick to reduce to its brutal absurdity. Here is Shylock with no more right to a cord with which to hang himself than had Antonio to a bandage for his wound. These quibbling ironies are for the layman among the few delights of law. Something of the villainy the Jew taught them the Christians will now execute; and Shylock, as helpless as Antonio was, takes on a victim's dignity in turn. He stays silent while his fate, and the varieties of official and unofficial mercy to be shown him, are canvassed.[15] He is allowed no comment upon his impoverishing for the benefit of "his son Lorenzo" or upon his forced apostasy. But could eloquence serve better than such a silence?

---

14. See Furness for an elaborate, illuminating and witty comment upon the situation.

15. It is hard to see why Antonio's taking the money to pass on to "the gentleman that lately stole his daughter" and providing that, for his half-pardon "he presently become a Christian", should be so reprobated by some critics. If we have less confidence today than had Antonio in the efficacy of baptism, have we none left in the rightfulness of reparation? Not much in its efficacy, perhaps. Antonio, one must insist, does not mean to keep any of the money for himself. One hopes he never lapsed into self-righteousness in recalling this. Nothing is said, however, about the original three thousand ducats!

PORTIA: Art thou contented, Jew? What dost thou say?
SHYLOCK: I am content.

With the three words of submission the swung pendulum of the drama comes to rest. And for the last of him we have only

I pray you give me leave to go from hence;
I am not well. Send the deed after me,
And I will sign it.

Here is the unapproachable Shakespeare. "I am not well". It near banality and achieves perfection in its simplicity. And what a completing of the picture of Shylock! His deep offence has been against human kindness; he had scorned compassion and prayed God himself in aid of his vengeance. So Shakespeare dismisses him upon an all but ridiculous appeal to our pity, such as ailing child might make that had been naughty; and we should put the naughtiness aside. He passes out silently, leaving the gibing Gratiano the last word, and the play's action sweeps on without pause. There can be no greater error than to gerrymander Shylock a strenuously "effective exit"—and most Shylocks commit it. From the character's point of view the significant simplicity of that

I am not well

is spoiled; and from the point of view of the play the technical skill with which Shakespeare abstracts from his comedy this tragic and dominating figure and avoids anticlimax after is nullified.

The Return to Comedy

The tragic interest is posted to oblivion cavalierly indeed. Seven lines suffice, and the Duke's processional departure. The business of the rings is then briskly dispatched, and made the brisker by the businesslike matter of the signing of the deed being tacked to it. Thence to Belmont; and while Lorenzo and Jessica paint its moonlit beauty for us, Balthasar and his clerk have time to change costume and tire their heads again for Portio and Nerissa. They have evidently, as we saw, none too much time; for Launcelot is allowed a last—and an incongruously superfluous—piece of clowing. But the musicians can play ahead for an extra minute or two if hooks and eyes refuse to fasten, and no one will notice the delay. The last stretch of dialogue is lively; a comic quartet coming after the consort of viols, and it asks for a like virtuosity. The play ends, pleasantly and with formality, as a fairy tale should. One may wonder that the last speech is left (against tradition) to Gratiano; but one practical reason is plain. Portia and Bassanio, Antonio, Lorenzo and jessica must pace off the stage in their stately Venetian way, while Gratiano's harmless ribaldry is tossed to the audience as an epilogue. Then he and Nerissa, now with less dignity than ever to lose, skip quickly after.

Act-Division and Staging

However well the First Folio's five-act rule may fit other plays, and whatever, in Elizabethan stage practice, division into five acts implied, there is ample evidence that *The Merchant of Venice* was meant to be played without an effective break. The scenes, and the padding in them, that give time for Portia and Nerissa to change clothes, are one sign of it. The first of these is padding unalloyed, and very poor padding at that. For the second, Shakespeare finds better and plesanter excuse; but in part, at least, we owe that charming duet between Lorenzo and Jessica to this practical need.[16]

A case of a sort can be made out for the division in the Folio. Granted five acts, this fourth and fifth are manifest; the beginnings and finishings of the first three make useful milestones in the story, but others every bit as useful could be set up. It is worth nothing that this act-division does nothing to elucidate the complex time-scheme of our anxious editors; but the Folio's expert play-divider would be no more bothered by that problem than Shakespeare had been. Nor was he concerned to end his acts memorably; the second leaves Aragon in our minds and the third ends with Jessica and Lorenzo's and the play's worst

16. The two scenes are, to a line, of the same length. Add to the one the opening of the trial-scene, and to the other, for safety's sake, twenty bars or so of music, and we have the time allotted for the change of costume.

scene.[17] There might, how-ever, be good enough reason in the Elizabethan theatre for making an act's first scene arresting and for letting its last tail away; for they had, of course, no curtain to lower upon a climax, and after an interval interest would need quick re-kindling. No producer today, one hopes, will want to lower a picture-stage curtain at such points. Nor, if he is wise, while his stories are working to their joint crisis will he give us pause to think by what strange leaps in time and speace they travel.

But surely there are many signs that—however, for convenience sake, it is to be acted, with or without pause—Shakespeare has conceived and constructed the play indivisibly. There is the alternating between Venice and Belmont, and the spinning-out of the Portia story to fit with the other; neither device gains by or countenances act-division. There is the unhesitating sweep of the action up to the trial-scene, and indeed beyond it. One can parcel it up in various ways—the Folio's and half a dozen others—and on various pleas; but will any one of them make the story clearer; will it not, on the contrary, do something to disclose its confusions? Prose and blank verse, rhymed couplets and a quartrain are used indifferently for tags; so these form no consistent punctuation. There is no scene, not even the trial-scene, that ends with a full close, until the play ends. There is, in fact, no inherent, no dramatic pause in the action at all; nor can any be made which will not be rather hindrance than help to a performance.

Well-paced acting will take the play straight through in the traditional, vague two hours. But if, for the weakness of the flesh, there must be pauses, division into three parts will be a little less awkward that into two. If you do not stop before the trial-scene you cannot, of course, stop at all; the play will be virtually over. You may reasonably pause at the end of the Folio Act III. This alone, though, will make very unequal division.

---

17. Furness sees dramatic point in the second act ending with Bassanio on the doorstep. I suggest that Nerissa's tag is meant to keep Belmont a little in our minds during the strenuous scene between Shylock and Tubal which follows; but that, if anything, it tells against an act-pause falling here, rather than for it.

For an earlier pause, the moment of Bassanio's departure from Venice will serve.[18] This splits the first three acts of the Folio all but exactly in two. Delay the pause another scene and we shall have done with Morocco. The second part would then begin with the tale of how Shylock took his loss and our first news of Antonio's losses, and would develop this interest till the eve of the trial. Incidentally it would hold all the inordinate time-telescoping; a helpful quickening, this, to its pause. But these divisions and the choice of them have no other validity than convenience; the play must be thought of as an integral whole.

Needless to say that the confusion of scene-divisions in most modern editions (a very riot of it when Jessica is eloping) is not Shakespeare's; nor is the expert of the Folio responsible, nor even Rowe, who contents himself with marking the moves from Venice to Belmont and back.[19] For a century editors disputed as to when *Venice, a street*, shifted to *A room in Shylock's house*, or to *Another street* or to *Before Shylock's house*, and chopped up the action and checked its impetus, when one glance at Shakespeare's stage, its doors and balcony and traverses, shows with what swift unity the play and its playing flow on. And whatever picturing of Venice and Belmont a producer may design, this swift-flowing unity he must on no account obstruct. Let that be clear.

But there is little difficulty in the play's production, once its form is recognized, its temper felt, the tune of its verse and the rhythm of its prose rightly caught. The text is very free from errors, there are no puzzles in the actual stagecraft. The music may come from Elizabethan stock, and the costuming is obvious. Nothing is needed but perception and good taste, and from the actors, acting.

---

18. There is, as we have seen, a possible contracting of the action here that gives a summariness to the last few lines and suggests (to the modern ear, truly) a "curtain".

19. Lord Lansdowne's Jew held the stage in Rowe's time; and for this reason, it may just possibly be, he does not trouble to bring the play into closer relation with his own theatre.

Othello

Shakespeare, as his habit was, took a ready-made story to work upon. It is as if, for a start, he feels a need to tie his exuberant imagination to something he can rank as fact. Cinthio's is a convincing story; its characters are clearly drawn, and it is, in its spare fashion, very well told. There was much to attract him in it: the romantic setting in Venice and Cyprus (he has never cared for commonplace back-grounds); the exotic figure of the Moor (of rarer stuff than Shylock), and the "Machiavellian" Ensign. It deals, moreover, the degradation of love between man and woman, a subject in which about this time he was finding varied material, both for tragedy and for such so-called comedies as *Troilus and Cressida and Measure for Measure.* The story itself he by no means improves in the course of compressing it into drama; he omits, indeed, some of its most striking touches, and, towards its crux, so jeopardizes its very credibility that all his craftsman's skill is needed to save this from collapse. But he endows Cinthio's outlined characters with an extraordinary actuality and vitality; Desdemona and Emilia, Othello himself, Iago, Cassio, Roderigo and Bianca making a group in this respect unrivalled in the rest of his work. And he charges the sordid matter of his original with poetry to make it the high tragedy we know.

The Story and the Play

He makes changes he could have avoided, but the purpose of them is clear. In the story Desdemona and the Moor-although she has married him against her parents' wish—have lived together in harmony and peace for some time. Shakespeare prefers an elopement for his starting point, since this gives an initial impetus to the action. He invents also the Cyprus war and its sudden crisis. Here is increased impetus, some evidence of Othello's soldiership, a background of notable event, and a pretext for transporting Desdemona to the isolation of a far island where she will be defenceless and he all-powerful. The Turks and their "mighty preparation" having served his purpose, he gets rid of them with a (dramatically) cynical ease. A "Third Gentleman's"

> News, lords! Our wars are done.
> The desperate tempest hath so banged the Turks,
> That their designment halts...

with Othello's as summary

News, friends; our wars are done. The Turks are drowned...

suffice. But it is not simply that he has no further use for them. They would be a positive hindrance to him now. For Iago must be set to work without more delay, and an Othello braced to action might prove intractable material. Jealousy thrives best in a stagnant soil.

The initial elopement must not be allowed to suggest a second tragedy of "violent delights" leading to "violent ends", for we are to have no such show of youthful folly. To prevent this the characters of Othello and Desdemona themselves are firmly outlined from the first; his austere dignity; the calm with which—mere girl that she is!—she faces the majestic Senate, confutes her father and wins her cause. And while Shakespeare cannot, without unduly slackening the play's action, produce the effect of the harmony and tranquillity of life in which the story discovers them, to replace this he sends them separately to Cyprus and, after bare escape with their lives—from the very tempest than so bangs the Turks, thus put to double use—reunites them in such an ecstasy of happiness that, cries Othello,

> I fear,
> My soul hath her content so absolute,
> That not another comfort like to this
> Succeeds in unknown fate.

Among other changes, the Captain's wife disappears.[1] Three wives

---

1. The Furness Variorum gives us five pages of footnotes upon Iago's description of Cassio in the first scene of the play as

→

would be one too many. In her place—conjured out of a single phrase in the story concerning a courtesan he was about to visit—we have Bianca, whose frailty, with its affectations of virtue, is set both against Desdemona's innate chastity and Emilia's coarser honesty, the play's pattern of womanhood being thus varied and enlarged. And Bianca is put to appropriate use in the scene in which Othello, eaves-dropping, takes what he hears of Cassio's light talk of her for further proof of Desdemona's guilt.

In the story the Ensign's wife ("a young, fair and virtuous lady; and being of Italian birth, she was much loved by Desdemona, who spent the greater part of every day with her"[2]) knows that is going forward, refuses all share in it, but dare not speak out for fear of him. For a combination of reasons Shakespeare cannot accept this. Such a theme demands elaboration and, elaborated, might prove engrossing, making the minor character the more interesting of the two. Nor could he well place an immobilized Emilia of this quality beside the passive Desdemona; he needs contrast here, not likeness. So he retains the intimacy, but changes the nature of it, makes them waiting-woman and mistress, and in every way contrasts them.[3] He contrasts his Emilia with Iago also; the growth of her loyal affection with his frigid treachery, her blindness to what is passing with his sharp wit.

To this end the episode of the handkerchief, as the story has it, is reshaped. The happy trait of the "*eccelentimente di mano*", which lets the wicked Ensign himself filch the handkerchief from Desdemona's girdle, is sacrificed. Iago, instead, has, says Emilia,

→ a Florentine,
A fellow almost damned in a fair wife...

in face for the fact that Cassio, as it turns out, has no wife. But the explanation is surely simple enough. Shakespeare, when he wrote the line, meant to follow the story in this respect. Later, for good reasons, he changed his mind and gave Bianca to Cassio for a mistress instead, omitting, however, to alter the text of this first scene. And Cassio was "almost damned" because every fellow with a fair wife is, in Iago's estimation, a predestined cuckold.

2. I quote, here and elsewhere, from the translation in the Furness Variorum.

3. But Emilia is a waiting-gentlewoman. No rigid class-distinction is involved.

> a hundred times
> Wooed me to steal it...

and, having at last picked it up, she gives it him and adds a covering lie to the fault. No more than this is left of the silent complicity of the story, though enough even so—coarse-grained as she is made, and for all Shakespeare's own dramatic "*eccelentimente di mano*"—to do some damage to Emilia's credit with us. The episode now serves as one more illustration of Iago's talent for using other hands to do his work for him. Roderigo, Cassio, Emilia, Bianca too; when he is in the vein they are his cat's-paws all. Not until, his affairs going awry, he gives Cassio that swordslash in the dark, does he, we may remark, *do* one single thing himself. And even this, and even the subsequent stabbing of Roderigo, as will later appear, he bungles.

Again, the Captain in the story knows that the handkerchief he find in his room is Desdemona's, and he attempts to return it to her; and, later, his wife is seen by the Moor at her window copying its embroidery, even as Bianca is asked to copy it. This goes well enough in a story. But clearly Cassio cannot be allowed to know. The play's closeknit action and its generalizing of location will make access to Desdemona seem easy, and his respect for her would never let him knowingly give her handkerchief to Bianca.

The Ensign's little daughter, whom Desdemona loves, is omitted. Iago is a fond father! Did Shakespeare feel that such a gem of irony might outshine the rest?

Roderigo is Shakespeare's invention. His gulling provides the shadow of an underplot, some comic relief—he makes a ridiculous counterpart to the nobler victim—and something more dramatically valuable than either. For, colourless himself, he is the mirror in which can be reflected an Iago that the stress of the main action will hardly let us see; cynically at his ease, ostentatiously base, yet meretricious even in this, and reckless too. Cinthio's Ensign—drawn like the rest in outline only, but firmly and precisely, without one false stroke—is patient, singleminded, veritably austere in his wickedness, and is victorious to the last, another story being needed to give him his deserts. But Iago must come by his within the compass of the play. And, for all his destructive cunning, here, from the beginning, is his own destruction implicit; in the cankering vanity, the innate malignity, crass appetite and mere itch to do evil, so vaingloriously displayed. It is in his coarse contempt for the "sick fool Roderigo" that his own fatal folly is visibly from the first, and the more rapidly ripens.

The capital changes, however, is that which converts the anonymous Moor into Othello, for with this it is that the whole brutal story is raised to the heights of tragedy. But, for all the gain, some loss is still involved. What, as Cinthio has it, could be better of its kind, after "the wicked Ensign" has resolved to wait patiently "until time and circumstance should open a path for him to engage in his foul project", than its unwitting opening by the Moor himself, who seeks and again and again questions the deprecatory villain, and waits in torture for the disclosure "which was to make him miserable to the end of his days", or than—while he is still convinced of her guilt—his demented grief for the murdered Desdemona and slowly gathering hatred of the man he had employed to murder her? But those lagging agonies, made so significant in the story—where also the very sparseness of the telling of them sets our imagination to work to fill the gaps—would provide too slack a mechanism altogether for Shakespeare's theatre, with its primary need (in his eyes) for continuing and continuous action.

Ay, that's the way;
Dull not device by coldness and delay

says Iago, when he has at last worked out his plan. And it is very much as if Shakespeare, with these dramatic drawbacks to the story in mind, were telling himself the same thing.

There is yet another capital difference between story and play. The story lacks all conflict. Cinthio's Moor is an ignorant, and—despite his bursts of rage—an unresisting victim throughout. The ignorance must be retained, or the plot, Iago's and the play's too, will collapse. Othello must be

tenderly led by the nose
As assess are.

By what replace, then, the conflict which in some sort seemingly all drama demands? Shakespeare gives us, between Iago and Othello—as between Moor and Ensign Cinthio does not—and emphasizes from the first, radical and acute contrast of circumstance and character. In everything the two are opposed. Iago is a nobody and has his way to make, has an abundant conceit of himself and smarts under neglect; there, indeed, is the immediate spring of his villainy. Othello—while Cinthio's Moor was simply "*molto valoroso...per essere pio della persona*"—is of royal descent, although he has had the tactful modesty to conceal this so far from republican Venice. Again, while Desdemona in the story says to her husband, "...you Moors are of so hot a nature that every little trifle moves you to anger and revenge", Shakespeare gives us an Othello calm beneath Brabantio's threats and abuse, in the matter of Cassio's brawl of iron self-control, and against that he sets the gadfly Iago, impatient from the first to be stinging.[4]

The play is half through before the sting is planted, and the two characters have been developed meanwhile in no very close relation to each other. But when this becomes intimate, the contrast between them is progressively heightened until a species of conflict is created, not of action, since the story forbids that, but of the very essence of the men. And as this is distilled before us, ever more intensely—can two such elements in humanity, we are brought to asking, so opposed, peaceably partake for long one share of the world together? Is not conflict, victory and defeat innate and inevitable in what they *are*? For

> He has a daily beauty in his life
> That makes me ugly...

That Iago says this, not of Othello, but of Cassio, says it incidentally, and that it somewhat belies, moreover, his diabolonian boastings, makes it none the less, but rather the more revealing. For of such intrinsic truths about themselves the most self-conscious men—and among these is Iago—will be the least aware. Out they slip to pass unnoticed. And here is a better reason for his hatred of Othello—as we see it in action; and what Iago does is ever better evidence of the man than what he says—than all the vaunted "reasons" his intellectual vanity sets him seeking.

---

4. One of the most remarkable things about Salvini's Othello—so I was told by William Poel, who saw and studied it—was the restraint in which he held himself until Iago's poison had begun to work in him. It made one think, said Poel, of a sleeping volcano. And when at last—and not till the play was half over—the passionate force in the man did begin to stir, the effect was terrific.

His task demands a force beyond his braggart "wit". He finds this in the loosing of some need of his very being to reduce the nobility confronting him to baseness. He must, so instinct tells him, if he himself is to survive. Within a set arena great goodness and great wickedness cannot coexist for long; one must yield to the other, or the bounds of the arena be broken. There can be no compromise. Shakespeare gives us, then, in place of conflict of action, this conflict of being. The fortress of good, to which siege is laid, is defencelessly unaware of its own goodness, as true goodness is. We watch it falling, stone by stone.

But nobility must be brought even lower than the baseness which attacks it, if the triumph of evil is to be complete; and this dictates the culminating change from story to play. The Moor of the story stands callously by while the Ensign clubs Desdemona to death. That is horrible. But Othello is made to fall from his ideal heights to deeper damnation still, and to do the deed himself. How is this possible? Shakespeare sets himself the task—to which Iago's task inheres—of showing us, and convincingly, the process of the spiritual self-destruction which can make him capable of such a deed, to which his physical self-destruction after is the mere sequel. For, like all great tragedies, it is a tragedy of character. And it is epitomized at the end in the mockery of that one terrible paradox,

> O, thou Othello, that wert once so good,...
> What shall be said to thee?

That wert once so *good*!

> Why, anything;
> An honourable murderer, if you will...

An honourable murderer! The soldier Othello saying it of himself. That was not within Cinthio's range.

The Shaping of the Play

It has been often enough remarked that in the action of Othello there is, for Shakespeare, an unusually near approach to classic unity.[5] "Had the scene opened in Cyrus", says Johnson, "and the preceding incidents been occasionally related, there had been

5. *The Tempest*, however, makes a nearer one.

little wanting to drama of the most exact and scrupulous regularity". But this (with due respect to Johnson) makes a misleading approach. There is no aiming at regularity and falling short of it. What unity there is—and it is very defective—is simply the outcome of an economy of treatment peculiar to the needs of the play. Unity of theme, that we have. As to unity of place; this is vaguely and implicitly established for several successive scenes within the bounds of Othello's residence. But Bianca and Roderigo—Bianca particularly—are most unlikely intruders there, where a while before Othello and Desdemona have been domestically disputing over the loss of the handkerchief. And time is given no unity of treatment at all; it is contracted and expanded like a concertina. For the play's opening and closing the time of the action is the time of its acting; and such an extent of "natural" time (so to call it) is unusual. But minutes stand for hours over the sighting, docking and discharging—with a storm raging, too!—Of the three ships which have carried the characters to Cyprus; the entire night of Cassio's undoing passes uninterruptedly in the speaking space of four hundred lines: and we have, of course, Othello murdering Desdemona within twenty-four hours of he consummation of their marriage, when, if Shakespeare let us—or let Othello himself—pause to consider, she plainly *cannot* be guilty of adultery.[6]

Freedom with time is, of course, one of the recognized freedom of Shakespeare's stage; he needs only to give his exercise of it the slightest dash of plausibility. But in the maturity of his art he learns how to draw dramatic profit from it. For this play's beginning he does not, as we have noted, contract time at all. Moreover, he allows seven hundred lines to the three first scenes when he could well have done their business in half the space or less, could even, as Johnson suggests, have left it to be "occasionally related" afterwards. The profit is made evident when later, by contrast, we find him using contraction of time, and the heightening of tension so facilitated, to disguise the incongruities of the action.

---

6. Other explanations have been offered: one, that Othello is driven to suspect Desdemona of fornication with Cassio before her marriage. But this is frivolous.

He can do this more easily if he has already familiarized us with the play's characters. And he has done that more easily by presenting them to us in the unconstraint of uncontracted time, asking us for no special effort of make-believe. Accepting what they are, we shall the more readily accept what they do. It was well, in particular, to make Iago familiarly lifelike. If his victims are to believe in him, so, in another sense, must we. Hence the profuse self-display to Roderigo. That there is as much lying as truth in it is no matter. A man's lying, once we detect it, is as eloquent of him as the truth.

The contraction of time for the arrival in Cyprus has its profitable dramatic purpose too. Shakespeare could have relegated the business to hearsay. But the spectacular excitement, the suspense, the ecstatic happiness of the reuniting of Othello and Desdemona, give the action fresh stimulus and impetus and compensate for the break in it occasioned by the voyage. Yet there must be no dwelling upon this, which is still only prelude to the capital events to come. For the same reason, the entire night of Cassio's undoing passes with the uninterrupted speaking of four hundred lines. It is no more than a sample of Iago's skill, so it must not be lingered upon either. Amid the distracting variety of its coming and goings we do not remark the contraction. As Iago himself is let suggest to us:

> Pleasure and action make the hours seem short.

Then, upon the entrance of Cassio with his propitiatory *aubade*, commences the sustained main stretch of the action, set to something more complex than a merely contracted, to a sort of ambiguous scheme of time, which is not only a profitable, but here, for Shakespeare turning story into play, an almost necessary device.[7] After which we have the long last scene set to "natural" time, the play thus ending as it began. The swift-moving, close-packed action, fit product of Iago's ravening will, is over.

Enter Othello, and Desdemona in her bed

—and, the dreadful deed done, all is done. And while the rest come and go about him:

---

7. To be examined more closely. See p. 146.

Here is my journey's end...

he says, at a standstill, and as in a very void of time. And as the "natural" time at the play's beginning let us learn the better what he was, so relaxation to it now lets us mark the more fully the wreck that remains.

THE SCENES IN VENICE

The three opening scenes move to a scheme of their own, in narrative and in the presentation of character. The first gives us a view of Iago which, if to be proved superficial, is yet a true one (for Shakespeare will never introduce in character misleadingly) and a sample of his double-dealing. Roderigo at the same time paints us a thick-lipped, lascivious Moor, which we discover in the second scene, with a slight stimulating shock of surprise at the sight of Othello himself, to have been merely a figment of his own jealous chagrin. There also we find quite another Iago: the modest, devoted, disciplined soldier, who though in the trade of war he has slain men, holds it "very stuff o' the conscience to do no contrived murder", and "lacks iniquity" to do himself service. The third scene takes us to the Senate House, where Brabantio and his griefs, which have shrilly dominated the action so far, find weightier competition in the question of the war, and the State's need of Othello, whose heroic aspect is heightened by this. His dignity is next matched, in another kind, with Desdemona's. And again we receive that slight shock of surprise—so stimulating to our interest in a character—when the

maiden never bold;
Of spirit so still and quiet that her motion
Blushed at herself...

of Brabantio's piteous pleading proves, for all that, to be as resolute and unafraid. Here is the twinned, confident nobility which is to be brought low. And Iago, conspicuously silent throughout the scene (Othello's orders to him at its beginning and end make both him and his silence conspicuous), surveys the two, and may seem to be sizing up his task—which, a moment later, with the snivelling Roderigo for listener, he begins by resliming them with the foulness of his mind, as a snake will with its slime the prey to be swallowed.

The scenic mobility of Shakespeare's stage permits him up to this point to translate his narrative straightforwardly into action. We pass, that is to say, from Brabantio's house, which Desdemona has just quitted, to the Sagittary, where she and Othello are to be found, and from there to the Senate House, to which he and she (later) and Brabantio are summoned. And the movement itself is given dramatic value—by its quickening or slackening or abrupt arrest. We have the feverish impetus of Brabantio's torchlight pursuit; Othello's calm talk to Iago set in sequence and contrast to it; its encounter with the other current of the servants of the Duke upon their errand; the halt, the averted conflict; then the passing-on together of the two parties, in sobered but still hostile detachment, towards the Senate House.

Note also that such narrative as is needed of what has passed before the play begins is mainly postponed to the third of these opening scenes. By then we should be interested in the characters, and the more therefore, in the narrative itself, which is, besides, given a dramatic value of its own by being framed as a cause pleaded before the Senate. Further, even while we listen to the rebutting of Brabantio's accusation of witchcraft by Othello's "round unvarnished tale" we shall be expecting Desdemona's appearance, the one important figure in this part of the story still to be seen. And this expectancy offsets the risk of the slackening of tension which reminiscent narrative must always involve.[8]

THE ARRIVAL IN CYPRUS

Shakespeare now breaks the continuity of the action: and such a clean break as this is with him unusual. He has to transport his characters to Cyprus. The next scene takes place there. An unmeasured interval of time is suggested, and no scene on shipboard or the like has been provided for a link, nor are any of the events of the voyage recounted. The tempest which drowns the Turks, and rids him of his now superfluous war, and has more thrillingly come near besides to drowning the separated

---

8. Emilia—who is *not*, as stage usage will have it, among Desdemona's attendants; why should she be?—Only acquires importance much later.

Othello and Desdemona—something of this he does contrive to present to us; and we are plunged into it as we were into the crisis of the play's opening:

> What from the cape can you discern at sea?
> Nothing at all. It is a high-wrought flood;
> I cannot, 'twixt the heaven and the main,
> Descry a sail

—a second start as strenuous as the first. The excitement offsets the breaking of the continuity. And the compression of the events, of the storm and the triple landing, then the resolution of the fears for Othello's safety into the happiness of the reuniting of the two—the bringing of all this within the space of a few minutes' acting raises tension to a high pitch and holds it there.

Shakespeare prescriptively makes his storm out of poetry, expands Montano's more or less matter-of-fact

> A fuller blast ne'er our battlements:
> If it hath ruffianed so upon the sea,
> What ribs, of oak, when mountains melt on them,
> Can hold the mortise?

into the melodious hyperbole of the Second Gentleman's

> For do but stand upon the foaming shore,
> The chiding billow seems to pelt the clouds;
> The wind-shaked surge, with high and monstrous main,
> Seems to cast water on the burning bear,
> And quench the guards of the ever-fixed pole

descending, however, for Cassio's arrival, and the news he brings, to simpler speech; although the verse with its compelling rhythm—touched, to keep the whole in key, with such an occasional richness of phrase as that which ends Montano's call to the rest to come and scan the sea for a sight of Othello's ship,

> Even till we make the main, and the aerial blue,
> An indistinct regard

—this is retained. And it lifts again to hyperbole in Cassio's mouth, yet, be it noted, to a quite different tune, for the celebrating of Desdemona's safety:

> Tempests themselves, high seas, and howling winds,
> The guttered rocks, and congregated sands—
> Traitors ensteeped to clog the guiltless keel,
> And having sense of beauty, do omit
> Their mortal natures, letting go safely by
> The divine Desdemona

and of his hopes for Othello's:

> Great Jove, Othello guard,
> And swell his sail with thine own powerful breath,
> That he may bless the bay with has tall ship...

The scene-painting ends here; for Iago, Desdemona and Emilia appear, and Shakespeare concentrates upon character in action again. Yet these last lines have not been merely decorative. Cassio's fealty to Othello, and his reverence for Desdemona sound in them; points pertinent both to the man and the story. And if treacherous Nature may have spared her for her beauty's sake, we are warned the next instant by the sight of her

> in the conduct of her bold Iago...

that man's treachery will not.

The scene's vehemence abates. The storm is forgotten. The verse, deflated of metaphor, flows easily along; and its ease and simplicity benefit Desdemona's own dignity in simplicity and her courageous outward calm. As fittingly, when Iago asserts himself, the verse fractures and disintegrates, after a little, into prose.

But Othello's own safety, still in question, is too important in the story to be left for more postscriptory treatment. So Shakespeare now simulates suspense by giving no less than a ninety-lane stretch of the scene to showing us Desdemona's silent anxiety, which he frames, for emphasis, by contrast, in a bout of artificially comic distraction. The clue to his intention lies in her

> I am not merry; but I do beguile
> The thing I am, by seeming otherwise.

Our attention is centred on her. The chatter and the laughter—hers in forced accord with the rest—and Iago's scurril rhyming are but an incogruous accompaniment to her mutely eloquent fears; and they do not—this we see—by any means beguile her from them. Once the surface of the merriment is pierced by the long-repressed escaping

There's one gone to the harbour?

the sharpness of its anxiety measurable by the comprehending Cassio's kindly reassuring

Ay, madam.

The idle diffuseness of the dialogue, too, by contrast with its recent compression, of itself helps interpret her sense of how time lags while she waits for news.

Iago emerges from the picture (the action must be thought of in terms of Shakespeare's stage[9]) for his malignly vigilant soliloquy:

> He takes her by the palm. Ay, well said, whisper; with as little a web as this, will I ensnare so great a fly as Cassio...

and her share in the scene is reduced to illustrative dumb show; but since she is the subject of the soliloquy she sill will hold our attention. The scene's action is here momentarily split, so to speak, into two, its force isolated in the menacingly prominent figure of Iago. Upon his dry explicatory prose the brilliant interruption of the *Trumpet within* tells the more startlingly. Then, with his, Cassio's and Desdemona's combined swift response:

> The Moor! I know his trumpet.
> 'Tis truly so.
> Let's meet him, and receive him.
> Lo, where he comes!

---

9. For his soliloquy he will advance to the front of the main stage; Desdemona and the rest will go towards or into to inner stage, the pictorial effect being of a fully rounded statue placed before a basrelief.

—the whole coheres again, and leaps, unconstrained, to life and movement.

The suspense is over, the tension relaxes. Othello appears; and after the

> O, my fair warrior!
>   My dear Othello!

of their reuniting, comes the nobly fulfilling music of

> I gives me wonder, great as my content,
> To see you here before me. O my soul's joy!
> If after every tempest come such calms,
> May the winds blow till they have weakened death!
> And let the labouring bark climb hills of seas,
> Olympus-high; and duck again as low
> As hell's from heaven!...

Here is the scene's third and superlative use of the imagery of the sea. It recalls, too, Desdemona's earlier

> downright violence and storm of fortunes...

They have come through both; but only, as we already know—and there is Iago surveying them to remind us of it—into a more treacherous calm. Othello's sequent

> If it were now to die,
> 'Twere now to be most happy; for, I fear,
> My soul hath her content so absolute,
> That not another comfort like to this
> Succeeds in unknown fate

gives us the already aging, disillusioned man: Desdemona, in her youthfulness, is confident for happiness:

> The heavens forbid
> But that our loves and comforts should increase,
> Even as our days do grow!

And he, inarticulately possessed by love for her, shuts out all but that with a thankful "Amen". For a last minatory jar to the harmony we have the low snarl of Iago's

O, y'are well tuned now!
But I'll set down the pegs that make this music,
As honest as I am

—and the preparation of the tragedy is complete.[10]

IAGO COMPASSES CASSIO'S DOWNFALL

Iago sets to work without delay; and for long to come now he will seldom be absent from the scene, since, fittingly, the action is centred on him, woven round him, even as he himself, spiderlike, weaves its plot. But the attempt upon Othello will be no trifling matter, and Shakespeare lets us see him proving his quality first upon lesser and less dangerous game. His vague plan "engendered" in Venice—

After some time, to abuse Othello's ear...

with scandal about Cassio and Desdemona—is consequently now shaped for a start to a prompter disgrace of Cassio, to an immediate profit that;

To get his place...

—so much to go on with!

We have sampled his protean gifts already with the transforming of the raucous cloaked figure beneath Brabantio's balcony into the frank, conscientious soldier, this again into Roderigo's coolly sceptic mentor in vice. From which nearest seeming semblance of himself it is that he now starts again, to turn, even more easily, jolly companion with Cassio, then moralist with Montano, before Othello to be once more the loyal soldier, and so on and so forth—swift to respond to the occasion's demand on him. He buys his way ahead with unstinted false coin. But the display is divided by soliloquies in which his naked mind can be seen and the course he is steering shown us, and, since he steers from point to point only, by no less than four.

---

10. Note that if the editors in general are right—and hardly disputably they are—to follow the lineation of the Quartos, with its

That e'er our hearts shall make.
O you are well tuned now...

then, the scansion dictates this dovetailed and much elided "O, y'are..." and the unescapable snarl in it.

Roderigo is to be his instrument; and upon the instructions which emerge from the web of words he habitually weaves about this feeblest of his victims—

> Watch you to-night; for the command, I'll lay't upon you....do you find some occasion to anger Cassio, either by speaking too loud, or tainting his discipline; or from what other course you please....Sir, he is rash and very sudden in choler; and, happy, with his truncheon may strike at you. Provoke him, that he may...

—upon this precise priming of our expectation Shakespeare can afford the halt in the action of the Herald's proclamation.

The proclamation in itself severs several subsidiary purposes. It helps settle the characters in Cyprus. The chances and excitements of the arrival are over. Othello is in command; but the war is over too, and he only needs bid the people rejoice at peace and his happy marriage. It economically sketches us a background for Cassio's ill-fated carouse. It allows a small breathing-space before Iago definitely gets to work. It "neutralizes" the action for a moment (a Herald is an anonymous voice; he has no individuality), suspends its interest without breaking its continuity. Also it brings its present timelessness to an end; events are given a clock to move by, and with that take on a certain urgency.[11]

Now comes

Enter Othello, Desdemona, Cassio, and Attendants.

The *Attendants*, which is the Folio's addition, add a touch of ceremony to this brief passage across the stage. But while it

11. But a clock whose hands move to order, so to speak. The Herald refers to "this present hour of five." A dozen lines later Iago says, " 'Tis not yet ten o' th' clocks". Modern editors isolate the Herald's speech as a separate scene; and the cleared stage before and after it justifies this, and overcomes—over-overcomes, one may say—the incongruity of the leap in time. The Quartos as usual, make no such indications. The stage is twice cleared, in fact; the effect is made. What need in print to call attention to the matter? It is only worth remarking that the editor of the Folio, inserting scene-divisions, establishes one before the speech, where no incongruity of time is in question, but not after, when, if the point could have trouble him, it is.

is no more, the few lines it allows for, with their easy cadence—

> Good Michael, look you to the guard to-night.
> Let's teach ourselves that honourable stop,
> Not to outsport discretion

—are economically made to speak of the effortless discipline which shows the good soldier in Othello, of his own temperance and self-discipline, of his affection too, as they flow on, for Cassio; "Michael" twice over. Shakespeare sounds the quiet note of the normal while he may; the strenuous action to come will tell the better against it.

Upon Othello's verse and the melodious echo of its final rhymed couplet impinges Iago's brisk prose, and his gross talk of Desdemona strikes a yet more flagrant contrast to the uncalculated dignity of the little wedding procession we have seen pass by. Cassio in his devout admiration of her—the more incredible, by these repeated signs of it, any notion of their adultery!—Is coldly unresponsive, would positively protest (we may feel, and the actor can indicate) but for his manly reluctance—upon which Iago impishly plays—to be branded Puritan. It is a like shame-facedness, a dearly-to-be-requited dash of petty moral cowardice, which betrays him a moment later in the matter of the "brace of Cyprus gallants" and "the stoup of wine".

The technical utility of Iago's sixteen line soliloquy, which fills the gap between Cassio's departure to "call them in" and his return with them and Montano, is to allow time for the "rouse" which will bring him back a step or so advanced in tipsiness already. For, since we are to have his repentance set out at length, we do not need to see the full process of his undoing besides. Shakespeare may seem to be short of pertinent material here. We are told that the feeble Roderigo has been fortified for his provocative task with a little Dutch courage too; this apart, no more than within a minute, we shall see for ourselves. But the soliloquy brings us at this ripe instant into naked touch again with Iago's quick, confident mind. And, cast for speed and impetus (by contrast with the surrounding prose) is easily flowing verse, with its final couplet—

> If consequence do but approve my dream,
> My boat sails freely, both with wind and stream

—it whips up the scene to the spirited pitch at which Cassio's exuberantly hilarious

> Fore God, they have given me a rouse already

is to capture it.

A tavern would, of course, be the suitable place for the carouse which follows, and the action could quite easily be transported there. But Shakespeare prefers to concentrate it all in this convenient nowhere in particular, so that it may come and go around Iago, its General in Command—who need not, therefore, now, nor for the rest of the long scene, quit the stage, nor have to relax his hold on it our us, until this battle is won and his next planned. The essentials of a tavern are as easily transported here; and a joke about the English being "most potent in potting" and a couple of ditties "learned in England" will—with an English audience—assure the illusion.

There is an edge to the foolery. As Cassio grows ridiculous in his cups Iago covertly mocks him, fanning his own jealous enmity too, with repetition of the respectful "lieutenant", "good lieutenant" (for how little longer will he need to call him so!), luring him to the jocular patronage of

> the lieutenant is to be saved before the ancient...
> this is my ancient...

—more food for enmity there! This flares but with Montano for one incautious moment in the contemptuous

> You see this fellow, that is gone before...

flung after his "good lieutenant's" unsteady departure to set the watch, to be as quickly masked again, however, beneath kindly, comradely—but how piosonously seasoned!—Reprobation:

> He is a soldier fit to stand by Caesar
> And give direction; and do but see his vice...

Another drop here into somewhat laden verse lends the passage sententious gravity; and the artless Montano is prompt to respond. For a signal of what is now imminent, Roderigo, drifting tipsily into the scene, is shot off upon his errand, is here and is gone—so swift can Iago be at a crisis—while Montano takes breath between sentences. And in another minute the mine has been sprung, and riot is afoot, with Montano also, by brilliant afterthought, involved.

Amid clamour and clangour, shouts, swords and the "dreadful bell" outtopping all, Othello appears, attended as before—by *Gentlemen with weapons*, say the Quartos; this helps depict him ruler of Cyprus. It is the second time that, by a sword or so, he, the soldier, stops, not forwards, a fight. Calm restored, be begins his sternly quiet questioning: first of Iago, who looks "dead with grieving", and so is plainly a witness, not a partaker, yet answers the "Who began this?" with a frank "I do not know"—leaving the culprits scope to damnify themselves the more; next of Cassio, too shamed to speak; then of Montano, disabled by his wound. Then it is Iago's turn again, and he has only—how conveniently!—to speak the truth. He gives it convincing clarity and circumstance, falsifies it ever so slightly. It is not the whole truth, that is all. Othello's sentence follows:

I know, Iago,
Thy honesty and love doth mince this matter,
Making it light to Cassio—Cassio, I love thee;
But never more be officer of mine.

Its place in the story besides, the episode serves the unfolding of his character. Here is the heroic calm still, but with a dangerous stirring beneath:

Now, by heaven,
My blood begins my safer guides to rule;
And passion, having my best judgment collied,
Assays to lead the way...

Iago and the broken Cassio are left alone. There is a moment's silence (marked after the tumult and the coming and going of guards and onlookers) while Iago quizzically surveys his handiwork. No stage direction is needed to indicate this. It is written into the text, with its breaking by the feline.

What, are you hurt, lieutenant?

—he still, most considerately, calls him "lieutenant".

There is nothing of the tragic hero in Cassio. He is as human in his repentance as in his folly, somewhat ridiculous—most enjoyable so to Iago—in the facility of his despair and the amplitude of his self-reproach, in such hyperbole as

> O thou invisible spirit of wine, if thou has no name to be know by, let us call thee devil.

Iago, making sure by one shrewd question that his own tracks are covered, lets all this wear itself out; then, "in the sincerity of love and honest kindness", gives him the fatal advice, gratefully accepted, to importune Desdemona to plead for him with Othello, and, not omitting another cryptically ironic "lieutenant" or two, sends him away somewhat comforted. He has steered back to the main lines of his plan:

> After some time, to abuse Othello's ear...

with means now provided.

The soliloquy which follows:

> And what's he then that says I play the villain?...

is a nodal point in the play, and it adds an essential to the viability of Iago's character. Until now he has been self-seeking; and Cassio's lieutenancy is surely in sight. But how will Desdemona's ruin profit him? It is evil for its own sake that he starts pursuing now; and out of her very goodness he will

> make the net
> That shall enmesh them all

—with which enrichment of wickedness opens a darker depth of tragedy by far.[12]

Here too would plainly be a striking finish to this long scene. But Shakespeare provides Iago instead with another exhilarating bout with Roderigo, who returns sobered—he also—by his beating, crestfallen and peevish. A few platitudes appease him. Iago has no further use for him; he has served his turn.

---

12. This soliloquy is more fully discussed in the section on the play's characters, p. 233.

But the despised little nincompoop will trip up his betrayer yet. That is the significance of his reappearance. He is dispatched to billet and bed. Iago, we note, needs no rest. The sun is rising. He also departs, briskly confident of adding to a good night's work a better day's.

THE ATTACK UPON OTHELLO

For relaxation before the tense main business of the tragedy begins we next have Cassio in the early morning bringing musicians to play beneath Othello's window (a pleasant custom, and here what delicate amends!), to this being added the grosser, conventional japes of the Clown. The few minutes so spent are offset by the unexpectedly close knitting of the main action when this begins again. For Iago finds no need to "set on" his wife to

move for Cassio to her mistress...

Cassio having saved him thus much trouble by making bold (he is sadly humbled, so to appeal to the waiting-gentle-woman) to send in to her himself. And she comes to report that Desdemona, unasked, is already speaking for him "stoutly". The economical compression strengthens the tensions of the scene, and the fortuitous furthering of Iago's ends bodingly suggests to us besides that the luck is with him.

For two last strokes of preparation we have Cassio, with the weak man's impatience, bent on importuning Desdemona to do for him what he has been told she is doing already, begging Emilia to gain him the

advantage of some brief discourse...

with her, alone, and a passing sight of Othello, at his general's task, Iago beside him, effectively promoted lieutenant already.

Then we see Cassio with Desdemona; but not alone. Emilia is there, it is before Emilia that she promises to help him. Upon them, after a—for us—expectant minute or so comes Othello. Iago has not, needles to say, drawn him "out of the way" as he told Cassio he would, but back here to find the two; Emilia's unexpected presence, he can show, a slight vexation to him. And it is in the midst of these indeterminate coming and goings that his muttered

Ha! I like not that

so effectively sows the seed—this tiniest of seeds—of tragedy.

The Ambiguity in Time: A Parenthesis

It is from this point, too, that the action passes into the ambiguity of time which has troubled so many critics. Compression of time, by one means or another, is common form in drama, and we have just seen it put to use in the speeding through a single unbroken scene of the whole night of Cassio's betrayal. But now comes—if we are examining the craft of the play—something more complex. When it is acted we notice nothing unusual, and neither story nor characters appear false in retrospect. It is as with the perspective of a picture, painted to be seen from a certain standpoint. Picture and play can be enjoyed and much of their art appreciated with no knowledge of how the effect is gained. But the student needs to know.

We have reached the morrow of the arrival in Cyprus and of the consummation of the marriage. This is plain. It is morning. By the coming midnight or little later Othello will have murdered Desdemona and killed himself. To that measure of time, as plainly demonstrated, the rest of the play's action will move. It comprises no more than seven scenes. From this early hour we pass without interval—the clock no more than customarily speeded—to midday dinner-time and past it.[13] Then comes a break in the action (an empty stage; one scene ended, another beginning), which, however, can only allow for a quite inconsiderable interval of time to judge, early in the following scene, by Desdemona's "Where should I lose that handkerchief, Emilia?"—the handkerchief which we have recently seen Emilia retrieve and pass to Iago. And later in this scene Casio gives it to Bianca, who begs that she may see him "soon at night". Then comes another break in the action. But, again, it can involve no long interval of time; since in the scene following Bianca speaks of the handkerchief given her "even now". Later in the

---

13. Midday is not specified, but it was the usual dinner hour.

scene Lodovico, suddenly come from Venice, is asked by Othello to supper; and between Cassio and Bianca there has been more talk of "tonight" and "supper". Another break in the action; but, again, little or no passing of time can be involved, since midway through the next scene the trumpets sound to supper, and Iago closes it with

> It is now high supper-time and the night grows to waste...

The following scene opens with Othello, Desdemona and Lodevico coming from supper, with Othello's command to Desdemona:

> Get you to bed on the instant...

and ends with her good-night to Emilia. The scene after—of the ambush for Cassio—we have been explicitly told is to be made by Iago to "fall out between twelve and one", and it is, we find, pitch dark, and the town is silent. And from here Othello and Emilia patently go straight to play their parts in the last scene of all, he first, she later, as quickly as she can speed.[14]

These, then, are the events of a single day; and Shakespeare is at unusual pains to make this clear, by the devices of the morning music, dinner-time, supper-time and the midnight dark, and their linking together by the action itself and reference after reference in the dialogue. Nor need we have and doubt of his reasons for this. Only by thus precipitating the action can it be made both effective in the terms of his stagecraft and convincing.

---

14. The suggestion is, moreover, that in point of time, these two last scenes overlaps; and, since the scene of Cassio's ambush moves so swiftly and that of Desdemona's murder, to begin with, so slowly, this suggestion can be brought home to the audience. Quite early in the first of the two we have Othello's

> Strumpet, I come!...

And, during the scuffling and confusion, the stabbing of Roderigo, Bianca's bewailings, Emilia's scoldings, he is already—and the precipitancy of his departure will have implied it—with Desdemona and about his deadly work. By the scene's end, therefore, and Iago's

> Emilia, run you to the citadel...

(which we shall not have forgotten when we hear her next knocking at the bedroom door) it is too late.

If Othello were left time for reflection or the questioning of anyone but Iago, would not the whole flimsy fraud that is practised on him collapse?

But this granted, are they convincing as the events of that particular day, the very morrow of the reunion and of the consummation of the marriage?[15] Plainly they will not be; and before long Shakespeare has begun to imply that we are weeks or months—or it might be a year or more—away from anything of the sort.

> What sense had I of her stolen hours of lust?
> I saw it not, thought it not; it harmed not me;
> I slept the next night well, was free and merry;
> I found not Cassio's kisses on her lips...

That is evidence enough, but a variety of other implications go to confirm it; Iago's

> I lay with Cassio lately...

Cassio's reference to his "former suit", Bianca's reproach to him

> What, keep a week away? Seven days and nights?
> Eight score eight house?...

More pointedly yet, Lodovico's arrival from Venice with the mandate of recall, the war being over—by every assumption of the sort, indeed, Othello and Desdemona and the rest are living the life of Cinthio's episodic story, not at the forced pace of

---

15. Determination to find possible gap in the action by which Iago's attack on Othello is entirely postponed by some weeks or months can only be rewarded by doing violence to the slight break in continuity between Emilia's offer to conduct Cassio to Desdemona with a "Pray you, come in", and Desdemona's reception of him with the

> Be then assured, good Cassio, I will do
> All my abilities in thy behalf.

And nothing can be plainer, by Elizabethan stagecraft, than a thus much interrupted) passage here from outer stage to inner, with Othello's passage across the outer stage—

> These letters give, Iago, to the pilot...
> This fortification, gentlemen, shall we see't?

—for a connecting link.

Shakespeare's play. But he wants to make the best of both these calendars; and, in his confident, reckless, dexterous way, he contrives to do so.

Why, however, does he neglect the obvious and simple course of allowing a likely lapse of time between the night of Cassio's disgrace and the priming of Othello to suspect Desdemona and her kindness to him—for which common sense, both our own, and, we might suppose, Iago's cries out? The answer is that there has been one such break in the action already, forced on him by the voyage to Cyprus, and he must avoid another.

The bare Elizabethan stage bred a panoramic form of drama; the story straightforwardly unfolded, as many as possible of its incidents presented, narrative supplying the antecedents and filling the gaps. Its only resources of any value are the action itself and the speech, and the whole burden, therefore, of stimulating and sustaining illusion falls on the actor—who, once he has captured his audience, must, like the spell-binding orator he may in method much resemble, be at pains to hold them, or a part of his work will be frequently to do again. Our mere acceptance of the fiction, of the story and its peopling—we shall perhaps not withdraw; we came prepared to accept it. Something subtler is involved; the sympathy (in the word's stricter sense) which the art of the actor will have stirred in us. This current interrupted by the suspension of the action is not to be automatically restored by its resumption. Our emotions, roused and let grow cold, must be roused again—and swiftly too, if, as in this play, emotion is to be a screen for liberties taken with the logic of the story's conduct. And the effects of such forced stoking will stale with repetition, until, if the actor in difficulties be tempted to coarsen the process too much, in its crudity it may fail of effect altogether.

Hence the help to the Elizabethan actor, with so much dependent on him, of continuity of action. Having captured his audience, he can the better hope to hold it. The dramatist may profit too. He will be spared the bridging of gaps by accounts of events intervening; secondary or superfluous matter, low in tension. Shakespeare hereabouts evades this aspect of the voyage to Cyprus and its inconveniences by ignoring them, and by restarting the divided action amid the stimulating—and effacing—anxieties of the storm. But such another—and necessarily a not too similar—device would be hard to find. Were he, moreover, to allow that likely lapse of time before the attack on Othello's confidence is even begun, it would but suggest to us as we watch the equal likelihood of an aptly scheming Iago letting at least a day or two pass between each assault to give his poison time to work. And with that the whole dramatic fabric would begin to crumble. Here would be Cinthio's circumspect Ensign again, and he would leave the action stagnating, with more gaps to be bridged, more intervening events to be accounted for, if ever so cursorily, the onrush of Othello's passion checked and checked again, and he given time to reflect and anyone the opportunity to enlighten him! Give Othello such respite; and if he then does not, by the single stroke of good sense needed, free himself from the fragile web of lies which is choking him, he will seem to be simply the gull and dolt "as ignorant as dirt" of Emilia's final invective, no tragic hero, certainly.

Shakespeare has to work within the close confines of the dramatic form; and this imposes on him a strict economy in the shaping of means to end and end to means, of characters to the action and the action to the characters. If Othello's ruin is not accomplished without pause or delay, it can hardly, under the circumstances, be accomplished at all. This predicates an Iago of swift and reckless decision (qualities that, again, the compression of time both demands and heightens) that will both win him his barren triumph and ensure his downfall. Then, again, Othello's precipitate fall from height to depth is tragically appropriate to the man he is—as to the man he is made because the fall must be precipitate. And that we may rather feel with Othello in his suffering than despise him for the folly of it, *we* are speeded through time as unwittingly as he is, and left little more chance for reflection.

Not, however, that continuity of action is of use simply for the sustaining of tension, nor that, continuity being kept, tension must not on occasion be relaxed; for if it were not—and fairly often—the strain, in any play highly charged with emotion, would become intolerable. But the dramatist can better regulate this necessary ebb and flow and turn it to account in the course of the action itself than if it is obstructed by repeated stopping and starting.

In all this, truly, Shakespeare treats time itself most unconscionably. But he smoothes incongruities away be letting the action follow the hourly calendar without more comment than in necessary, while he takes the longer one for granted in incidental references. And all is well while he sees that the two do not clash in any positive contradiction.

The change into ambiguity of time is effected in the course of Iago's first and decisive attack upon Othello. This is divided into two, with the summons to dinner and the finding and surrender of the handkerchief for an interlude. In the earlier part—although it is taken for granted—there is no very definite reference to the longer calendar, and Iago, until towards the end of it, deals only in generalities.[16] Not until the second part do we have the determinate "I lay with Cassio lately...", the story of his dream, the matter of the handkerchief, and Othello's own

> I slept the next night well, was free and merry;
> I found not Cassio's kisses on her lips...

with its implication of passing weeks or months after the morrow of the landing. But would it not also in reason be the better for the suggestion of some longer interval, during which Iago's doses of poison will have had more chance to work, than the dinner to "the generous islanders" can offer? But here arises again the question of continuity of action. A suggested interval would not only, from the standpoint of reason, seem to give the poison time to work but some antidote of good sense too. And from the standpoint of the play's action, such an interruption, actual or suggested, must lower its tension and dissipate interest, just when its main business, moreover, too long held back, is fairly under way. Shakespeare will certainly not feel called on to make such a sacrifice to the reasonabilities. Lowering it but a very little, he does break the tension upon Othello's and Desdemona's departure (Emilia left behind, the scene continuing, the continuity of action kept). He inserts the episode of the handkerchief. Treated by Iago, this will

---

16. There is, however, one earlier incidental sign that the longer calendar is already in Shakespeare's mind, Desdemona's reference to Cassio as

> A man that languishes in your displeasure...

—"languishes" certainly suggesting something more than a few hours of disgrace.

capture our interest. Then Othello returns, transformed from the man merely troubled in mind to a creature incapable of reason, "eaten up with passion..."; and a little of his emotion reflected in us will let us too lose count of time, obliterate yesterday in today, confound the weeks with the months in the one intolerable moment.

But the overriding explanation of what Shakespeare does here and at similar junctures is that he is not essentially concerned with time and the calendar at all. These, as with the actor and his behaviour, and other outward circumstances, must be given plausibility. But the play's essential action lies in the processes of thought and feeling by which the characters are moved and the story is forwarded. And the deeper the springs of these the less do time, place and circumstance affect them. His imagination is now concerned with fundamental passions, and its swift working demands uncumbered expression. He may falsify the calendar for his convenience, but we shall find neither trickery nor anomaly in the fighting of the intellectual battle for Othello's soul. And in the light of the truth of this the rest will pass unnoticed.

Examination of the Play's Shaping, Resumed

At no other moment than this, when she is pleading for Cassio with Othello, do we see Desdemona quite confidently, carelessly happy. She could beguile her fears for Othello's safe landing by laughing with the rest at Iago's sallies; but it was empty laughter. Into the ecstasy of their reuniting had stolen his boding

> If it were now to die,
> 'Twere now to be most happy...

Their first wedded intimacy was marred by the alarms of the broil. And when a little later she comes to call him in to dinner, the rift between them—though she does not know it—will have opened. Even with the tale of his headache and her

> I'm very sorry that you are not well

her gaiety has gone.

Shakespeare gives himself this single chance, then, of showing her, and Othello too, as they well might have hoped so happily to be. The picture is drawn in a few strokes; in her youthfully generous impatience of the discipline which makes Cassio "an example"; in the hinted sense of his—for her—eldrliness in the

> 'Tis as I should entreat you wear your gloves,
> Or feed on nourishing dishes, or keep you warm...

in his uxorious yielding and her sensitive response to the gently measured irony which covers it:

> I will deny thee nothing:
> Whereon, I do beseech thee, grant me this,
> To leave me but a little to myself

with the tender

> Be as your fancies teach you;
> Whate'er you be, I am obedient

—its pretty singsong only sharpening for us its unconsciously tragic presage. Her artless pride, too, in her new power of place as her "great captain's captain", shows in her bidding Cassio stay to hear her speak, with its confidence that then and there she can "bring him in". And her importunity seems so to publish her innocence that, as Iago stands watching the two of them—his first move, the muttered mock-impulsive "Ha! I like not that", already made—we may well ask ourselves whatever matter for a second he will manage to find.[17] Desdemona provides it him. For it is from her mischievously merry

17. The stagecraft hereabouts in presumably as follows: Desdemona, Emilia and Cassio are on the inner stage, where Cassio has been brought ("in") by Emilia for the beginning of the scene, for which the curtains will probably have been drawn back also. Othello and Iago enter on the outer stage. They re-enter rather; and the Quartos have them still accompanied by the gentlemen who went with them, a while since, to the fortification, and who will now, after a moment or so, vanish unnoticed. That the Quartos should not allow them an exeunt is nothing out of the way, and the only slight importance in their return is that it strengthens the continuity of the action. The outer stage now serves he purpose of a sort of ante-room (the modern editorial *Enter Othello and Iago at a distance* has no specific warrant; we owe it to The Theobald apparently), and this will account for Othello catching only a glimpse of Cassio as he leaves. It looks as if Othello was then meant to join Desdemona, momentarily at least, upon the inner stage while Iago remains in the "ante-room", removed from then at any rate, and free, while he watches them, to give expressive play to his thoughts.

What! Michael Cassio,
That came a-wooing with you, and so many a time,
When have spoke of you dispraisingly...

that he draws his

My noble lord...
Did Michael Cassio, when you woo'd my lady,
Know of your love?[18]

Iago, it will be remembered, is now playing for deadlier stakes than Cassio's lieutenancy. His net to "enmesh them all"; and while so far he has had no more precise end in view, the evil possessing him is no longer of the sort to be appeased by material gain. Nor has he, in fact, the means of inflicting such disaster on Othello. To whom could he betray him as he has betrayed Cassio? He must bring him to be the cause of his own undoing.

Before he provokes his passions Iago means to corrupt his mind. How to set about this? Not by direct assault; he cannot deal with him as with a Roderigo. Here too there must be self-destruction. The best he can do to begin with is to find some flaw in the moral defence, some little leak in the dike, and quietly contrive to enlarge it. Othello has unquestioning self-confidence. Yet he is no egoist; he translates this spontaneously into confidence in others. But the more unquestioningly it has been given the harder will any breach made in it be to restore; and to loss of confidence in the culprit will be added some latent loss of self-confidence too. He loved Cassio and his confidence in him was betrayed. He may forgive him; but not only can he never feel sure of him again, by just so much he will remain the less sure of himself. Here is a leak in the dike, which Desdemona by her pleading has already done something to enlarge; for Othello is yielding to her against his better judgment.

One way, and a swift one, to the corrupting of the mind is through a perverting of the imagination. Othello's is, even as his nature is, full-powered. But he has exercised it in spiritual

18. Additional evidence of his eavesdropping from the "ante-room" Had he been an open listener to their talk he would be asking a question of which he obviously already knew the answer.

solitude, and for that it is the less sophisticated and the more easily to be victimized by alien suggestion. Again, he must be induced to do himself the harm; and Iago, as the process is here illustrated and compressed, begins with words as bait; and, so to speak, he trails these words before him, sapping their integrity by questionable stress and intonation, by iteration lending them a cumulative power, setting imagination to confuse and falsify the plain thoughts which they should represent. It is a poetic practice bedeviled, and he is expert in it. And in the ensuing doubt and confusion he can the better operate.[19]

Forthwith, in answer to the sequent question he prompts Othello to ask him, he strikes the keynote of—

But for a satisfaction of my thought...

augmenting it with the pejorative

No further harm.

The combination vibrates in Othello's ear; and a rapidly reciprocated "thought...thought...think", with an echo of Desdemona's "honest" from her

I have no judgment in an honest face...

for reinforcement, issues in

What dost thou think?
Think, my lord?
Think, my lord?

By heaven, he echoes me,
As if there were some monster in his thought
Too hideous to be shown

—imagination both intrigued and balked. Iago's tacit pose provokes it further, and to the appeal:

if thou dost love me,
Show me thy thought.
My lord, you know I love you.

---

19. The student may find it convenient to have these passages of close analysis accompanied by the pertinent part of the text itself.

The feint at evasion can but halt before Othello's own unequivocal

I think thou dost...

and in a moment the opportunity is offered of

For Michael Cassio,
I dare be sworn—I think that he is honest

its shift from "sworn" to "think", doubling the dubiety of "think", making it the most provocative stroke yet.

The disintegrating play of word and thought continues. Iago, like a tricky wrestler, slips and dodges, evades and invites attack, nor lets himself be cornered until, upon the imperative

I'll know thy thoughts

he retorts with the defiant

You cannot, if my heart were in your hand;
Nor shall not, whilst 'tis in my custody

and coolly casts loose, sure that he at least has stirred Othello's imagination into a turmoil, riddled his mind with doubts.

He is skirmishing ahead behind this screen of word-play. Emerging, who still could be more disinterested, scrupulous, more benevolent than Iago? Trust in Cassio is inevitably flawed, with none but himself to blame. But no slur has yet been cast on Desdemona; unless an intonation in the sententious

Good name in man *and woman*, dear my lord,
Is the immediate jewel of their souls...

should strike Othello's sharpening ear. And the envenoming "jealously" is first insinuated, incidentally, as self-reproach:

it is my nature's plague
To spy into abuse, and oft my jealousy
Shapes faults that are not...

Confessing to our faults wins confidence. How, after that, should simplicity of heart suspect in fervent warning—

O, beware, my lord, of jealousy...

—the poisonous suggestion from which jealousy may breed?

Iago quickly slips back into the impersonal upon his homilectic "green-eye monster...". But the sting of the brutal "cuckold"—of the word itself and the very sound of it—will rankle, and to the invitation of the final "jealousy" Othello responds.

It is an encouragingly defenceless response; in the murmured "O, misery!", which Iago may rather surmise than hear, yet more so in the superficial confidence, the disdain, the apparently robust good sense of

> Why, why is this?
> Think'st thou I'ld make a life of jealousy...?

—as you, Iago, confess you do.

> 'Tis not to make me jealous,
> To say my wife is fair, feeds well, loves company,
> Is free of speech, sings, plays, and dances well...
> I'll see before I doubt; when I doubt, prove;
> And, on the proof, there is no more but this,
> Away at once with love or jealousy!

But it is all too positive; the protestations are too elaborate; that "jealousy" sticks in his mind like a burr, and will to the tip of his tongue. And for the first time "my wife" is specifically brought into the question. Nor does he take in the least amiss his friend Iago's interference in the matter. He ends, indeed, with a tacit invitation, something foolhardily like a challenge to him, to go further if he can. It is a challenge which Iago readily accepts.

Hereabouts, in terms of actual life, he might more wisely be breaking off this successful engagement, to return later to the attack with his gains consolidated, when the intellectual poison shall have spread, and the self-infecting fever of the imagination risen higher yet. Shakespeare, for reasons we have argued, does not commonly permit himself such gaps; but their admissible places are often traceable in the close-knit fabric by little—for a simile—knots and splicings where the threads change colour or thickness.

So here. Iago, thus encouraged (as he says) by his equanimity, by (as we see) Othello's ill-concealed trepidation, shows his "love and duty" to his "dear...lord" with a "franker spirit" indeed. Desdemona is no longer "my lady"; we have the bluntly familiar

Look to your wife....

instead, which quickly leads, by way of the insidious

I know our country disposition well....

(hint at the alien in Othello and the seed of much misgiving) to the first thrust home:

She did deceive her father, marrying you;
And when she seemed to shake and fear your looks,
She loved them most.

A twofold accusation; both aspects of it actually true; her very love for Othello turned seamy side without. A most apt thrust. And back to his mind must come—to ours also, for the moment was memorable—Brabantio's

Look to her, Moor, have a quick eye to see;
She has deceived her father, and may thee.

The very words; Iago had heard them.

The tormentor, from now on, has his prey intellectually broken in, and answering, compliantly or by recoil, to each touch on the rein, each flick of the whip; to such a show of unctuous devotion as the hardy mind would repel by a pitiable

I am bound to thee for ever

to the covertly derisive

I see this hath a little dashed your spirits

by the hollow

Not a jot, not a jot.

And he winces now at the very name of Cassio.

He must be brought to admitting his distress, to fettering it on himself, so to say. Iago reiterates, therefore, the

My lord, I see you're moved

and is repaid by he converting of that earlier, elaborate, dignified disclaimer into the feeble protest that he is not much moved...

while a return to the perplexity of

I do not think but Desdemona's honest

(but it is Desdemona now, not Cassio!) Shows that incipient poison to be still at work. How should Iago then resist the veiled sarcasm of

Long live she so! And long live you to think so!

The next opening Othello volunteers:

And yet, how nature erring from itself—

It seems to betoken a disquiet dilating more profoundly in him. Iago bodily takes advantage of it. Too boldly? he asks himself—when he has tarred Desdemona with

a will most rank,
Foul disproportion, thoughts unnatural...

—and he sidles into qualifying apologies, managing to make them, however, yet more damagingly to the point.

though I may fear
Her will, recoiling to her better judgment,
May fail to match you with her country forms,
And happily repent.[20]

But he need have felt no misgiving. Othello's

Farewell, farewell...

is friendly, although he will not be deceived by its ostensible carelessness, nor by the offhand.

If more thou dost perceive, let me know more...

20. "Will", in one of its sense, connotes carnal appetite. For us it has lost that meaning, so we lose here the effect of its use. Of what Iago means and would be understood to mean there is no doubt. But if Othello were to turn upon him he could plead the ambiguity of the word (Shakespeare continually plays upon it: for the most cited instance, see Sonnets 134-6) and take refuge in one of its politer senses. "Happily" the O.E.D. allows may stand for "haply".

Nor indeed can Othello sustain this. Despite himself there breaks from him the shameful

Set on thy wife to observe....

—hard upon its heels the curt

leave me, Iago

confessing the shame. And Iago himself must find it difficult to keep some colouring of excultation out of the obdedient

My lord, I take my leave.

Is he wise to return as he does instead of letting well alone? It is as if he could not keep his fingers off this instrument which now yields so fascinatingly to his touch. But he wants to make sure that in his absence the good work will go on, Cassio be held off, so that Desdemona in her innocence *may* "strain his entertainment", while Othello, primed just to this degree of suspicions, will watch them but say nothing—since, of course, a few frank words to either could still cut through the flimsy net. He meets, for response, with a stiff

Fear not my government.

But he is not deceived by the studied dignity of that.

Othello, the man of action, is not habitually introspective, and Shakespeare allots him this single true soliloquy. He is used neither to concealing nor analysing his own thoughts and motives, nor to conjecturing other men's. He is quite childishly impressed by Iago's cleverness at that—who

doubtless

Sees and knows more, much more, than he unfolds who

knows all qualities, with a learned spirit,
Of human dealings.

But he, his faith attacked, his imagination poisoned, his mind perplexed, and now alone, is a man spiritually rudderless and adrift. He surrenders first to panic:

> If I do prove her haggard,
> Though that her jesses were my dear heart-strings,
> I'ld whistle her off, and let her down the wind
> To prey at fortune

next, pathetically, to the humbling thought:

> Haply, for I am black
> And have not those soft parts of conversation
> That chambers have, or that I am declined
> Into the vale of years—yet that's not much....

then to precipitate despair:

> She's gone; I am abused, and my relief
> Must be to loathe her

—relief finding its immediate expression in such common-place sarcasms as the idealist turned misogynist will habitually have at call, talk of "this forked plague" and the like.

Then the mere sight of Desdemona—no more than that needed to dissipate these figments!—Seems to be about to make all well. Yet to her simple, happily intimate

> How now, my dear Othello!
> Your dinner, and the generous islanders
> By you invited, do attend your presence

he finds himself—despite himself—responding only with sardonically riddling evasions. The wedge of suspicion has been driven between them.

The soliloquy and this brief passage between the two form a trough in the waves of the action, allowing us a survey of Othello as Iago's first attack has left him; passions not yet fired, but mind and imagination bewildered and warped, confidence gone.

THE HANDKERCHIEF

The two depart to their "duty" dinner with "the generous islanders", and then follows the quick exchange between Iago and Emilia over the handkerchief. Thick-skinned Emilia's unscannable

> I am glad I have found this napkin....

is matched, as for contrast, against the gentle melody of Desdemona's parting line. Iago comes prowling, alert for Othello's return, to vent petty spleen on his wife because he finds her here instead (that much of safety valve he may allow himself); offering amends with a brutally indecent joke, quibbled away. Her indifference to such usage, her concern to gratify him! Her discrimination in dishonesty:

> What handkerchief?
> Why, that the Moor first gave to Desdemona,
> That which so often you did bid me steal.
> Hast stolen it from her?
> No, faith; she let it drop by negligence,
> And, to the advantage, I being here took't up...

and her shruggingly submissive departure at his curt bidding! Here is a pair united by very different bonds.

This makes but a forty-line interlude between Othello's departure, deeply disquieted, it is true, yet self-controlled still, and his return, a creature possessed. Nor does Shakespeare mitigate the inordinacy of the contrast by any pretended spinning-out of time or incidental change of subject, or shift of place. He does not even shift from verse to prose, and tension is fully sustained. But there is both surprise and substance in this episode of the handkerchief, and enough of both to secure our complete attention. So it serves equally as a solid division between the two capital scenes and as a firm bridge uniting them.

Its pettiness, besides, will throw into relief the toweringly tragic force of what is to come. Iago stresses this for us with his

> Trifles light as air
> Are to the jealous confirmations strong
> As proofs of holy writ: this may do something...

That it can be made to do what it does, a handkerchief found by chance and filched, that in such a trifle such deadly power can be lodged—men's lives at its mercy!—is, of course the dramatic point of its use. The poignancy of the tragedy gains by contrast with the pettiness. Further, a spice of sheer ill-luck is involved, and this relieves the severity of what has now become a tragedy of character, with its ordered cause and effect steadily pointing and leading to the justified end.[21]

Iago continues:

> The Moor already changes with my poison:
> Dangerous conceits are in their natures poisons,
> Which at the first are scarce found to distaste,
> But with a little act upon the blood
> Burn like the mines of sulphur.

This is the effective link between his late encounter with Othello and the one to come, and it shows signs of being arbitrarily compressed to make it so. "The Moor already changes..."—a hint here that Iago has come from watching him, just possible to suggest in action, amid this telescoping of time (if he came from the direction of Othello's departure), Emilia's ten lines to herself allowing for it. "Dangerous conceits..."—The repeated "poisons" may even point to an elision, the gap somewhat awkwardly closed. The sentence itself sums up Iago's scheming; and promptly with that "act upon the blood..." Othello reappears, by the very look of him to warrant the word.[22] Iago's elated, gratified

---

21. It is instinctive to compare the part played in the story by this episode with the piece of unalloyed ill-luck by which, in *Romeo and Juliet*, Friar John's journey to Mantua is stayed. By that and that only the play's catastrophe is precipitated. Shakespeare has much matured in art since then. In Cinthio's story the Ensign himself steals the handkerchief. In the play, to involve Emilia in the matter, she is let find it and hand it to Iago. That is a halfway step to accident, but no more. Nor does the business determine the catastrophe, only helps it on. Accident may find a place then, in tragedy, as it does in tragic life. But it had better not be pure accident, nor a decisive place.

22. It is to be noted than the Folio puts Othello's entrance after "I did say so", thus separating this from "Look, where he comes", to avoid which (apparently) modern editors are apt to put it after *that*. But both the Quartos squeeze their stage direction into the margin at "blood". One must not attach too much importance to such things nor found serious argument upon what may be a printer's vagary. But clearly, for the effect of Iago's "I did say so", Othello should, a brief moment earlier, have appeared upon the (inner?) stage.

I did say so:
Look, where he comes!

both rounds off this interlude and begins the second encounter between the two.

ANOTHER OTHELLO

Othello's silence as he stands there gains import from the sultrily ominous music of Iago's commenting

Not poppy, nor mandragora,
Nor all the drowsy syrups of the world,
Shall ever medicine thee to that sweet sleep
Which thou ow'dst yesterday.

Then, as he paces forward, to that bated

Ha, ha! false to me?

the jaunty

Why, how now, general! No more of that

is as the setting of a match.[23]

Iago's frigid sapience, those mocking precepts for the complaisant cuckold, are now flung back at him, translated into the agony of

I swear 'tis better to be much abused
Thou but to know't a little...
What sense had I of her stonel hours of lust?...
I found not Cassio's kisses on her lips...
I had been happy, if the general camp,
Pioneers and all, had tasted her sweet body,
So I had nothing known

—an agony which obliterates all else, all but itself and the moment, for us, if we feel with him, as for Othello; a factor of import, then, in the action's treatment of time.

---

23. The Quartos have a reiterated

false to me, to me?

The second "to me" may well be an actor's interpolation; there are, seemingly, a number of them in the play. Even so, it is some slight evidence—any being needed—that the line is meant to be throttled down in the speaking, not rung out clear.

But before he yields to his fury, Othello, in terms of what has been noblest to him in life, of

> the plumped troop and the big wars
> That make ambition virtue!...

takes tragic leave of what is noblest in himself. An instant later Iago's ironic concern is shocked into reality when the "waked wrath" of

> Villain, be sure thou prove my love a whore...

is loosed first of all upon him.

The sudden physical retaliation upon Iago is instinctive; he is not the author only, but the very instrument of torture. The cry for proof, even if it can only be of guilt, and for "ocular proof", is for some actuality which will displace these nightmare imagining before they riot into madness. The adjuration to Iago to

> abandon all remorse;
> On horror's head horrors accumulates;
> Do deeds to make heaven weep, all earth amazed...

reflects a vision of the abyss into which, if the thing is true, he sees that he himself may fall.

He has, it is evident, his man by the throat; and it is here that, for the first time, Othello loses self-control. Nor is it only that the old quiet authority of

> Keep up your bright swords, for the dew will rust them

has gone; the later warning to the night-brawlers:

> Now, by heaven,
> My blood begins my safer guides to rule...
> if I once stir,
> Or do but lift this arm...

could never have issued in trumpery violence such as this. Iago is stripping him of self-respect. When he next lifts his arm it will be to strike Desdemona.

This futile violence brings no relief, a moment's exhaustion only, which lets Iago recover his jolted wits, and turn his incessantly belauded honesty to good account. An indignant protest—

> Take note, take note, O world,
> To be direct and honest is not safe.
> I thank you for this profit...

—and a dignified essay at departure; and the ashamed Othello will certainly recall him. He remorsefully does; and by that will deliver himself yet more helpessly into his hands, faith in Desdemona wrecked, and none but the wrecker left for guide.

Here is, as it were, the end of one paroxysm of fever. Pending another, we see still at work the infection of mind in which the trouble was begun—

> By the world,
> I think my wife be honest, and think she is not;
> I think that thou art just, and think thou art not...

—at work now upon a weakened nature. Iago can safely administer more violent doses of poison:

> You would be satisfied?
> Would! nay, I will.
> And may: but how? How satisfied, my lord?
> Would you, the supervisor, grossly gape on—
> Behold her tupped?

and the racked cry of

> Death and damnation!

may compensate him somewhat for the indignity of his recent throttling. But the pure pleasure of inflicting pain so intoxicates him that for a second or two he is at a loss:

> What then? how then?
> What shall I say? Where's satisfaction?

And had Othello still sane eyes to see and ears to hear, the malicious savagery in the

> Damn them, then,
> If ever mortal eyes do see them bolster
> More than their own!...

Were they as prime as goats, as hot as monkeys,
As salt as wolves in pride...

could not but show him the man. Instead, himself bereft of reason, he demands

a living reason she's disloyal

and receives instead, in even grosser picturing, only more fuel for his frenzied imagining; and for "proof"—Iago deftly foisting in the word—a trivial tale of a handkerchief. And this the bankrupt mind welcomes with a pitiful

Now do I see 'tis true.

The essential work is done. And now, in a kind of antiphon to that farewell to the old Othello, is dreadfully conjured up a new:

Look here, Iago:
All my fond love thus do I blow to heaven:
'Tis gone.
Arise, black vengeance, from they hollow cell!
Yield up, O love, thy crown and hearted throne
To tyrannous hate! Swell, bosom, with thy fraught,
For 'tis of aspics' tongues!...
O, blood, blood, blood!

In it he blasphemes his so prized Christian baptism, kneeling

In the due reverence of a sacred vow...

to call upon a "marble heaven" to consecrate his revenge. Iago is equal to the occasion, falling upon his knees also, with magnificently histrionic irony, to partake this sacrament of evil, mocking its pagan piety the while. For by his practical doctrine evil is a servant, not a god, and the "wronged Othello's service" of his oath, his own.

Let him command,
And to obey shall be in me remorse,
What bloody business ever.

"Command", "obey"; he can afford to put it so; and note the

enticing reminder of the "bloody business". It is in cold blood that one part of the looked-for command is given—

> Within these three days let me hear thee say
> That Cassio's not alive

—and in covert delight received—

> My friend is dead; 'tis done at your request...

—you rid me, that is to say, of *my* rival and *your* friend. And with this profit on his investment in villainy Iago might wisely be content. But he has grown avid of evil for its own sake; and shall the splendidly lethal force that Othello is, now docile to his hand, be checked here? For a moment he fears so; until his feline

> But let her live

bring him the assurance of

> Damn her, lewd minx! O, damn her!
> Come, go with me apart; I will withdraw,
> To furnish me with some swift means of death
> For the fair devil

—suggesting, for the scene's end and its actors' *exeunt*, intents too terrible to be published to this light of day. Finally, two pregnant strokes:

> Now are thou my lieutenant.
> I am your own for ever.

Iago has won what he set out to win and more; and the double tongue, in that "I am your own..." through which so clearly rings an excultant "You are mine", proclaims the triumph of his double-dealing. But evil has him toiled as fast as he has toiled Othello, and he will trip and fall in the nets of his own weaving.

THE HANDKERCHIEF AGAIN

Enter Desdemona, Emilia and the Clown.

After the prolonged and close-knit tension some such unqualified relief as the Clown now brings with his antic chatter will be welcome. Twenty lines of it encase besides Desdemona's unconsciously ironic message to Cassio:

> Seek him, bid him come hither; tell him I have moved my lord in his behalf and hope all will be well.

Ten more give us her vexation at the mislaying of the handkerchief, and Emilia's underling's face-saving fib about it.[24]

Othello reappears. He head had been aching when she came to fetch him to dinner; hence her

> How is't with you, my lord?

He surveys her in enigmatic silence for a moment. To an unexpected tang of the sardonic in his answering

> Well, my good lady....
> How do you, Desdemona?

she opposes—as if they were well used so to rallying each other—the gently bantering mimicry of her

> Well, my good lord.

He has his fury on the curb now, but still he finds it "hardness to dissemble", and he approaches this test of the handkerchief fumblingly; at best his forthright nature is not apt at such wiles.

> Give me your hand...

—it is actually as if the mind, clogged with inhibited rage, could get no forther than the first syllable of the wanted word and thought. Her hand responsively in his stirs the old love and new hate mingled in him to queer sardonic figurings. Her innocent incomprehension leads him to the dead end of a sententious

---

24. The concluding

> but my noble Moor
> Is true of mind and made of no such baseness
> As jealous creatures are...

may seem, in critical cold blood, to be too immediately and pointedly apposite for likelihood. But in this it is, in its own way, of a piece with the general compression of the action; and its likelihood passes unquestioned with the rest.

The hearts of old gave hands;
But our new heraldry is hands, not hearts

but only for the effrontery—what else!—Of her

I have sent to bid Cassio come speak with you

to spur him promptly to a starting point:

I have a salt and sorry rheum offends me;
Lend me thy handkerchief

—crude, commonplace, all but comic.

Here, my lord.
That which I gave you.
I have it not about me.

She is vexed that she has not; yet for her it is but a handkerchief, so be sought for and sometime found. For him, fury seething in him, imagination luridly aglow, its loss becomes the very emblem of her guilt. And she can call—can she?—His anguished accusations

a trick to put me from my suit...

—her brazen suit that Cassio "be received again", which she can urge too by lovingly reproaching him with an

In smooth, you are to blame.

Lest he lose all power of dissembling and kill her then and there, he shakes her off and goes.

This scene is basically cast, and it must be acted, in a key of workaday domesticity[25]; and Desdemona's share of it, more particularly, should be viewed from that standpoint. It is noticeably detached, moreover, in tone and by an incidental touch or so, from yesterday's arrival and the swifter march of the action. Here they are, outwardly, as any comparable couple, married and settled, might be. Witness the knowing Emilia's comment on his outburst of ill-temper:

25. May not the whole play, indeed, be labelled a "domestic tragedy", Shakespeare's single essay of the kind?

> 'Tis not a year or two shows us a man.

Desdemona's bewildered

> I ne'er saw this before

and her later, chastened

> Nay, we must think men are not gods,
> Nor of them look for such observancy
> As fits the bridal.

She is more than vexed at the handkerchief's mislaying. But mislaying is not loss; and he is unwell, and she will not vex him needlessly. Besides, he is otherwise troubled already. Not until later, regretting even her mild part in their squabble—the milder, though, the more exasperating!—Does she argue that

> Something sure of state...
> hath puddled his clear spirit; and in such cases
> Men's natures wrangle with inferior things
> Though great ones are their object

by when, truly, she is, on reflection, puzzled and troubled enough herself to be searching for reassurance.

Was it singularly obtuse of her not at once to detect some menace in that queer scrutiny of her hand and queerer discourse? Here is, indeed, some light upon a factor in her character which contributes, if but passively, to her undoing. Desdemona is utterly unself-conscious. Othello's love for her, moreover, and hers for him, are a part now, she feels, of the natural order of things. They are in the air she breathes. She is uncalculating too, and it belongs to her happiness to be so. For her, with him, to think is to speak; and for him, with her, if the matter concerns the two of them, surely it must be the same. Whatever, then, may be behind his cryptic talk and conduct she will not readily imagine herself to be concerned. Nor in wifely wisdom, if she is not, will she aggravate an ill mood, whether by ignorantly probing or coldly disregarding it. She responds to its equivocal play with banter, with serious simplicity, lastly with a lightly impatient

> I cannot speak of this

—and proceeds to speak of Cassio.

Her suicidal persistence in pleading for him can be put to the account of her uncalculating candour too, of the frankness which is so flawless that, by Iago's evil logic, it may equally be flawless deceit. And here, when for once it is not quite single-minded, bad is made worse, not better.

For Cassio and the handkerchief become gages in a domestic tourney.

> That handkerchief
> Did an Egyptian to my mother give...
>   She dying gave it me,
> And bid me, when my fate would have me wives,
> To give it her...
>   there's magic in the web of it:
> A sibyl, that had numbered in the world
> The sun to course two hundred compasses,
> In her prophetic fury sewed the work....

—beneath the vehemence of this, of these mordant refrains from the tales of the days of his wooing that she had found so "passing strange", she flinches for a moment; it troubling her too, since the matter seems so to trouble him, that she has tripped into telling him a little less than the truth. But she recovers as quickly. She is no longer that wondering girl, nor a bride, even, but a wife confirmed in her status. The handkerchief is precious; but against this extravagant intimidation Venetian dignity and civilized good sense protest in a quietly admonishing

> Why do you speak so startlingly and rash?...
> Heaven bless us!...
> It is not lost; but what an if it were?

And if unhappily it prove to be, he may the better learn that when he is calm. But his peremptory

> Fetch't, let me see it

mere self-respect demands she face with a firm

> Why, so I can, sir but I will not now.

Then, suddenly, she makes the matter a trial of strength between them. Which is to prevail, reason or unreason?—with Cassio's case most unhappily chosen for an example of the reason he must show her.

> You'll never meet a more sufficient man.
> The handkerchief!
> I pray, talk me of Cassio.
> The handkerchief!
> A man that, all his time,
> Hath founded his good fortunes on your love;
> Shared dangers with you,—
> The handkerchief!
> In smooth, you are to blame.

She would soften the reproof by a caress, but with an enraged "Away!" he flings her off and is gone; hers, thus, the immediate victory, yet an ill one to win.

Emilia has some warrant for her sarcastic

> Is not this man jealous?

And if her conscience as she listened has been reproaching her for her own plain lie, her guiltier silence, Desdemona's well-meant evasions may have helped to ease it. A wife may excusably do as much to please a "wayward" husband as to placate an angry one, and a maid be less scrupulous than her mistress. But Desdemona, who asks no such petty victories, stays puzzled and troubled to the point that, Cassio now appearing with Iago, she quite forgets she has sent for him.[26]

She welcomes the distraction, and her generous mind recovers poise in her real concern for "thrice-gentle Cassio's" trouble. Iago deflects her from the thought that after all Othello's anger may somehow have its aim in her.

---

26. This will be the normal implication of

> How, now, good Cassio! What's the news with you?

But it is as possible that Shakespeare himself either momentarily forgot it, or—as is more likely—thought it more effective for Iago to bring him to her.

Can he be angry?
Something of moment, then: I will go meet him...

—for, while all is working well, explanations must be prevented.

It is this that she modestly and magnanimously enlarges into the

Something sure of state,
Either from Venice of some unhatched practice
Made demonstrable here in Cyprus to him...

as sufficient cause. So, without heed to Emilia's coarser wisdom and its warning, she will go seek him too and—"If I do find him fit...."—Yet again plead Cassio's cause; by which time in any case, Iago will have him safely out of the way which time, in any case, Iago will have safely out of the way.

She will now be absent from the action for a while, and the fine spirit she brings to it very markedly absent. But this short quiet passage, which is so expressive of her—selfless, high-minded, reasonable of heart—leaves her vivid to remembrance.

Promptly upon her going, and in sharp unlikeness to her, appears the little trull Bianca, the very woman that Iago is persuading Othello—his folly illuminated by the contrast—to believe Desdemona to be.[27] Her affectations find full display in the stale artifice of her

Save you, friend Cassio!...
What, keep a week away? Seven days and nights?
Eight score eight hours? And lovers' absent hours,

27. Bianca's appearance here illustrates an indefiniteness of place which fits well with uncertainty in time. The handkerchief has been lost somewhere within the bounds of Othello's dwelling. We are still upon that spot. What is Bianca, of all people, doing there? Cassio's surprised and irritated

What make you from home ?

goes halfway—the negative half—to counter the unlikelihood. As to time; he has been—this is explicit—"a week away" from her. Yesterday's landing, then, has quite gone by the board.

More tedious than the dial eight scores times!
O weary reckoning![28]

And in the squabble over the handkerchief, travesty of the one just past, we have jealousy reduced to its rightly ridiculous stature.

OTHELLO AT IAGO'S FEET

For the next scene's opening Bianca's pretty clinging to Cassio is succeeded by an Iago fastened to the heels of his wounded victim, so to say, and aggravating the wounds:

Will you think so?
Think so, Iago?

—the infected mind, under ceaseless sapping, is near exhaustion. Of argument there is no more need; the gross image will serve:

To kiss in private?...
Or to be naked with her friend a-bed
An hour or more...?

And the trumpery of the handkerchief—the word, once again, iteratred in his ear; Othello, with a feeble snatch at salvation, exclaiming,

By heaven, I would most gladly have forgot it

—is now to be turned to conclusive account. Each fresh stroke makes for the man's deeper debasing; and he welcomes them, asks for them:

Hath he said anything?
He hath, my lord...
What hath he said?
Faith, that he did—I know not what he did.

28. "Stale artifice" as she will utter it, coming when and where it does, and by contrast with the rest of the verse. Shakespeare could make the same sort of thing sound fresh enough in *Romeo and Juliet* and *A Midsummer Night's Dream*, when the play itself is dominantly cast in the mould of such artifice; and he gives it excellent comic effect in the later *As You Like It*. But here the imagery will sound, as it is meant to, flat and false. And so will Cassio's strained apology in the same kind.

What? What?
Lie—
With her?
With her, on her; what you will

—at which point he physically gives way, and collapses, babbling, *in a trance, at* Iago's feet.

It is a spectacular triumph. The humiliated Ancient has brought his General to this; the dignity, nobility, authority dissolved in these mere debris of a man. He must enjoy it for a moment, cannot but laud his venomous achievement with the ironic

Work on,
My medicine, work!

before he turns to a businesslike recovering—for further torture—of the stricken creature.[29]

Cassio appears (told by Desdemona to "walk hereabouts"); but after letting him show his concern Iago finds pretext to be rid of him. The sudden "no, forbear", betokens some fresh plan; and behind the smooth facade of

The lethargy must have his quiet course....
Do you withdraw yourself a little while,
He will recover straight: when he is gone
I would on great occasion speak with you

we may divine his brain at work on it.

Cassio gone, Othello recovering, he probably—if surprisingly!—does not intend his opening

How is it, general? Have you not hurt your head?

to bear the scabrous meaning, which still staggering and obsessed brain, by the reproachful

Dost *thou* mock me?

so pitifully lends to it. He will be the more amused to note how

29. Actors of Iago are accustomed to put their foot, for a moment, upon the prostrate body, even to give it a slight, contemptuous kick. This is wholly appropriate.

compulsively his medicine does work. He will note too that, as if from sheer exhaustion, Othello's rage seems to be flagging, since the cynical compliments, which he next metes out to him upon the certainty of his cuckoldom, rouse him to no more than a weary

O, thou art wise, 'tis certain.

The fresh trick he has now prepared, with Cassio once more for instrument and supplementary victim, will come the timelier, therefore. It is the most puerile of tricks: to provoke Cassio to talk scurril of Bianca and make the listening Othello believe it is of Desdemona. But Iago, grown foolhardy with success, begins now to jerk his puppets with contemptuous ease. He sets his ambush. Cassio will doubtless prove ready game, and he instructs Othello as assiduously as he might a child—who, indeed, cannot resist a preliminary peep from his hiding-place to whisper a

Dost thou hear, Iago?
I will be found most cunning in my patience;
But—dost thou hear?—most bloody.

In this passage to come Othello is brought to the very depth of indignity. Collapsed at Iago's feet, there was still at least a touch of the tragic in him, much of the pitiful. But to recover from that only to turn eavesdropper, to be craning his neck, straining his ears, dodging his black face back and forth like a figure in a farce—was ever tragic hero treated thus?[30]

Iago plays his game coolly and steadily, following his own good advice to "keep time in all", giving himself, however, the passing pleasure of pricking Cassio with a

---

30. Most actors of Othello, I think, have shirked this scene, wholly or in part; and Salvini (by the note in the Furness Variorum) justified its omission "on the ground that it is not in accord with Othello's character", that it belittled a man of such "haughty and violent temper" was not, in other words—we may fairly gather—in accord with Salvini's own dignity either. But that is, of course, the very point of it. From the dignity of the play's beginning Othello sinks to this, to rise again to the tragic dignity of its end.
The dodging in and out of hiding and the rest of the painfully grotesque pantomime is, of course, the most striking feature of the scene.

How do you now, lieutenant?

—the wounding word so seemingly needless a slip! He tantalizes the hidden Othello for a while with disconnected phrases and enigmatic laughter, which will make, besides, what he later does let him hear the easier to misinterpret. Bianca's unlooked-for return might well upset his calculations. But by good luck she has the handkerchief itself to fling back at Cassio with the most opportune

> A likely piece of work, that you should find it in your chamber, and not know who left it there! This is some minx's token, and I must take out the work? There—given it to your hobby-horse....

and her railing departure lets him send Cassio after her and so be rid of him, his unconscious part in the game satisfactorily played out.

Othello emerges, one thought predominant:

How shall I murder him, Iago?

He would have Cassio "nine years a-killing"; the "noble Moor" is stripped to savagery indeed. Desdemona must be kept in the current of his fury. Iago finds fresh obloquy for her; to be despised by her very paramour:

> And did you see the handkerchief?...to see how he prizes the foolish woman your wife! She gave it him, and he hath given it his whore.

He need not fear for her fate:

> A fine woman! A fair woman! As sweet woman!...let her rot, and perish, and be damned to-night.

Nevertheless from this moment Othello's torture becomes self-torture too. And the suffering that asks vengeance and the suffering that breads pity are at intricate war in him, rending him:

> my heart is turned to stone: I strike it, and it hurts my hand. O, the world hath not a sweeter creature......Hang her!.....but yet the pity of it, Iago! O, Iago, the pity of it,

> Iago!....I will chop her into messes. Cuckold me!

—his nature shown naked to us; no convention of verse or set prose intervening.

Pity, it would seem, might at least so far win as to open a way to the truth, were not Iago there, at his coolest, to steer, by occasional deft touches to the rudder, through this vortex. What smarter goad to a betrayed husband than the derisive

> If you are so fond of her iniquity, give her patent to offend; for if it touch not you, it comes near nobody

which does, in fact, move Othello to his ultimate

> Get me some poison, Iago; this night. I'll not expostulate with her, lest her body and beauty unprovide my mind again: this night, Iago.[31]

—for he cannot sustain these agonies longer. But Iago, though poisoning would be the safer plan, has a more pleasing picture in his eye: of Othello destroying with his own hands the beauty he had adored. How fittingly!

> Do it not with poison. Strangle her in her bed, even the bed she hath contaminated.

And Othello, not wicked at heart, yet with a wicked deed to do, snatches, as men will, at whatever vindication:

---

31. Having spun out *time,* for the sake of likelihood, Shakespeare now accelerates the *action* of the play; the distinction is to be noted. Cassio was to be dispatched "within these three days", while for Desdemona we have had so far nothing more precise than Othello's

> I will withdraw,
> To furnish me with some swift means of death
> For the fair devil

which followed hard upon Cassio's sentence. Now Desdemona is to die "this night", and Iago promptly promises news of Cassio's death "by midnight". The effect is that of the quickening flow of a river as it enters a gorge and nears a cataract; our interest quickness as we watch. No inconsistency is involved. That Othello, to be quit of the intolerable strain, and Iago lest his deceit be discovered, should each grow eager to precipitate the catastrophe accords both with circumstance and character.

Good, good! The justice of its pleases: very good!

the prospect of Cassio's death besides drawing from him an

Excellent good!

And upon this a trumpet sounds, and Desdemona appears with Lodovico, on embassy from Venice, ceremoniously attended.

By just such a trumpet call was Othello's own happy advent to Cyprus heralded, and we have heard none since. The scheme for his undoing was barely shapen then. This one finds him a man betrayed and self-betrayed, in moral ruin, Iago's creature, sworn to the murder of wife and friend. Yet at the sound, and the symbolic sight in Lodovico of Venice and her sovereignty, he becomes on the instant, to all seeming, the calm and valiant Moor again—frail though the seeming is too soon to prove. It is one of the salient moments of the play, and Shakespeare thus throws it vividly and arrestingly into relief.[32]

A Parenthesis: The Use of Lodovico: The Action Advancing of Its Own Momentum

With Lodovico's arrival the play enters a penultimate phase, worth brief consideration as a whole; of suspense, enriching of character, of full preparation for the long last scene. The horror of this has already been projected for us in the

32. Modern editions slightly obscure the intended effect by postponing the entrance of Lodovico and Desdemona until Iago has seen them and announced them to Othello, and so given him a second or two in which to recover his equanimity. But Q1 (commonly accepted here also for the spoken text in preference to the Folio) has

Ia. ...you shall heare more by midnight.
A Trumpet.
Enter Lodovico, Desdemona, and Attendants.
Oth. Excellent good:

What Trumpet is that same?

The sound of the trumpet and the simultaneous (or all but) entrance of Lodovico and Desdemona will thus surprise him in the very midst of his exulting over the murders to be done, and his effort to control himself will be given its full pictorial value.

> Get me some poison, Iago; this night. ...Do it not with poison. Strangle her in her bed. ...Good, good!...

and a lesser dramatist, bent on little else, might have cared merely to forge ahead to its consummation, tying off the main threads of the story as best he could by the way. Shakespeare, for all that he is now speeding the action to its end, is in no such haste.

Lodovico's coming weaves a fresh strand into the texture of the play. His mission, the recall to Venice, Cassio's succession—these are weighty matters; and he, bearing the mandate for them, is a figure of consequence. Despite the dire events in prospect then—Othello's murderous passion already breaking surface; Desdemona, vilely outraged, a woman in a daze—due ceremony must still be observed, the customary courtesies offered and accepted, cheerfully withal. Othello knows, the watchful Iago too, and we know, within how short a while the deeds to be done will savagely wreck this fine pattern of procedure. Meanwhile—life, as ordained, must go on.

But for the killing of Cassio—a bagatelle!—Iago's work is done. Until now we have been incessantly conscious of him urging events onward. Now, merely giving them an occasional deft touch or two, he can detachedly observe them, moving to their inevitable end. He comments regretfully—yet not hopelessly—upon their unhappy drift. It is an even more sinister aspect of him. He is pricked to activity again by the sudden reirruption of the absurd Roderigo, by the bringing home to him that he himself, even he, is lapsing into danger—and from such a quarter! He baits the fellow's death-trap with deliberate, economical care; it shall serve for Cassio's also. It is a deadlier, double-edged counterpart to the trick which undid Cassio before. It miscarries. Deprived for the first time of a cat's-paw, Iago has to handle the job himself, and he bungles it.[33] His own undoing has begun.

Thirdly, there is the so-called "brothel scene" and that of the "Willow Song". These are not necessary to the action at all; they are there to illuminate character. The first redresses a

---

33. It turns out that he has not even, as he supposes, rid himself of Roderigo.

much-disturbed balance, and restores to us an Othello who is neither mere bloodthirsty monster nor degraded puppet. The second brings us unforgettably near to a Desdemona defeated in "fortune" but not in goodness, and for the last time fully herself. The play would be impoverished indeed by the loss of these closing episodes of suffering and submission.

Analysis of the Action, Resumed

OTHELLO STRIKES DESDEMONA

By Lodovico's ceremonious solution, Othello's as ceremonious response—

> God save you, worthy general.
> With all my heart, sir.
> The duke and senators of Venice greet you.
> I kiss the instrument of their pleasures

(but note the oriental turn of phrase, a touch in it even of ironic humility)—the scene is set moving again upon a seemingly even keel. But beneath the compelled calm his rage will be surging only the more fiercely, we know. So does Iago, retired into watchful silence after his sardonically oracular reply to Lodovico's passing

> How does Lieutenant Cassio?

the

> Lives, sir

—for another hour or so.

Against this morbid calm—how like, how different from, the quiet dignity of our earliest sight of him—sounds out the happy melody of Desdemona's welcome to her "good cousin Lodovico", token of Venice and home to her, who "shall make all well", who, even better, comes to recall them from the exile to which she had so devotedly set out. Her innocedntly persistent "love I bear to Cassio" wrings from him a stifled

> Fire and brimstone!

while its contradiction in her joy at their return—Cassio to be left behind—he only ignores. For he is past reasoning; she besides as likely now to play the whore in Venice as here. His brain, indeed, racked by its efforts at self-control, seems near turning. His speech, when Desdemona nears him, degenerates to a jabbered

I am glad to see you mad

and upon her ruthful

Why, sweet Othello?

he strikes her.

She does not cry out. And this, with the amazed silence of the rest there, sets a seal upon the atrocious thing. Her only protest:

I have not deserved this

—then she weeps silently.

Lodovico's grave amazement shows in measured reprobation. But Othello, the blow struck, vindicates it—

O, devil, devil!
If that the earth could teem with women's tears,
Each drop she falls would prove a crocodile.
Out of my sight!

—and augments it with the cold cruelty of

What would you with her, sir?...
Ay; you did wish that I would make her turn:
Sir, she can turn, and turn, and yet go on,
And turn again; and she can weep, sir, weep;
And she's obedient, as you say, obedient,
Very obedient. Proceed you in your tears.

He comes, in this zest to insult and degrade her before the world, never nearer in spirit to the "demi-devil" who has ensnared him.

But the violent oscillation of thought begins again. As before between pity and rage, so now between the poles of

Concerning this, sir—O, well painted passion!
I am commanded home. Get you away;
I'll send for you anon. Sir, I obey the mandate,

> And will return to Venice—Hence, avaunt!
> Cassio shall have my place...

he sways, until—Desdemona dismissed—as if clutching for very sanity at anything of use and wont, he steadies to a

> And, sir, to-night,
> I do entreat that we may sup together;
> You are welcome, sir, to Cyprus...

and, after a final outburst (lunatic to his hearers; only we and Iago catch the connection):

> Goats and monkeys!

follows her.[34]

This long scene, with its fit of epilepsy, with Othello's degradation to eavesdropping and bloodthirsty savagery, with the outrage upon Desdemona, has been the play's most brutal and harrowing yet. It now ends with a quiet, gentlemanly colloquy between Lodovico and Iago; the one so shocked, disillusioned, grieved:

> Is this the noble Moor, whom our full Senate
> Call all in all sufficient? Is this the nature
> whom passion could not shake?...

—the other so regretfully making the worst of it:

> He is much changed...
> What he might be—if what he might he is not—
> I would to heaven he were!...
> Alas, alas!
> It is not honesty in me to speak
> What I have seen and known.

---

34. But *do*, we, across five hundred lines of speaking time, catch the connection with Iago's

> Were they as prime as goats, as hot as monkeys...

Not, it is possible, very exactly. But the phrase is a memorable one, and Othello's remembrance of it may sufficiently stir our own. To Lodovico it suggests, with the rest of the wild talk, that he may be off his head. He very nearly is, as the matter of the next scene, to which this phrase is a keynote, will more amply show.

Two men of the world, deploring such behaviour. But what more—in a difference to between husband and wife—what more than deplore it can they do?

THE "BROTHEL" SCENE. DESDEMONA AT IAGO'S FEET: EMILIA AROUSED

Othello's share in this next scene is, we noted, superfluous to the play's action; yet how impoverished would the picture of him be by the loss of it![35]

He has followed Desdemona. In contrast to the tepid end of the last scene we are admitted into the midst of a sharp cross-examining of Emilia by an Othello whom her pluck, roused for the first time, can at least set twice thinking. But here is the pathos of the matter. This questioning comes too late. He has pledged himself to a besotted belief in Desdemona's guilt. Denial of it now only tortures and enrages him; it is the offer of a comfort he can no longer take, the reminder of a happiness he has lost. Coming from Emilia it is witness to a conspiracy to deceive him; from Desdemona, it only show her the more hardened in guilt. Committed to his error, he only asks to be sustained in it, and hardened for what he has sworn to do.

So he does his best to shake Emilia's denials, and, when he cannot, relapses upon the sneer of a

That's strange

—which yet (since his happiness, if lost, is not forgotten) has a tang of wistfulness in it.[36] Whereat Emilia, good fighter that she is, seizes the slight chance:

I dare, my lord, to wager she is honest,
Lay down my soul at stake...

---

35. It is comparable in this respect to the scene in *King Lear* between Lear in his madness and Gloucester in his blindness. By neither is the action advanced; the characters are enriched by both.

36. The second sentence of his attack on her will read better if it is left a broken one:

Yes, you have seen Cassio and she together—

some opprobrious verb implied, a present participle probably. This will also help to restore the "she" to its nominative, and remove a minor editorial difficulty.

and hammers her daring home, leaving him without retort, but for a conclusive

Bid her come hither. Go.

We wait, when he is alone, for some sign that the tide of evil in him may be turning. But all that comes is the

> She says enough; yet she's simple bawd
> That cannot say as much. This is a subtle whore;
> A closet lock and key of villainous secrets:
> And yet she'll kneel and pray: I ha' seen her do it.

Though he can suffer still and regret, he is too weary-minded now to rid himself of the spell.[37]

Emilia, though unbidden, return with Desdemona, as if she foresaw danger threatening, and takes her dismissal reluctantly. Then twenty-five words suffice for a vivid prelude to what is to come, and even the action they demand is made plain in them:

---

37. It is customary, seemingly, to read this speech as if Emilia were bawd and whore both. But it is Desdemona, surely, whom Othello assails as whore. This is to be the starting point of his coming scene with her. It is certainly her and not Emilia whom he has seen "kneel and pray". Hence the later, sardonic

Have you prayed to-nigh, Desdemona?

To gibe at Emilia for praying is sheer dramatic waste.
As to how to identify the
This is a subtle whore...

with Desdemona, that is simple enough. We are momentarily expecting her appearance by the way Emilia has departed. Any competent actor can combine the "this" with a gesture which will unmistakably apply to her.

Let a difficulty be admitted in the
closet lock and key of villainous secrets...

which does seem to connect in thought with the orders to Emilia to "shut the door" and (later) to "turn the key". But Othello's mind is still flinging violently an arbitrarily between one subject and another: and the connection is hardly close or definite enough to invalidate the more dramatically appropriate reading.

My lord, what is your will?
          Pray, chuck, come hither.
What is your pleasure?
          Let me see your eyes;
Look in my face.
          What horrible fancy's this?

—the distantly proud humility of her response to his summons; her approach at his bidding with eyes downcast, since if he feels no shame for the blow struck she feels if for herself and him too; her eyes as obediently lifted, she sees in his for the first time that which appals her.

"I'll not expostulate with her," he had told Iago, "lest her body and beauty unprovide my mind again...". But he cannot, he finds, forbear. So he first, in self-defence, smirches to himself that "body and beauty" by picturing her as a whore in a bawdyhouse, traded to him for a turn. The sight of her on her knees, looking so "like one of heaven" that the devils themselves might fear to seize her, the very cadence of her protesting

Your wife, my lord, your true and loyal wife

exclaim against the perversity. He must then needs mesh himself yet deeper in it. Damned once for adultery, she shall "double damn" herself by swearing she in innocent. For her sin against him he will take vengeance. Her sin against herself, her goodness and beauty, and against his faith in them—that breaks his heart. He has only to believe she is innocent when she swears it; but this is the one thing he can no longer do. Nor can he reason and explain; he is as a man hypnotized, possessed. Raised here to the pitch of poetry, it is in substance the commonest of cases. Two beings who have, as have these two, reached intimate communion, cannot, once this is broken, fall back upon a simply reasonable relation.[38] His collapse in tears lets her approach him. She tries to find him excuses for his treatment of her. But what

---

38 Cf. the scene between Hamlet and Ophelia, built upon much the same psychological basis.

can now bridge the gulf opened between them?[39]

Only slowly has she gathered, does she force herself to understand, what is the "ignorant sin" he will have it she has committed. And not until, emergent from his self-conscious suffering, his eyes on her again, he catches that "committed" with its unlucky connotation of adultery, does he—iterating it, as other words have been set iterating in his hot brain; swinging it round him like a weapon—deal her blow upon blow:

> What committed!
> Impudent strumpet!...
> Are not you a strumpet?...
> What, not a whore?

—blows more grievous by far than that which must physically mark her still. But these she does not take meekly, resists them, rather, with an explicit and religious pride—

> No, as I am a Christian:
> If to preserve this vessel for my lord
> From any other, foul unlawful touch
> Be not to be a strumpet, I am none

—which only drives him back, hardened, upon the brutal sarcasms of his brothel imagery. Resummoning the bewildered Emilia, he leaves her.

---

39. What she says of her father here—

> if you have lost him,
> Why, I have lost him too

—is not meant to indicate that she already knows of his death. Shakespeare would not let her refer to it thus, "in passing", even at such an otherwise distressed moment as this. We learn of it later, after she is dead herself, from her uncle Gratiano, brought into the action, most inconspicuously, for, it would seem, this sole purpose. Brabantio having been too important a factor in the play to be left unaccounted for at the end. Nor, at this juncture, would Shakespeare want to add a "second string" to Desdemona's suffering. The nearer to the play's end we come, the more important it is to sustain the singleness of the tragic motive. All she means, then, by "I have lost him too" is that (as we know) her father has cast her off.

Her flash of defiance extinct, she is left spiritually stunned. Her hurst may be measured by the wan humour of her answer to Emilia's troubled question how she does:

> Faith, half asleep

—too deep a hurt for her not to welcome a moment's stupour, not to make light of it, if she but could. She awakes, as out of sleep, to certainty of loss, sees herself in the cold light of it. What is left her but to weep?—And weep she cannot. Sensible to some fatally pending consummation of this inexplicable evil, the dire end to all their joy:

> Prithee, to-night
> Lay on my bed my wedding sheets: remember...

But she sends too for the shrewd, practical Iago. While she awaits him indignation surges in her

> 'Tis meet I should be used so, very meet!

—which melts under his velvet touch to the rueful simplicity of

> Those that do teach young babes
> Do it with gentle means and easy tasks;
> He might have child me so; for, in good faith,
> I am a child to chiding.

Nor, a moment later, kneeling there, begging him to intercede for her, is the conscious of any abasement before the two, dependents as they are.

Candour is of the very essence of Desdemona's character, a spontaneous candour, uncalculating, inconsistent; open then to all suspicion. Here what she does and says is as the reflection of passing clouds in a clear mirror. One avowal succeeds another. Each shows her differently, and all with truth.

Childishly, she cannot bring herself to repeat the "name" that Othello has called her. It is at the sound of it, rapped out by the less fastidious Emilia—

> He called her whore...

—and upon Iago's so reasonably pertinent enquiry:

Why did he so?

that she at last breaks into tears. Emilia is so filled with wrath and so lost in the satisfaction of venting it, that the solution—

> I will be hanged, if some eternal villain,
> Some busy and insinuating rogue,
> Some cogging, cozening slave, to get some office..

—which she hits upon within an inch, still escapes. Her.

For Iago this is another, and a gratuitous triumph. When Othello fell convulsed at his feet, he had taken pains for that. But to have Desdemona humiliated there too, and imploring his help, is an unlooked for pleasure. He sovours it complacently.

The trumpets summon to supper. Desdemona must dry her eyes and once more play the regnant hostess at Othello's side. Iago watches her go, Emilia tending her. Surely he has achieved his end. But he turns to be confronted by an absurdly angry Roderigo.[40]

RODERIGO AGAIN

Amid these crowding events we may well have—even as it seems for the moment has Iago—all but forgotten his existence; the more comically outrageous, then, the incongruity between Othello's fall, Desdemona's agony and the tale of his own wrongs, into which he so portentously launches:

> I do not find that thou dealest justly with me

—into the horrors of this pending tragedy thrusts Roderigo, demanding justice!

But we laught at him unfairly. He knows of no troubles but his own; and there is something pathetic in being so ridiculous

40. Another instance of the usefulness of indeterminate locality. Roderigo has not much more business in a room in which Othello and Desdemona have recently been so intimately alone than had Bianca in a similar vicinity. But—unless we are reminded by scenery—we shall not consider this. And the effect to be made here depends upon Iago's sudden turn from his cold survey of the pathetically submissive figure of Desdemona to encounter Roderigo's coxcomb revolt. It would be lost by an exit, a cleared stage, or re-entrance.

in oneself. His case against Iago is strong. He has been most patient. It is time he took a high hand. He has summed up his grievances, sought choice expression for them, studiously—it is evident—rehearsed it, and for once he means to do the talking:

> Every day thou doffest me with some device, Iago; and rather, as it seems to me now, keepest me from all conveniency, than suppliest me with the least advantage of hope. I will indeed no longer endure it.

He finds himself most magnificently overriding Iago's protests. The fellow is his social inferior, after all, and no better than a pimp:

> The jewels you have had from me to deliver to Desdemona would half have corrupted a votarist: you have told me she hath received them and returned me expectations and comforts of sudden respect and acquaintance...

So, despite being tempted into one rather shrilly feeble parenthesis—

> Very well? Go to? I cannot go to, man; nor 'tis not very well!...

—he reaches his peroration in fine form:

> I will make myself known to Desdemona. If she will return me my jewels I will give over my suit and repent my unlawful solicitation; if not, assure yourself I will seek satisfaction of you.

Iago gives a second or so to the assembling of the implications of this admirable combination of penitence and thrift, and then quickly comments:

> You have said now

—as indeed Roderigo has, and pronounced his own doom.

For the time being there is only Iago's tiger smile to tell us this, although it should suffice. The revealing soliloquy is postponed to a later scene, until the plan now concocting behind the smile shall be actually in action, the ambush set. It will then be speeded through, as at that moment it must be. This both avoids delay here, and denies to the disposing of Roderigo and Cassio the fierce thought given to Othello's ruin. For Iago, flushed with success and scornful of these minor victims, is recklessly improvising now.

But he takes the floor—and the balance of the scene shifts at once—with a magnanimous

> Why, now I see there's mettle in thee; and even from this instant to build on thee a better opinion than ever before...

and overrides Roderigo in turn, and ignores his ill-temper and saps his resolves, and cajoles him and manoeuvres him with the old adroitness. Within a little he has the repentant libertine converted to prospective assassin. Yet Roderigo

> will hear further reason for this.

Reason and Roderigo go well together.

DESDEMONA DIVESTS HER—FOR DEATH

Between the devising of this first of the midnight murders and its execution we have a scene of ordered calm; of ceremonial courtesy, of Desdemona's divesting her for sleep.

Enter Othello, Lodovico, Desdemona, Emilia and Attendants.

They come from the supper to which we heard the trumpets summon them. It will hardly have been a spontaneously gay repast, as a certain evasiveness in Lodovico's urbane

> I do beseech you, sir, trouble yourself no further

may imply. Each line of these few is lightly pregnant; and an edge to the tone of it, the colouring of the phrase, the actor's look or gesture will tell us what is astir beneath the tension. Othello(it is Emilia''s later comment)

> looks gentler than he did...

—she did not hear, then, his brutal command to Desdemona;

> Get you to bed on the instant; I will be returned forthwith: dismiss your attendant there: look it be done

(the dry anonymity of the "your attendant there" emphasizing their menace) pendant to his as urbane determining of Lodovico's chivalrous courtesy by bowing him on their way together with an undeniable

> O, pardon me; 'twill do me good to walk...
> Will you walk, sir?

So they depart, their escort after them.

In the passage which follows all action whenever, save for the wonted nightly "unpinning", is arrested; there is no other such in the play. Of action of every sort, and of violence and distress of speech, we have so far had plenty. This prepares, in its stillness, and in the gentle melody of the songs, for the worse violence and the horror to come, and is, as we have noted, a setting against which no shade of Desdemona's quiet beauty can be lost.

The strain of self-control before Lodovico relaxed, she finds herself suddenly steeped in sheer physical fatigue. She repeats Othello's orders to her—

> He says he will return incontinent:
> He hath commanded me to go to bed,
> And bade me to dismiss you

—without comment. And her response to Emilia's alert, alarmed

> Dismiss me!

is but the listlessly submissive

> It was his bidding...

Yet the morose

> I would you had never seen him!

draws a quick

> So would not I: my love does so approve him,
> That even his stubbornness, his checks, his frowns,...
> have grace and favour in them.

Spiritless? It is not that. But if his love has failed her she must find refuge in her love for him.

Upon her weariness fancies and memories play freely. Reminder of the wedding sheets (imaging—so she had meant them to—the end as the beginning of their wedded joy) begets the fancy to be shrouded in them some day. From that evolves the memory of her dead mother, and of the maid Barbara and *her* "wretched fortune", and the song which "expressed her fortune"; and this recalls Venice, and for Venice stands the handsome, grave Lodovico.

The sad rhythm of the song, as she sings it, soothes her mind, if it leaves her senses still morbidly acute:

> Hark! Who is't that knocks?
>
> It is the wind

answers matter-of-fact Emilia. And she can note now such petty matters as that her "eyes do itch" and ask lightly if that "doth...bode weeping, and even half-humorously shake her head over

> these men, these men!

We are seeing the last of Desdemona, but for the midnight moment in which she will wake only to the horror of her death. So, for a finish to the scene, and a completing of her character, Shakespeare stresses the trait in it which has incongruously proved to be the fittest material for this tragedy, the goodness—the too absolute goodness—of a fibre of which Iago's enmeshing net has been made.

It is Brabantio's daughter who now speaks; the daughter of a great house, strictly, isolatingly reared, and conserving—launched into the world—a gently obstinate incredulity of its evil:

> Dost thou in conscience think—tell me, Emilia—
> That there be women do abuse their husbands
> In such gross kind?

and it will be in some incredulity of such innocence that Emilia so circumspectly answers,

> There be some such, no question.

But she is glad of the chance to cheer her mistress with a little salty humour, to agree that "by this heavenly light" she would not wrong her husband, since

> I might don't as well in the dark

and then to treat these tenuous ideals with the hardening alloy of some good coarse common sense. But Desdemona stays unimpressed:

> Beshrew me, if I would do such a wrong for the whole world

and, what is more,

> I do not think there is any such woman.

Emilia, her tongue once loosed, waxes eloquent upon wedded life and how to live it. Sound, practical doctrine! Expect little, overlook much; but threaten, and give, tit for tat. And as we listen, and watch Desdemona indifferently listening, and mark the contrast between the two, there may slip into the margin of our minds the thought: better indeed for her had she been made of this coarsers clay. But then she would not have been Desdemona.

IAGO BEGINS TO BUNGLE

When Desdemona and Emilia have departed,

Enter Iago and Roderigo.

This is the play's penultimate scene. It is thrown (as usual) into contrast with the quiet colloquy just ended; and the high organic tragedy of the scene to come will in turn stand contrasted with its turmoil. It is besides a counterpart to that other night scene which marked the arrival in Cyprus with Cassio's disgrace, and is thrown into contrast with that too. For while the chief puppets are the same, Iago no longer manoeuvres them with the same enjoyable ease; and the stakes in the game are more desperate, no mere thrashing and the cashiering of Cassio, but, by one means or another, death for them both, and quickly, lest puppets turn dangerous. His capital scheme has moved faultlessly towards fruition. But even now what might not happen to stay Othello's hand, or to turn it, or Cassio's, against him? For full success, all the threads must be knotted up and cut together. Well, the "young quat" Roderigo's ire can be turned to the cutting of two at one stroke, since

> whether he kill Cassio,
> Or Cassio him, or each do kill the other,
> Every way makes my game...[41]

He calculates as shrewdly as ever, but more summarily; he plays high and recklessly still. This scene is the last, moreover, of which he directs the action; and its crowding, feverish movement after the long-sustained scheming, comes as the breaking of a dam. But, ominously, he bungles the stroke which, Roderigo having bungled his, could still rid him of Cassio. By now even *his* nerve is strained. The crisis wrings from him too that strange involuntary

> if Cassio do remain,
> He has a daily beauty in his life
> That makes me ugly...

although, as if surprised by such a thought, he quickly obliterates it beneath the more matter-of-fact

> and, besides, the Moor
> May unfold me to him: there stand I in much peril...

And it is a nakedly brutal scene, in which the first murderous harvest of all the complex trickery and treachery is so summarily reaped.

Ironic flattery of his "good rapier" will not make Roderigo a very competent murderer, but the "satisfying reasons" demanded have at least stiffened that once-sentimental lover to the pitch of a callous

> 'Tis but a man gone

and a cowardly thrust in the dark. He gets in return yet better than he gives; and, after a few moments grovelling agony an one last terrible flash of enlightenment, here will be the end of

---

41. The Quartos have "game", the Folio "gaine". The Folio may in general be the better text, but the suggestion of gambling certainly fits the mood of the scene.

him.[42] He had done Iago's schooling some credit; one pities the poor wretch, nevertheless.

Cassio, retaliating on Roderigo, is in turn served out by Iago—who, however, having made no clean job of it, prudently vanishes.[43] The noise brings Othello out upon the balcony above. He has heard Cassio's voice; he knows it well. But in the silence that has fallen and the darkness, his straining ears only catch after a moment Roderigo's low repentant moan:

O, villain that I am!

—a shamefully swift relapse from villainy![44] Cassio's cry, however:

O, help, ho! light! a surgeon!

reassures him—his betrayer dying if not dead—and he exults to the perennial infatuate refrain:

'Tis he. O brave Iago, honest and just,
That has such noble sense of thy friend's wrong!
Thou teachest me...

Up to this moment it has been just possible, we may have felt, that Othello, swinging between rage and suffering, might

---

42. Later it turns out otherwise. We learn in the last scene that

even but now he spake
After long seeming dead...

and witnessed against Iago. But I suspect this to have been an afterthought on Shakespeare's part. In this scene certainly there is no hint that he is not dead, every evidence that he is.

Incidentally Q2 has, when Iago stabs him, *thrusts him in*. The direction implies that there were not (when this edition was viable) two men available to carry away the body at the scene's end, Cassio's chair having the prior claim.

43. After "But that my coat is better than thou knowest" he does not waste time in thrusting at Cassio's padded doublet, but slashes below it at his groin. Iago's aim would be better and the stroke a fairly fatal one had he not to keep his face hidden. Even so, Cassio can exclaim, "I am maimed for ever...My leg is cut in two!"

44. Othello's "It is even so" of the Folio, could be read—the voice mistaken for Cassio's—as savagely sarcastic comment, and perhaps effectively. The Quartos' "Harker, 'tis even so" simply gives continuity to his speech and serves to keep our attention as much upon him as upon the two figures below.

somehow purge himself of the evil in him. But Iago has set the example, and the wild beast has scented blood:

> Minion, your dear lies dead,
> And your unblest fate hies: strumpet, I come!...

And to the stuttering, choking fury of the crowded last couplet—

> Forth of my heart, those charms, thine eyes, are blotted;
> Thy bed, lust stained, shall with lust's blood be spotted.

—he goes to do the deed prepared. Desdemona is doomed.[45]

As he vanishes Cassio calls out again, and this time Lodovico and the hitherto unknown Gratiano appear.[46] We hear them

---

45. Another passage which producers of the play and actors of Othello conspire to omit, on the ground, presumably, that, as in the eavesdropping upon Cassio, his behaviour here lacks dignity. But that, of course, as with the eavesdropping, is the very point of it. In the course of the play Othello is swung, and ever more widely, between the conviction that he is taking righteous vengeance on Desdemona and the primitive savagery which this rouses in him—and without which, it well may be, he could not so overcome his own anguish as to take it. In this stuttering, chocking outbursts he drops nearer to the savage than ever yet; from it he will have risen, at our next sight of him, to the tragic height of

> It is the cause, it is the cause, my soul...

46. If the stage for which *Othello* was written boasted not only the centre balcony, *i.e.*, the upper stage, but one over each of the side doors as well, I think that almost certainly Lodovico and Gratiano appeared upon one of these. But the centre one alone would be wide enough to allow them to enter it by one side an instant after Othello has left it by the other without seeming to be in awkward proximity to him. There is nothing against this in their own

> To come *in* to the cry...

or in Iago's appeal

> What are you there? Come *in* and give some help

the "in" being merely a figure of speech; if it were not, "out" would be the appropriate world. In either case they seem to be meant to respond by descending to the lower stage: and while they pass momentarily out of sight in doing so, Iago can the better dispatch (as he thinks) the wounded Roderigo. He then confronts them below with his

> What may you be? Are you of good or evil?

mistrustfully whispering;

> Two or three groan: it is a heavy night:
> These may be counterfeits: let's think't unsafe
> To come in to the cry without more help

—and there they stay, and nothing more happens for the moment. Cassio's cries are now reduced to an exhausted "O, help!", Roderigo is still repentantly groaning. Then Iago returns, "in his shirt", like one roused from his lawful slumbers, carrying a light, alert and helpful; just such a ready change worked in him as went with that first swift passing from beneath Brabantio's balcony to the Sagittary, from Roderigo's side to Othello's.

He seems not to recognize Cassio; how should he look to find him here? When he does his commiseration is heartfelt:

> O me, lieutenant! What villains have done this?

—for he cannot at the moment finish his bungled job, since, he notes, there are onlookers now. But he can at least do swift justice upon the one villain who

> is hereabout
> And cannot make away.

And the prostrate Roderigo is welcome to see his face as he stabs him, for he will take care not to miss his stroke this time. He finds, indeed, some pleasure in thus winding up accounts with his dupe. And he easily drowns the aghast shriek:

> O damned Iago! O inhuman dog!

with a stentorianly indignant

> Kill men i' the dark! Where be these bloody thieves?

Roderigo, he may well suppose, will trouble him no more.[47]

For an instant, as he stands there by the body, nothing stirs.

> How silent is this town!

he says; an accusing silence which he breaks with an echoing

---

47. See, however, p. 197, note 42, and page 222, note 61.

Ho! Murder! Murder!

Those prudent onlookers approach—Lodovico he recognizes, the other is less distinguishable—and he can now, with them to witness, give undivided care to Cassio, his stricken comrade, his very "brother"; grief wrings the word from him.

He makes sure that Cassio has no clue to his assailants. Bianca's appearance, and her hysterical collapse at the sight of her lover, offer her to him for a scapegoat. The lifeless Roderigo, recognized and well wept over, may be turned to more account yet.[48] And while he mentally assembles the factors for some fresh, plausible fiction, he is here, there and everywhere, binding Cassio's wound, summoning a chair for him, seeing him safely into it and away. He is as ready and quick as ever; but possibly too quick, somewhat emptily ready. It is easy to browbeat Bianca, and he does so with gusto, arraigning her before these Venetian dignitaries Lodovico and Gratiano:

> Stay you, good gentlemen. Look you pale, mistress?
> Do you perceive the gastness of her eye?
> Nay, if you stare, we shall hear more anon.
> Behold her well; I pray you, look upon her:
>
> Do you see, gentlemen? Nay, guiltiness will speak,
> Though tongues were out of use.

---

48. There may be, I think, textual error here in Iago's repetition of Bianca's

Who is't that cried?

He can scornfully echo her; I see no other reading, nor very much dramatic point in that. It is possible, therefore, that Iago's original sentence is lost and that this replaces it.

That Shakespeare has every thread here clear in his mind is shown by Gratiano's telling Cassio that he has been to seek him. It will have been to inform him of his promotion to governor. Gratiano, who brings also the news of Brabantio's death, is a later arrival from Venice than Lodovico. It is the last of these compressions of the action, and very inconspicuously made. Not besides that while there are several references to the governorship, the last, in Cassio's presence at the end of the play, he is never told of it directly. As with Brabantio's death, of which Desdemona is never told, Shakespeare does not want at this juncture to give a subordinate matter primary importance.

All very menacing! But of *what* he is to accuse her he has evidently no idea; he is searching as he speaks. Emilia's arrival and the need to repeat the tale of her give him the liar's valued chance to tell the economized truth. He pursues the Bianca trail:

> Prithee, Emilia,
> Go know of Cassio, where he supped to-night.
> What, do you shake at that?

But Bianca, by now, is in fighting trim, and can answer Emilia's

> Fie, fie upon thee, strumpet!

with a smart

> I am no strumpet, but of life as honest
> As you that thus abuse me.

Each boasts and counterboasts her respectability until Iago cuts them short with

> Emilia, run you to the citadel,
> And tell my lord and lady what hath happed.

Another blunder, thus to send her posting off! Might she not come in time to stop the murderous work afoot then? But his final

> This is the night
> That either makes me, or foredoes me quite

(he stays behind the rest to confide it to us), the old confident swagger marred for the first time by a strain of doubt, speaks of some sense in him that his "divinity of hell" may not have armed him quite invincibly after all.[49]

THE END

The events of the first three scenes of the play, we noted, could be presumed to pass in just about the time it took to act them, and this was time enough for an exhibition of the chief characters

---

49. At two points in this scene the question can be raised of the comparative effect to be made by implied as against actually exhibited action.
When Othello departs with that savagely menacing contd. ...

concerned. Then came a speeding of events and drastic compression of time. Now, since Lodovico's coming, the action been only normally compressed, the scenes strung loosely along, *within* them little or no time-compression; and within this long final scene there is to be none at all. For Othello, indeed—who is never absent from it, upon whom its entire action centres—it is as if, once his sworn deed is done, time and life itself lose all momentum. We have seen him, time and life itself lose all momentum. We have seen him, after one storm, joyfully make port. Here, after another, is the ship slowing—his own imagery—to her "journey's end".

Strumpet, I come!...

to what extent does he leave us thinking of him, as the bustling scene proceeds, on his way to kill Desdemona? The thought, I believe, will persists; because her fate is the capital issue, while the recovery of Cassio and the dispatching of Roderigo, with which the actual action is occupied, are secondary ones. But action exhibited will always command primary attention. This thought of Othello, therefore, will occupy no more than the margin of our minds; it will form a latent though very living, link with our next expected sight of him.

When Emilia is bid "run...to the citadel" and hastens off, the sight, coupled with this latent thought of Othello, may stimulate the question whether she can overtake him, cannot at least arrive in time, even whether (in an alertly minded audience) Iago has not therefore blundered by sending her. But the thought of her on her way will not persist with us as did the thought of Othello on his, if only because the now succeeding action involves Othello and Desdemona themselves and her murder and will obliterate thought of all else. The intended effect, indeed, is that it should. Then, when she knocks at the door we shall recall her hastening off, and the question is stimulated, with the tacit comment: Too late, after all!

But is it legitimate, and is it consistent with Shakespeare's ever most practically minded exercise of this art to provide for these secondary effects, which, it would appear, a given audience may not appreciate, fully or perhaps at all? The answer surely is: yes, as long as they *are* secondary and the primary are neither sacrificed to their success nor will be prejudiced by their abortion. They can be compared to the inner parts of a piece of orchestral music. At a first hearing only an expert may detect them and appreciate their enrichment of the whole. The rest of us may need half a dozen hearings. But the more there is to discover the greater will be the interest; and this can be as true of a play as of music.

The scene falls into three sections: the first filled by Desdemona's murder, the second by the discovery of Iago's guilt and the killing of Emilia, the third by Othello's orientation to his own end. The murder is soon accomplished, and it is but the consummation of what has gone before. From then until he kills himself he takes little more than a passive share in the action. It eddies without him: but he has lost all purpose, and even the attack upon Iago is half-hearted. Montano (though "puny whipster" he is not) easily gets his sword from him. So the bulk of the scene is given to a survey of the spiritual devastation that has been wrought in him. Bit by bit, the "noble Moor" who was "all in all sufficient", is revealed to himself and the others as a gull, a dolt, "as ignorant as dirt", the "good" Othello is a savage monster; and the soldier, firm and renowned in action, yet guilty of *this* action, is reduced to futile gestures and inarticulate bellowings of remorse. It is a terrible, shameful spectacle, of which Shakespeare spares us nothing, which, indeed, he elaborates and prolongs until the man's death comes as a veritable relief, a happy restoring of him to dignity.

Enter Othello with a light, and Desdemona in her bed.[50]

Of all the contrasts in the play between the end of one scene and the opening of the next, or the disappearing and reappearing of a character, none is more striking than this, than the passing from the alarms of Roderigo's murder and Cassio's wounding, from the reciprocal scoldings of Bianca and Emilia, to the sublimity of Desdemona's sleep, and from our last sight of Othello, clothed with fury, lusting for her blood, to his entry here, as a priest might come to do sacrifice, bearing his light, uttering his oracular

It is the cause, it is the cause, my soul:
Let me not name it to you, you chaste stars!
It is the cause.

---

50. According to Q2. Q1 also has *with a light*; but the Folio omits it, and editors have, in consequence, preferred to have a light already burning in the room. This is not quite such a small error as it may seem. The intention in Q2 plainly is that Othello shall enter with the light illuminating his face; and the steadiness with which he carries the (presumably) naked candle does much to emphasize the abnormal calm which gives dramatic distinction to his appearance.

He is calm as water is when near to boiling, or the sea with a surge of storm beneath. Exalted in his persuasion that it is justice he deals and not vengeance, he regains a satanic semblance of the nobility that was. He had feared "lest her body and beauty" might "unprovide" his mind. The spell of them is working in him, the first cold image of

> that whiter skin of hers than snow
> And smooth as monumental alabaster

quickening, through vision of the living light beneath, to a full sense of them; this pursued beyond to the charnel

> Be thus when thou art dead, and I will kill thee,
> And love thee after...

—the initial perverting of the mind finding such final issue; as too in the bitter

> I must weep,
> But they are cruel tears...

as in the blasphemy of

> This sorrow's heavenly;
> It strikes where it doth love.

Desdemona wakes; and, as she would at any time—must have, it will seem, so many times—calls drowsily,

> Who's there? Othello?
> Will you come to bed, my lord?

A poignant incongruity: he, wrought and intent, ready to kill; she but slowly shaking free from the sleep which weariness has sent and innocence not denied her, passing rather, indeed, from sleep to nightmare, to the incredible sight of him with eyes rolling, passion shaking his "very frame", to incredible talk of crime and killing and guilt, until, her heart palsied, she gasps,

> why I should fear I know not,
> Since guiltiness I know not; but yet I feel I fear.

Bewildered, she fences against his fierce

> Think on thy sins

and threat of death with pretty quibbling conceits—so unreal it all still seems to her—until he beats the futile weapon down with an ultimate

Peace and be still!

She is awake now and collected, and wifely compliance joins with womanly dignity:

I will so. What's the matter?

The handkerchief! That this ridiculous trifle should be her death warrant, that her plain provable denial now comes too late to outweigh the "strong conception" of her guilt this madman has been brought to "groan withal"—here the play's tragic irony is sharpened to its keenest point. Add the final instance following, in which wickedness and folly together are able to "turn her virtue into pitch", her peculiar goodness, that uncalculating candour, to her harm. Cassio's death, when she hears of it, means her undoing, since her witness to her innocence will be denied her. It is in innocence that she connects the two:

My fear interprets then. What, is he dead?...
Alas, he is betrayed, and I undone!

—that blind innocence!—And her tears are a terrified child's. But Othello's distorted mind can only read in it more evidence of her guilt.[51]

It is in cold deliberate anger that he kills her. We are spared none of the horror, neither her panic struggles, nor the hangman humanity of his

---

51. "My fear interprets then..." This is the reading of the two Quartos. It contributes to a more regular, and perhaps, therefore, a more authentic line than is the Folio's "O, my fear interprets". (An initial "O", breaking the metre, itself hints at an actor's interpolation.) The meaning is, I take it—though the one reading does not make it clearer than the other, nor either very clear—that her present vivid fear interprets for her at last Othello's bewildering anger at the loss of the handkerchief, the blow, the impudent strumpet" and the rest. Desdemona's gentle courage has been, throughout the play, a striking feature of her character. It goes with her candour and lack of suspicion, her blindness to the evil enmeshing her.

Nor dead? not yet quite dead?
I that am cruel am yet merciful;
I would not have thee linger in thy pain:
So! so![52]

The abrupt knocking at the door and Emilia's insistent voice can set his wits alertly on the defensive even while the fully sentient man barely yet comprehends what he has done. His

She's dead...
Ha! No more moving?
Still as the grave...
I think she stirs again. No...

---

52. There is a reading hereabouts in Q1, which is now generally rejected but which nevertheless invites comment. The accepted Folio text for the moment of the smothering runs

Des. Kill me to-morrow, let me live to-night.
Oth. Nay, if you strive.
Des. But halfe an hour.
Oth. Being done, there is no pawse.
Des. But while I say one prayer.
Oth. It is too late. *Smothers her.*
Ameilia at the doore.
Aemil. My Lord, my lord? What hoa?
My Lord, my Lord...

Q1. besides the omission of "Being done, there is no pawse", and such slight changes as to *He stifles her* and *Emillia calls within*, has, after "It is too late",

Des. O Lord. Lord. Lord.

Since Dyce reproved Collier for admitting this to the edited text (Furness Variorum: footnote, p. 274) on the grounds that the effect involved was, first "not a little comic" and secondly "disquietingly vulgar", no other editor appears to have raised the question. But it is worth consideration at least. For the effect (saving Dyce's opinion) would at least be neither comic nor vulgar, and might prove to be very poignant indeed. Imagine it: Desdemona's agonized cry to God, and as the sharp sound of it is slowly stiffed, Emilia's voice at the door rising through it, using the same words in another sense. A macabre duet, and unaccountable enough to call from Othello a most distraught

What voice is this?...

shows a mind working detached—and the more swiftly—within senses still benumbed. It is with the

> If she comes, in she'll sure speak to my wife...

that he stumbles—the intimate word itself piercing him—into the light of the irrevocable fact; to cry out then in amazed agony:

> My wife! my wife! what wife! I have no wife.

The deed done, the passions so tortuously wrought up to its doing begin to unravel. From the wreck of the Othello that was emerges a man who is both the victim and the creature of the deed.

His grief is an ingenuous as a child's:

> O, insupportable! O, heavy hour!

the man's awed sense of guilt is as unmeasured:

> Methinks it should be now a huge eclipse
> Of sun and moon, and that the affrighted globe
> Should yawn at alteration.

It is a furtive criminal that draws the curtains round the bed to admit Emilia with a bantering

> What's the matter with thee now?

and a callous one that answers her

> O, my good lord, yonder's foul murders done!

with the bland mockery of

> What, now?

And through the sombre

> It is the very error of the moon:
> She comes more near the earth than she was wont
> And makes men and

speaks a spirit accursed.

The news of Cassio's escape rekindles his fury. It is quenched on the instant by the sound of that voice from the dead:

O, falsely, falsely murdered!

—Desdemona's; she is in Emilia's arms, faintly proclaiming (as for answer to the horror-struck "O, who hath done this deed?" She gasps out her pitifully preposterous "Nobody; I myself...") *his* guiltlessness too. A last corroboration of her other perjuries, if he will! Then, with the soul-searing

Commend me to my kind lord...

she is dead indeed.

The man's riven mind seems, for a moment, in the evasive

Why, how should she be murdered?...
You heard her say yourself, it was not I

to be self-contemptuously sounding, under Emilia's accusing gaze, the depths of the ignominy of a acquittal thus opened for him, to reject it by frenetically, exultantly invoking an eternal vengeance now upon the gentle dead:

She's like a liar gone to burning hell:
'Twas I that killed her.

Whereupon, with volcanic Emilia, it is quick blow for blow, given and taken; for him the foul word to vindicate the brutal deed—

She turned to folly, and she was a whore...
Cassio did top her...

—from her plain "devil...devil". Yet out of the coarse melee rises his challenging

O, I were demned beneath all depth in hell,
But that I did proceed upon just grounds
To this extremity

soars too, in anguished remembrance, the ecstatic

Nay, had she been true,
If heaven would make me such another world
Of one entire and perfect chrysolite,
I'ld not have sold her for it.

It is not however these splendid protests that strike Emilia, but the cursory

ask thy husband else...
Thy husband knew it all

which slips out besides; this leaves her for an instant breathless. Then she finds herself re-echoing, her first stupidly echoed "my husband!" And again, with horror doubled and redoubled, as every echo of it draws from Othello the ever more horrible truth. And she cries to the unhearing dead:

O, mistress, villainy hath made mocks with love!

Horror comes to a head, and clarifies:

My husband say that she was false?
He, woman:
I say thy husband; dost understand the word?
My friend, thy husband, honest, honest Iago.

Reckless of consequence, she deals a deliberate hammer blow:

If he say so, may his pernicious soul
Rot half a grain a day! He lies to the heart...

Although Othello, baited and exasperated, the murderous blood still hot in him, draws sword on her now, a choking dread is rising in him. She defies him and his lowering

Peace, you were best.

And it is she who stoutly check and silences him and holds him there, a culprit, while she vociferates to all who may hear to come and arraign him.

A Parenthesis: The Play's Finishing

The finishing of the play is technically not a very simple task. There are the customary conventions to fulfil. Iago's treacheries must be disclosed, and not only to Othello; they must be published to the rest of this mimic world also. Such a methodical completing of the story seems on a stage such as Shakespeare's, where illusion is uncertain, to confirm its credibility; it resembles the old-fashioned "proving" of a sum. This outcry from Emilia will assemble everyone concerned. If story were all, the threads could now be combed out and tied up expeditiously enough. But the play is a tragedy of character; and Othello's—even though no spiritual salvation will dawn for him—is not be left in mere chaos. The dramatist's task, then, is to restore him as much to himself, and to such a consciousness of himself, as will give significance to his end, and to do this convincingly without pursuing the action beyond appropriate bounds.

Consider, for comparison of treatment, other such Shakespearian partnerships in death. Romeo and Juliet die from simple mishap, divided by a few minutes of time; and the completing of the story follows as a long—and rather tiresome—anticlimax. This is early work. *Othello, Antony and Cleopatra, Macbeth*; these are all three mature, and in each case the method of the ending fits story and characters appropriately together. Between Antony's death and Cleopatra's action is interposed that lends hers an importance matching his, even as in life the two are matched; and this can be very suitably done since the scope of the story is so wide. Lady Macbeth, on the other hand, has been reduced, well before hete play's end, to the wraith of the sleep-walking" scene; and she dies actually "offstage". But from the moment of Duncan's murder she has been a slowly dying woman, the battlefield is no place for her; and her death, made much of, might, the action close-packed as it is, inconveniently outshine Macbeth's.

As to Othello and Desdemona; if he is to be restored to dignity his death must not come as an anticlimax to hers. Yet, as in cause, so in effect, it must closely depend on hers. Shakespeare makes, then, no break in the action; and he keeps Desdemona's murdered body the motionless, magnetic centre of it, silently eloquent until the end. Again, Othello cannot be let actively dominate the scene until his end is imminent. It would never do, for instance, to have him personally dragging the truth from Iago, Emilia or Cassio, tritely reversing in epitome the process of his deception. To avoid such recapitulation, Iago, before he appears for the second time as prisoner, has already "part confessed his villainy", and will obstinately refuse to say more, while Cassio will not appear till then, when there is nothing much left for him to say. For a channel of disclosure we have the impetuous Emilia, who herself has it all to learn, for an instrument the handkerchief, which she set on its fatal course.

Nor can Othello himself do justice on Iago. As requital for Emilia's death it would be inappropriate; he does not care whether she lives or dies. And to kill him a moment before he kills himself would be a discounting of the effect of his own end. What initiative is left him, then, until the time comes for him to do justice on himself? It follows that the tensions of the scene must be sustained for the most part without him. Yet he must never be deprived of his pre-eminent place in it. The dramatic task involved is by no means an easy one.

Analysis of the Action, Concluded

To the Folio's

Enter Montano, Gratiano and Iago

the Quartos add, *and others*; and there is gain in the sudden irruption of half a dozen or more figures, from among which Emilia picks out, even before we may, the one that counts, with her keen

O, are *you* come, Iago?...[53]

Yet he is her husband; and he must clear himself. Desperately she bids him

Speak, for my heart is full.

But her fiery challenging brings instead only sourly evasive admissions, and to the damning

My mistress here lies murdered in her bed...
And your reports have set the murder on

no answer at all, except (amid the appalled murmurs) for Othello's suddenly weary, strangely empty

Nay, stare not, masters: it is true indeed.

And for a helpless moment it even seems as if, the deed irrevocable, Othello, the man he is, with vengeance on a guilty wife—

53. The Folio's later speech-heading "*All*" gives countenance to the Quartos' "*and others*", since it can hardly be meant to indicate Montano and Gratiano alone.

woman's voice alone swearing her guiltless—not unpardonable, here might be coming an end to the whole matter.[54]

It is the mone woman who will not have it so. While Montano and old Gratiano deplore the thing done, Emilia, with her

Villainy, villainy, villainy!...

is flinging herself on the track of the true doer, frantically, incoherently flogging her every faculty into use:

I think upon't: I think: I smell't: O Villainy!
I thought so then: I'll kill myself for grief:
O villainy, villainy!

As cool as she is frantic, Iago marks a danger signal in that "I thought so then...", and he orders her home, out of the way. He will mark another in her stricken

Perchance, Iago, I will ne'er go home

—since she is ready now for the worst. But Othello's sudden collopse in inarticulate agony takes all eyes and ears, and for the moment she is stayed. His savage rage dissolved in savage grief, she finds relief from her own anguish in the sight of his, satisfaction even:

Nay, lay thee down and roar;
For thou hast killed the sweetest innocent
That e'er did lift up eye.

And they unite in grief for the dead Desdemona. Even Othello's exculpatory

O, she was foul!...

laments her; and in the echoing

'Tis pitiful....

compunction wells again. And Gratiano's gentle

---

54. It should be noted, however, that Lodovico, the man of authority, is not present.

Poor Desdemona! I'm glad thy father's dead...

takes no account of guilt or innocence. He and the rest there stand and gaze.

Only Iago holds frigidly, vigilantly apart, the sight of him so reminding us that where he is evil is brewing still. Then Othello's

but yet Iago knows...

turns every eye on him again.

That she with Cassio hath the act of shame
A thousand times committed...

—this, with its frenzied "thousand times" raising the scene to fever pitch again—

Cassio confessed it;
And she did gratify his amorous works
With that recognizance and pledge of love
Which I first gave her...

Iago can tell what is coming, and there is no stopping it. He has a wary eye on Emilia—

I saw it in his hand:
It was a handkerchief...

—and, when he sees the light of this break on her, a dangerous one. But there is a deadlier power left in that "trifle light as air"—and a livelier danger to *him*—than he would suppose; witness for response, upon a note she has never sounded till now, Emilia's deep searching

O God! O heavenly God![55]

55. The Q1 reading; the Folio (also, substantially Q2) having

Oh Heaven! oh heavenly powers!

The difference, at this point, is not a slight one; Q1 striking the far stronger note. It is generally admitted that the text of *Othello* bears many marks of the 1605 "Act against Swearing" (and one has but to glance at the Concordance, with its two entries under "God" and its long list under "heaven"). The line in the Quarto has, therefore, that much inferential claim, to be what Shakespeare first wrote. contd......

This handkerchief, then, has been the instrument of Desdemona's death; she the cat's-paw to handle it; her pleasuring of Iago, her petty lie, her silence, all means to the appalling end. And God above has permitted this. What shall she do?

Iago, alert to a fresh force in her, gives her full warnings; first with a sharp

Zouns, hold your peace.[56]

(But " 'Twill out, 'twill out..." she cries; her strong spirit crying through her); then, after a moment, with a cold and clear

Be wise, and get you home.

And would she be so wrong to be wise? She can no longer mend the matter. What profit therefore now in pinning guilt upon Iago—and he her husband after all? She can read besides in his look what will befall her if she does. She might well choose to be wise. But if she cannot restore Desdemona to life, to honour and her innocent name she can. Therefore, without need to question what she shall do, she answers that cold, clear "Be wise..." as clearly with a resolute, deliberate

I will not

—and, for the dead Desdemona's sake, faces her fate.

Then and there Iago draws his sword. It is not the most plausible of ways, this, one would suppose, to confute Emilia. But guile, failing, turns into foul abuse, and "honest Iago" into the trapped beast, fangs bared. To which monster it is that Gratiano makes gentlemanly protest:

Fie!
Your sword upon a woman!

But a more important argument in its favour is its challenging intent, so closely akin to Laertes' "Do you see this, O God?"; to Macduff's "Did heaven look on and would not take their part?" (which should surely read "God", the whole scene hereabouts being enfeebled by repeated "heavens"); and, of course, to more than one passage in *King Lear*—where, however, Shakespeare escapes difficulties with the Censor by expressly "paganizing" the play. But this challenging attitude towards divinely permitted evil is characteristic of the mature tragedies.

56. Q1 also.

Emilia speaks on. If the words are to be her last she will leave nothing in doubt:

> O thou dull Moor! that handkerchief thou speaks't of
> I found by fortune and did give my husband...
> She give it Cassio! No, alas, I found it,
> And I did give't my husband

—nor minimize (witness the stressed and repeated "my husband") her own blind partnership in the villainy. With all eyes on two of them. Iago is kept at bay. But when—coming, indeed, like a very clap of it!—The tremendous

> Are there no stones in heaven
> But what serve for the thunder?

turns attention to Othello, he slips through the defence, wreaks vengeance on her and is gone.

But for kindly old Gratiano, Emilia would fall and die there unheeded; and, after a moment's care of her, even he leaves her for dead. The rest have still only eyes for Othello, whom Iago's escape leaves balked, silenced, motionless, yet with such giant menace in the very look of him that Montano must wrest his sword away, and, General though he be, set drastic guard over him till the fugitive can be caught and justice done. So sentries are set without the door; and they leave him there, disarmed and imprisoned, alone with the dead Desdemona and the dying Emilia.

He sinks into impotence:

> I am not valiant neither,
> But every puny whipster gets my sword.
> But why should honour outlive honesty?
> Let it go all

—into an oblivion which even Emilia's dying words do not pierce. She, dragging herself to Desdemona's side, her mind wandering—back to the refrain, the "Willow, willow, willow", which was her mistress' last sad gift of herself to her—can yet rally strength to take the death-witnessed, never-doubted oath:

> Moor, she was chaste; she loved thee, cruel Moor;

> So come my soul to bliss, as I speak true;
> So speaking as I think, I die, I die.

But it is all unregarded that she dies.

His mind is elsewhere. He says to himself,

> I have another weapon in this chamber;
> It is a sword of Spain, the ice-brook's temper;
> O, here it is. Uncle, I must come forth.

Whereupon he proceeds to play a grimly comic little practical joke upon Gratiano, who is on guard without, armed with the sword Montano had secured. The old man's voice protests confidently:

> If thou attempt it, it will cost thee dear;
> Thou hast no weapon...

Othello is actually wielding his new-found one as he answers with boyish cunning:

> Look in upon me, then, and speak with me,
> Or, naked as I am, I will assault thee.

And when Gratiano innocently does so, there stands the prisoner, formidably rearmed.[57]

If he meant, as it will seem, to pursue Iago, the impulse is dead in him already. But his soldierly dignity must be retrieved from that momentarily humiliated depth of "I am not valiant neither...," even if to the

> I have seen the day
> That with this little arm and this good sword
> I have made my way through more impediments
> Than twenty times your stop...

he must now add a bitter

> O, vain boast!

57. A typically Shakespearean device: to follow the tragic moment of Emilia's death by this semi-comic trick, so both separating it from the tragedy still to come, and heightening this by contrast.

He stands there an awe-inspiring figure still, in outward seeming still the Othello who had but to lift his arm for the best of them to sink in his rebuke. But the fire within is cold, the purpose gone:

> Be not afraid, though you do see me weaponed;
> Here is my journey's end, here is my butt
> And very sea-mark of my utmost sail...

wan echo, this, of the ardent

> O, my soul's joy!
> If after every tempest come such calms...

of the whelming

> Like to the Pontic sea,
> Whose icy current and compulsive course...

—the mighty and untamable sea that has been throughout the image most consonant to his nature.

Then he turns to the dead Desdemona:

> Now, how dost thou look now?[58]

and takes, with Gratiano for witness (whose grave compassion will exemplify our own as we listen), another and very different farewell of her. The up-wrought

> whiter skin of hers than snow
> And smooth as monumental alabaster

becomes a simple

> O, ill-starred wench!
> Pale as thy smock!

For his murderer's look which so terrified her we have now

> When we shall meet at compt
> This look of thine will hurl my soul from heaven,
> And fiends will snatch at it

58. And he must, I think, pull back the curtains of the bed, and, if need be, raise the body, so that the dead face can be plainly seen.

and, for his mortal assault on her with its "Strumpet...strumpet!", the timid touch of his finger on her breast or cheek, and the dull

> Cold, cold, my girl!
> Even like thy chastity.

It is their last communion: her visionless gaze, his unavailing words.

With a quick twist his thoughts pursue Iago:

> O, cursed, cursed slave!

to be flung back upon his own maddening guilt:

> Whip me, ye devils,
> From the possession of this heavenly sight!...

(his macabre

> Be thus when thou art dead, and I will kill thee,
> And love thee after...

has ripened into this). It is his last and stormiest fit of such passion

> Blow me about in winds! roast me in sulphur!
> Wash me in steep-down gulfs of liquid fire!...

It subsides into the deep, measured diapason of

> O, Desdemona! dead Desdemona: dead!

—the irrevocable indeed in that last word, and in a softly added

> Oh, oh!

dumb suffering and remorse.[59]

---

59. The Folio reading. Most editors here follow the Quartos'

> *O Desdemona, Desdemona* dead. O, O, O.

(Q2 replacing Q1's comma after the second "Desdemona" by a semi-colon).

Too much importance must not be attached to minor phrasing or to punctuation, which may in fact be either the prompter's of the printer's. But the Folio reading here happens to be substantially preferable, both in its repetition of "dead" (the added emphasis being of much dramatic

contd.....

In the ensuing silence Lodovico appears, escorted, and embodying once more the majesty of Venice itself. Montano is with him, and behind them is the captured Iago, disarmed and guarded. The wounded Cassio comes too, carried in a chair. And the scene which follows has the semblance of a tribunal, over which Lodovico authoritatively presides.[60]

He addresses the one culprit indirectly, considerately, commiseratingly:

> Where is this rash and most unfortunate man?

and Othello accepts disgrace:

> That's he that was Othello: here I am.

He treats the other as fittingly:

> Where is that viper? bring the villian forth

and the two are confronted.

Iago is silent, and his face a mask. Hence (at one remove

---

value) and for the weightier rhythm and melody, which help to make the line the solemn apostrophe I think it is meant to be instead of giving countenance to yet another mere outcry.

It is interesting to compare this whole passage with that in which Lear apostrophizes the dead Cordelia. We have the same intimate simplicity of phrase. Death, and the death of one so dear, is no matter for rhetoric. And even for Cleopatra, attired in all her splendour, Charmian finds the simplest of terms: "a lass unparalleled". And Macbeth when the news of his wife's death is brought him, can find no words whatever. How far we are in all these from Romeo's grief, and almost as far from Horatio's "flights of angels".

60. From now until the beginning of Othello's last speech Lodovico should dominate the scene. Actors of Othello are too apt to believe that, even from "It is the cause, it is the cause, my soul...", to the end, the responsibility rests upon them. But Shakespeare has been careful to relieve them from such a strain, and the scene itself from the monotony involved. Emilia's masterful intervention, Iago's attack on her, his flight and her death provide such relief. And now, for a while, Othello remains an all but passive figure, and, for a little, before his

> Soft you; a word or two before you go...

is an all but silent one. By which passivity the dramatic value of his last speech, when he does make it, is notably increased.

of thought) Othello's baffled

> I look down towards his feet: but that's a fable...

A swift stroke at the pinioned creature—

> It that thou be'st a devil, I cannot kill thee.

—should answer the question one way or the other. But at Lodovico's peremptory

> Wrench his sword from him

he is for the second time disarmed; and Iago, though he wince, can vaunt diabolically enough:

> I bleed, sir, but not killed.

The tension is relaxed by Othello's rueful, sardonic:

> I am not sorry neither: I'ld have thee live;
> For, in my sense, 'tis happiness to die.

This kindles the compassionate reproach of Lodovico's

> O, thou, Othello, that wert once so good,
> Fallen in the practice of a damned slave,
> What shall be said to thee?

which finds answer in the terse

> Why, any thing;
> An honourable murderer, if you will;
> For nought I did in hate but all in honour.

An honourable murderer! Is there more to be said?

Lodovico continues his inquest. Each there has his part in it, and by an individual touch or two helps to sustain and diversify the fabric of the scene. The wounded Cassio's response to Othello's single-syllabled, abased avowal of intent to murder him, is but a grieved

> Dear general, I never gave you cause.

As unaffected a

> I do believe it, and I ask your pardon

recalls—if nothing could restore—the old frank comradeship between the two.

And what more cause had this other?

> Will you, I pray, demand that demi-devil
> Why he hath thus ensnared my soul and body?

Does Iago even know the answer? "I hate the Moor", rabidly, senselessly, profitlessly; a search through the ruin of his tricks and lies would add nothing real to that. And in the light of the consequences—for him also—such an answer must seem almost less tragic than absurd. Incorrigibly he wraps himself in the shreds of his satanic conceit, as self-deceived in this, it may be, as were his victims in their "honest" Iago:

> Demand me nothing; what you know, you know.
> From this time forth I never will speak word.

And if the ordeal will be sharp, the hardihood of vanity is great.

Lodovico's shocked

> What, not to pray?

Gratiano's exasperated

> Torments will ope your lips

are, at each extreme, the habitual human response to such contumacy. Othello's indifferent

> Well, thou dost best

speaks of weary readiness to have done with it all.

But he must be held to life's business still; so the magistral Lodovico, showing him some respect, insists:

> Sir, you shall understand what hath befallen,
> Which, as I think, you know not...

The last is heard of the paltry handkerchief. He confirms Emilia's judgment:

> O, fool! fool! fool!

Then the rest turn, as men will with grave matters concluded, to talk more volubly of the lesser. Here it is of the

letter
Found in the pocket of the slain Roderigo...

and of "another discontented paper", and of the trick played on Cassio which led to his disgrace, and of Roderigo's wonderful recovery. And how much more of the sort would there not be to say, but that Lodovico once more gives orders.[61]

Othello must to prison. As they prepare to conduct him there he speaks:

Soft you; a word or two before you go...

The old quiet authority is his again in fullest measure; a touch of irony added here. Before *they* go. Give orders now who may, he will not. Then:

---

61. This diverting of our attention at such a moment from Othello to the papers found in Roderigo's pocket has been a matter of distress to certain commentators. Koester, in particular, to quote from the Furness Variorum, finding here "in the needlessness of these letters, and in the fact that they rehearse only what is already known to the audience, a proof that the scenes, in which the events related in these letters occur, were omitted in the representation."
But it is of course, only another example—of which the play holds several—of preparing for a passage of supreme tension, such as Othello's last speech will be, by one in which the tension is slack. That Shakespeare did not think of the letters and of Roderigo's recovery until he suddenly found he had need of something of the sort—of this there are signs. Was the letter that "imports the death of Cassio" written by Iago? When?—not to mention why? And was he, the tried soldier, such a bungler with sword and dagger that he could not competently dispatch the already wounded Roderigo?
But these are idle arguments. The dramatic purpose of the passage is plain enough: to take our attention temporarily from Othello, so that when he recaptures it he will do so the moie impressively. Material for such a passage much not be of first importance, or the tension will not be slackened; nor, at such a critical moment, can it be of merely extraneous interest, or our attention will be dissipated. The Roderigo-Iago-Cassio complication, with a final reference to the handkerchief, seems, then, to fill the need and suit the occasion fairly well. And far from the inconsistencies involved and the pedestrian style being evidence that Shakespeare did not write the passage, admit its dramatic utility, and they could perhaps better be pleaded as evidence that he did.

> I have done the state some service and they know it...

—his one dispassionate comment upon his downfall from what he was. For the rest, let them speak the truth of him, and of those "unlucky deeds"; and the mild detachment of the phrase tells them that he himself knows it, as a man may when nothing is left him of either hope or fear. They are to speak

> Of one that loved not wisely but too well;
> Of one not easily jealous, but being wrought,
> Perplexed in the extreme...

It is the truth.

> of one whose hand,
> Like the base Indian, threw a pearl away
> Richer than all his tribe of one whose subdued eyes,
> Albeit unused to the melting mood,
> Drop tears as fast as the Arabian trees
> Their medicinal gum...

No longer cruel tears; and the crude horror of the deed done already tempered a little—Nature's healing sadness would be at work. But not in him. He knows better than they can tell him or Venice decide what is due to an Othello, traitor to his Christian self, from him who is now that self again; and this they shall see. Therefore,

> say besides, that in Aleppo once,
> Where a malignant and a turbaned Turk
> Beat a Venetian, and traduced the state,
> I took by the throat the circumcised dog,
> And smote him, thus

—twice they have disarmed him, but he had kept a dagger hidden.

Gratiano and Lodovico cry out at the sight. Cassio does not; his comment comes later:

> This did I fear, but thought he had no weapon;
> For he was great of heart

—homage to his lost hero overriding prescribed disapproval.

Othello, the while, lies dead, with the dead Desdemona in his arms:

> I kissed thee ere I killed thee; no way but this,
> Killing myself, to die upon a kiss.

The simple rhyme and the simple sentiment harbour peace in oblivion.

But Lodovico turns our eyes once more upon Iago:

> O, Spartan dog,
> More fell than anguish, hunger, or the sea.
> Look on the tragic loading of this bed;
> This is thy work...;

In Iago's stressed silence, as he looks, is the last stroke of the action. His face is an inscrutable mask. What lies behind that but the stupidity of evil?

Act and Scene Division

Q1 and F1, near of a date in their printing, which was some eighteen to twenty years subsequent to the play's writing and staging, agree—but for a slip or so, fairly patent as such—upon its act and scene division.

The scene-division is in any case indicated in the action itself by the "cleared stage".[62] Localization, except for the first three scenes and the last, is less than precise. But the action demands this.[63]

As to the act-division; this has (exceptionally) sufficient purely dramatic validity, is sufficiently a part of the play's articulation, for it to be at least claimable—despite the twenty-year lag—as Shakespeare's own. Act I is indubitably a unit of action. Act II may be accounted one also, if not so completely, since Iago's "By the mass, 'tis morning..." and Cassio's later "The day had broke before we parted..." link II and III closely together. Act V has unity of subject. It compasses all the murderous consequences of Iago's scheming, and in it the whole action is wound up. There seems only to be no good reason why Acts

---

62. The trivial complication concerning the Herald is noted in its place.
63. Cf. p. 174, note 27; p. 190, note 40.

III and IV should be divided as they are—or indeed at all—unless it be to make up the classic count of five. If this should be the purpose, the division is doubtless as good a one as may be. It shares the total matter of the two acts approximately in halves, and the flow of the action can be said to move more swiftly and fatally towards catastrophe—and markedly so—in Act IV than in Act III.

But act-division may be made to mean, in the actual staging of a play, more than one thing; a short formal pause of relaxation, or a prolonged interval in which the audience can move about and the sympathetic contact established with the actors will be broken, or anything between the two; and the effect upon the performance will be very different. What the practice of the theatre was, either at the time of the play's writing or of its printing twenty years later, we do not know. Five acts smacks somewhat of the respectability of editing and printing, and F1 has certainly imposed the formula upon some plays that Shakespeare himself never so shaped. But it does not follow that he never so shaped any. *Henry V* at least, in fact, he did. Nor does it follow that three acts or four may not have suited him as well if that suited his subject. He and his theatre were not bound to the classic rule for its own sake, and it can have meant little to his audience. Why indeed—so free was he—should he plan his plays to any so unyielding a measure as "acts" at all? To some significant pattern, inevitably, his play must be shaped. If this allowed for a relaxing pause or so convenient to actors and audience and of benefit to its performance, so much the better. And if in time the five acts became an established formula for the theatre as for the printed page, and four interrupting intervals in a performance promised to be too many, the superfluous ones had only to be formalized, even to vanishing point—Shakespeare and his immediate inheritors were masters enough in a theatre of their own making for that; and that, I suggest, is how they would view the matter.

The producer of Shakespeare's plays today, in this as in more important questions, must distinguish the essential from the incidental. Where direct evidence is lacking as authority for what he aims to do he must fall back on circumstantial, judging the worth of it. He must, on occasions, badly deduce the particular from the general; this being his own general knowledge of the essentials of Shakespeare's art, his title to produce the plays at all. He need not claim to be impeccably correct in what he does. He cannot wait for positive proof over this or that disputed point; he must do something. In the small matter of this play's act-division his course is, however, both easy and pretty plain. He should not, very certainly, introduce act-divisions of his own devising; nor does he need to, with four already provided, which are on the whole more likely to be Shakespeare's than not. He need not, on the other hand, give the value of a prolonged interval to what may have in Shakespeare's own theatre counted merely as a formal pause. Nor if—the evidence being what it is—he overrides an act-division altogether (say, that in particular between Acts III and IV) will he commit any deadly sin; for he can plead that he is but emphasizing the general continuity of action, which is one of the "essentials in ordinary" of Shakespeare's art.

The Characters

IAGO

If Iago present something of a problem to the critic, so did he to Shakespeare. It was not a question first of imagining the man and then of finding the appropriate thing for him to do. What was to happen had already in the main been settled—by Cinthio; Shakespeare's task was to devise a character who could take his allotted share in this, convincingly and effectively.

Cinthio is in no difficulty. He warrants his "wicked Ensign" capable of every necessary crime simply by describing him as "a man of the most depraved nature in the world", and thereafter telling us that this or the other happened in the tone of one who—the events being over and done with—fears no contradiction. But the dramatist is by no means so taken at his word. His characters, under our scrutiny, must convince us of the likelihood of what they do even as they do it, while every word they speak is compulsory evidence of what they are. Carried through on such terms, the Ensign's task in the story—Iago's in the play, and Shakespeare's—can be no easy one.

Out of Cinthio's Moor Shakespeare moulds to his own liking the heroic Othello, confident, dignified, candid, calm. He sets up an Iago in total contrast to him; a common fellow, foul-minded and coarse-tongued, a braggart decrying in others the qualities he himself lacks, bitterly envious, pettily spiteful, morbidly vain. He has abounding vitality, a glib tongue and a remarkable faculty of adapting himself to his company, as we see when the cynical swagger which so impresses Roderigo—that portentous "I am not what I am" and the like—turns to sober soldierly modesty with Othello. Since Iago in the course of the play will attitudinize much and variously, and not only before his victims but to himself, will exhibit such skill and a seemingly all but supernatural cunning, Shakespeare, for a start, gives us this unvarnished view of him, of the self, at any rate, that he shows to Roderigo, whom he despises too much to care to cheat of anything but money.

We could take it, too, that this opening view of Iago, the first impression he is to make, was meant to be the true one, if only because Shakespeare, in first presenting a character, never deliberately misleads us, is accustomed, rather, to sketch in its chief features, then and there, as unmistakably as possible, so as to leave us in no doubt from the start as to the sort of man or woman he is.[64] He likes, moreover, to state his case—so to say—as soon and as clearly as possible. And here, in the first two scenes, in the contrast between the men, and in the boasted hate and its masking, are the main factors of the play already defined and set in motion. We shall, besides, soon become aware that a play is in the making differing in important aspects from its neighbour tragedies. With Macbeth, with Antony, amid the clashes of *King Lear*, the destructive force is one of the nobler human ardours turned to evil, and the battleground—as so notably with Hamlet—is the hero's soul. Here the evil impulse is externalized in Iago; and if Othello's soul be a battleground, he himself puts up to fight on it. Nor can the jealousy which undoes him be properly called a degrading of the love it supplants; it is an aberration rather, and an ignoble one. Iago inoculates him with it, as with a disease,

---

64. I can think of no instance to the contrary. It will be partly, of course, a question of economy. He has much to do with his characters—their talk and action make up his sole medium—and not overmuch time in which to do it. He cannot afford to turn them first in one direction, then in another, and so complicate his task.

and after the feeblest of struggles against it—he is lost.[65] Othello is not, therefore, a spiritual tragedy in the sense that the others may be called so. It is only the more painful; an all but intolerable exhibition, indeed, of human wickedness` and folly, which does not so much purge us with pity and terror as fill us with horror and with anger that such a shoddy creature as Iago, possessed by his mountebank egoism, his envy and spite, should be able unresisted to destroy an Othello and bring Desdemona to her death. This incongruity is the keynote of the tragedy, and Shakespeare, therefore, strikes it clearly to begin with. And the actor who tries, here or later, to present Iago as a sort of half-brother to Milton's Satan only falsifies both character and play.

To begin with he is not planning Othello's ruin at all. While he protests that

> I do hate him as I do hell pains...

yet for an aim:

> I follow him to serve my turn upon him...

and he admits that Brabantio's anger can at most only

> gall him to some check...

Roderigo do not more than

> poison his delight...
> And though he in a fertile climate dwell,
> Plague him with flies...

Spite; nothing deadlier! And when later, left alone, he asks himself how he may best serve his turn upon him, it will be by filching Cassio's place; and simply to this end it is that he intends

> After some time, to abuse Othello's ear
> That he is too familiar with his wife.

It will not doubt gratify his malice merely to see Othello vexed by jealously (that being, it seems, the one sort of barb by which

65. Cf. Leontes, whom Shakespeare, writing later, treats as a purely pathological case.

his own hide might be pierced); and a finer-drawn second thought ensues, another vista is opened in the

> and to plume up my will
> In double knavery...

—to flatter and foster, besides, that is to say, his egregious conceit of his own wickedness.[66] But he is still aiming in the main at his own material advantage. Well for him, it will seem in retrospect, had he looked no further and known when to "cash in" on a success. For within a while, by his plausible tongue and his gangster's skill, he will most brilliantly have manoeuvred Cassio into disgrace, and still be "honest Iago" to all the world, his victim included. And there is the lieutenantry ripe and ready to fall to him. But by then he must be appeasing the hunger of his quite profitless hate for Othello. Here are deeper waters. Success exhilarating him, he plunges in, to find that seemingly he can navigate them as brilliantly. He wins his will, and no hate could be more fully satisfied. But it is at the price of his own torture and death; no part of the programme, this! There is this tragedy of Iago to be consider too, though it will hardly appeal to our pity.

---

66. Bradley, after much debate, finds in the "plume up my will..." the master-key to Iago's mind, his inmost motive. To agree one must add, I think, that Iago is hardly aware of it—nor Shakespeare. This is not necessarily the paradox it may sound. An imaginative author, steeped in his subject, will sometimes write more wisely than he knows. One need only insist, then, that Shakespeare is not here intentionally presenting us with any such master-key; for if he were he would give the phrase an appropriate saliency, whereas it is so placed in the speech that it cannot well be made either arresting or memorable. In the "double knavery" does come the first hint of the will to do evil for its own sake (as well as for the profit of it) that carries Iago both to triumph and disaster, but one cannot recognize the tune from this single note heard in passing.
Bradley was a most enlightened critic and one hesitates to differ from him. But his habit of treating the characters in a play as if they had once lived actual lives of their own (he says elsewhere, for instance, that Iago's intellect cannot be compared to Napoleon's; but one must not, surely, even begin to compare an imaginary Iago to a real Napoleon, while it lends his pages great vitality, is apt to blind him to mere dramatic technicalities such as this.

What is the secret of his success—and failure? If it rests, as is likely, in his being what he is, he cannot tell us, and we listen to those many soliquies in vain. Of his opinions and desires and of what he means to do they will tell us truly; but as to what he *is*, less than another can the man who lives by deceiving others know the truth about himself. We observe and must judge for ourselves. He vaunts his doctrine of "reason", and seemingly wier ears than Roderigo's have approved that

> 'tis is ourselves that we are thus or thus. ...If the balance of our lives had not the one scale of reason to poise another of sensuality, the blood and baseness of our natures would conduct us to must preposterous conclusions...

—as, in fact, the blood and baseness of Iago's nature ultimately do. He owes it, then, to his intellectual vanity to make a show of finding good reason for wreaking his hate on Othello. But it is a very poor show. He cannot trouble even to decide whether he thinks that Othello has cuckolded him or no.

> I know not if't be true,
> But I, for mere suspicion in that kind,
> Will do as if for surety.

Suspicion of "the lusty Moor" (about the last epithet, incidentally, to apply to Othello) is, however, of itself so encouraging, that he returns to it, yet to admit besides in the very next breath that

> The Moor, howbeit that I endure him not,
> Is of a constant, loving, noble nature;
> And I dare think he'll prove to Desdemona
> A most dear husband...

—to which incongruous testimony he tags a fantastic notion of fastening upon Desdemona himself since

> I do love her too,
> Not out of absolute lust...
> But partly led to diet my revenge...

next contributing to this mental chaos a sudden parenthetic

For I fear Cassio with my night-cap too...

(the recent, frank, merrily gallant kiss of greeting offered Emilia twisted to that account!). Needless to say we hear no more of his "love" for Desdemona or fear of Cassio. And his suspicion of Othello's lechery, stoked up to

the thought whereof
Doth like a poisonous mineral gnaw my inwards;
And nothing can or shall content my soul
Till I am evened with him, wife for wife...

collapses, inconsequently and ridiculously, then and there, into

Or failing so, yet that I put the Moor
At least into a jealousy so strong
That judgment cannot cure...

By the light of his reasoning, then—this being a specimen of it—Iago would not seem likely to get very far. Nor is his judgment of Othello's character oversound. Nor, when he turns to Desdemona—with

That Cassio loves her, I do well believe it;
That she loves him, 'tis apt' and of great credit...

—does he come nearer the mark; and even as to Cassio he is astray. And the soliloquy's ending, its

'Tis here, but yet confused...

suggests that he is not wholly unaware of all this himself. It is not "reason" that serves him, though he would like to think it did. We note, too, that his projects are continually changing. It is on the spur of the moment that he is at his best, when he trusts to its inspiration.

Swinburne, refining upon Hazlitt, calls Iago "a contriving artist in real life", and the phrase is illuminating. Here indeed is the key—and was there need of any other?—to the problem Shakespeare set himself when he decided that his heroic Othello was not to be destroyed by an opponent of the same calibre, but dragged down by an Iago. He will not, that is to say, exalt such wickedness. That Iago himself should do so—the clever, but essentially stupid fellow, the common man of common mind—is quite another matter. But how equip such a one for his task, with genuine capacities denied him? By endowing him with the intuition of the artist, and the power of counterfeiting them. And Shakespeare will have a further need, which an artist Iago can satisfy, of a villain pursuing wickedness for its own sake.

The artist in leading-strings, writing or painting or making music to order, may be a happily harmless creature enough. Love of his art for its own sake turns him egoist. This is inevitable. In normal human love for a person, a country or a cause, we find egoism and devotion combined, the egoism storing up no more force than will be spent in devotion. But the artist's devotion to his evolving work is to something that is still a part of him, and his egoism will thus be fed and fed until the completing of the work discharges him of its burden. Being ill-fed or over-fed, it may grow diseased and monstrous. The force of a passion so self-fulfilling as to be self-forgetful is likeliest, perhaps, to carry him cleanly through the adventure; and this, at its most powerful, can so mobilize his faculties that their functions will seem to fuse—imagination and thought and skill working together as one—to an incommunicable magnifying of their power. The artist-egoist, minding nothing but his art, can, of course, be as harmless a creature—unless to himself and his friends and relations—as the artist in leading-strings, and his work may have its peculiar value. But set such an occult and lawless force operating in real life, and it can prove dangerous indeed; this force in Iago, for instance, of a love of evil for its own sake, vivified by the artist's powers, pursued with the artist's unscrupulous passion.

The medium in which Iago works is the actor's; and in the crude sense of pretending to be what he is not, and in his chameleon-like ability to adapt himself to change of company and circumstance, we find him an accomplished actor from the beginning. These rudiments of the art of acting most people learn to practice a little—and harmlessly—in real life; but Iago is an expert to the point that pretence is second nature to him. In his earlier manoeuvring, moreover, he is on familiar ground. "Honest Iago", with his sympathetically parasitic faculty of being all things to all men, knows, without thinking, how his fellow soldiers Cassio and Montano (Roderigo is a nonentity), the Cyprus gallants and Othello will think and act when events pass—with a very little help from him—as they do. So all goes well. Then, under their stimulus of success, and triflingly perhaps of wine,[67] his inherent hatred of Othello begins to pulse more urgently, and then it is that the artist in Iago takes effective command. For his profit in Cassio's ruin, already achieved, is forgotten, and it is the thought of Othello's that obsesses him, profitless though this may be. Here is the artist who will do he thing for its own sake, and out of sheer delight in the doing let himself be carried beyond all bounds of "reason" and prudence. Desdemona shall be ruined too, though he has no hatred for her. And, beaconlike, there at once flashes on him—as inspiration visits the artist—a solution to the problem that his reason left so confused. An error to speculate, as his own nature bade him, upon Cassio's treachery to his friend, Desdemona's to Othello. It is the very virtues of the virtuous that can best be turned against them. While Cassio, therefore,

> this honest fool
> Plies Desdemona to repair his fortunes,
> And she for him pleads strongly to the Moor,
> I'll pour this pestilence into his ear,
> That she repeals him for her body's lust;
> And by how much she strives to do him good,
> She shall undo her credit with the Moor.
> So will I turn her virtue into pitch;
> And out of her own goodness make the net
> That shall enmesh them all.

Iago feels—as at such a moment the fervent artist will—that a very revelation has been vouchsafed him, sent direct from the Devil himself, so exhilarating is it. And Shakespeare has found, in part at least, the Iago he needs. And the way is now open to the play's tragic end.

But given the unqualified purpose, what of the task itself

67. That which hath made Cassio drunk hath made him bold. Lady Macbeth had the same head for liquor.

and the means? To undermine Othello's faith in Desdemona! What part can Iago play which will best let him attempt that? Of the hectoring admonition which serves with Roderigo there can naturally be none, nor much, to begin with at any rate, of the frank comradely helpfulness which is bait for Cassio. Can any sort of frontal attack, indeed, be made on that superb authority? Somehow, then, he must find his way behind the defences, and from there, in the friendliest fashion, help Othello to achieve his own ruin. Hate, moreover, dictates this, since there is no ill worse than self-inflicted ill. But how insinuate his way into that very sanctuary of Othello's being where love for Desdemona is lodged? How discover in his own base nature enough understanding of Othello's to admit him there? How qualify for the playing of this part?

Play-acting is pretence, and as an art it is more than that. The actor is the dramatist's mouthpiece, and as an artist he is something besides. His share in their mutual work is to give bodily life to what has until then existed only as thought recorded in words. The career of a character in a play from its imagining to its presenting on a stage has something in common with the begetting and birth of a child, and the particular shares of the parents in their off-spring may both seem as obvious and prove as hard to analyse. But an actor will acquire certain specialized and somewhat anomalous faculties. Being neither mere mouthpiece nor mere puppet, he interprets a character—the material the dramatist gives him—in the terms, more or less disguised, of his own personality. Yet it will not be his true personality. He cannot, strictly speaking, know more of the character than the dramatist has told him, and this, though it be the essential part, can never be much. But he must seem to know much more, and in many ways, if we are to think of the two as one. Yet this need be but seeming. He need acquire no knowledge but apparent knowledge, cultivate in this respect no ability but to seem able, nor build up, of this composite pèrsonality demanded, anything but a painted facade. Note that it is not a question of trivial knowledge or poor ability, still less of evil or good, but of knowledge and ability merely reflected as in a mirror—which reflects the best and the worthless alike. The actor's is, above all, the faculty of sympathy; found physically in the sensitive ear, the receptive eye, the dancer's body that of itself responds, emotionally in the tears or laughter ready at call, and intellectually in a capacity not only seemingly to absorb some product of another's thought, but to reproduce the effects of understanding it without necessarily having understood it in the least. The mirror upheld to nature is a long-accepted image for the art of the theatre. As the art matures the mirror is brough to reflecting from beneath the surface; and in the character and skill of an Iago is pictured to us—a reflecting from art back to life again—how bedded in human nature and active in real life and actor's faculty can be. In real life also it *may* be innocuously exercised; the worst to be urged as a rule against the parasite intelligence—to which dishonourable status the loss of artistic sanction reduces the actor's—a certain complacency in futility. But with hate to give it purpose, it can be made, as Iago makes it, an instrument of deadly corruption.

He has most sensitive material to work upon. Othello—it is the countervailing trait to his soldierly calm—is as quick in response to a touch or a hint as the high-mettled barb he would ride. And if Iago wisely cannot, neither has he need to accuse Desdemona directly and brutally. A little eavesdropping gives him for a starting point matter which is in Othello's mind already, a known answer to his artless question whether Cassio knew of the wooing. From there he feels his way—as delicately at first as an insect by its tentacles—into that field of the man's affections in which he means to make havoc; and he surreptitiously takes and ever so slightly twists the form of the matter he finds there and reflects it back to Othello, who sees his own thought again as in a distorting mirror, receives back thoughts and words obscured and perverted. He cannot dominate Othello yet, but he can misinterpret him to himself.

The finer the nature the more fragile its defence; when thicker skins would be but chafed, the poison permeates Othello. For a measure of his susceptibility: it needs but the provocative intonation of that single word "Indeed" to set him questioning, and again questioning, insistent to be answered, and to leave him to self-questioning. Here is the intuitively feared requital for the "content so absolute" of his reunion with Desdemona; no halfway for him between that and a very helplessness of doubt.

And Iago, admitted to intimacy, can not proffer, for bad example, his own failings in jealousy and suspicion, but—his parasite mind feeding on Othello's, his coarse spirit gaining percepton from contact with Othello's fine spirit—can soon learn to detect rifts in the texture of its confidence made ready for his widening that Othello will then himself the more effectively widen again. "By heaven," he exclaims, "he echoes me"; and words and thoughts are indeed flung back and forth between them until it would be hard to say whose they first were. And note how Iago seizes on the vague misgiving in the unfinished thought of Desdemona's nature "erring from itself—" to shape and colour it into a vivid image of her, rank of "will" and could of mind; it is such a verdict on her very love for him that he renders back to Othello, to be digested and turned about, and to re-emerge, its stigma on them both, in the bitter "Haply, for I am back..."

In this passage of less than two hundred lines we are shown Othello's moral disintegration. But it owes its compressed form and continuity to dramatic convenience only. Actually to be imagined is a protracted, many-sided, disjunctive process of chicanery, in which Iago gathers, mainly from Othello himself, how best to cheat him, a complexity which Shakespeare clarifies and orders into the form of a few minutes' talk, into no greater a space than the action allowable can animate.

Iago is enjoying himself. He has the artist's faculty for doing well whatever he takes pleasure in doing, and for no soldier reason than that. He is even amusing himself. The trick with the handkerchief—"This may do something"—should prove a pretty one. He has yet to see the effect of his poison on Othello. It will doubtless soon begin to "Burn like the mines of sulphur", but he can hardly look suddenly to find his obliging self in the clutch of that "waked wrath", and being shaken as a rat by a dog.

He is a passionless creature. Cinthio gives his wicked Ensign some motive for evil-doing in jealousy, and a love for Desdemona ignored and so "changed into the bitterest hate". But Shakespeare admits neither love nor lust into Iago's composition, nothing so human; shows him to us, on the contrary, frigidly speculating upon the use such indulgence might be to him, and as frigidly deciding: none. Even his hate is cold, and will be the more tenacious for that, its strength not being spent in emotional ebb and flow. His endeavours then to respond suitably to Othello's outburst—the flamboyant "Take note, take note, O world..." and the kneeling to echo and to mock the oath by "yond marble heaven"—are simply histrionic, and overdone at that. And this, made plain to us, might be plain to Othello, were he not "eaten up with passion". For of intellectual excitement Iago *is* capable, and, elated by swift success, he begins to runs risks. That stirs his cold blood; it is all that does. And the pleasures of the game, as it develops, and multiplying. He has the noble Moor stripped now, but for a rag or so, of his nobility; no stimulus to savagery seems to be too strong for him. Iago can, consequently, admit more of himself into the part he is playing, can, in the actor's phrase, "let himself go", while the actor faculty enables him still to keep a cool enough eye upon whither he is going. He can thus vent the full foulness of his mind, in itself a relief and a pleasure: and there is the sheer pleasure of seeing Othello suffer and madden beneath the spate of it. And his daring pays. The success of the enterprise betters all expectation. Not merely is Cassio's death to be granted him—and he had schemed for no more than his disgrace—but at that zestful crisis, with the artist in evil in him strung to perfect pitch, one timely phrase assures him of Desdemona's thrown in too.

But in the very ease and abundance of his success, in his complacent enjoyment and exploitation of it, looking neither ahead nor around, lie the means to his ultimate ruin. To harry the distraught Othello until he actually collapses at his feet in a fit, then to rally he unlucky cuckold and condescendingly urge him to "be a man"; to be able to jerk him, like a black puppet, back and forth from his eavesdropping—what could be more amusing? And having once had to defer for his ends to each changing shade of Othello's mood, now to find the victim swaying to every sinister touch, even to be able—artist is evil as he is—to devise that felicitous strangling of Desdemona "in her bed, even the bed she hath contaminated"—this is gratifying too. There are secret satisfaction besides. To see Desdemona struck and be the hidden force behind the blow, to deplore Othello's conduct and be the unsuspected prompter of it; this is meat and drink to thwarted, perverted vanity. And that the blind fools who have ever galled him by their patronizing praise should be deaf to the irony in his

> Alas, alas!
> It is not *honesty* is me to speak
> What I have seen and known

—he finds egregious pleasure her.

Then comes, as an unlooked-for gift, the most delectable episode in his clandestine triumph. He has seen Othello collapsed at his feet; now it is Desdemona kneeling there, innocently begging the humble Ensign to rescue her from the very misery—did she but know it, worse!—into which he, even he, has plunged her. He savours her anguish, gently encourages the pitiful delusion. Could his tortuous "Divinity of hell" be more gracious to him—yet, fittingly, and as invariably under surfeit of good luck, more beguiling? For in the cold, complacent arrogance of his success he disregards and dismisses with a dozen contemptuous words, with a final "You are a fool: go to", the threat that, at this very moment, emerges so plainly and sounds so insistently in Emilia's questing anger. Here again shows the radical stupidity of the man, that other aspect of the adroit, intuitively extemporizing artist-actor-charlatan, who until now has played his deadly part so well. He misjudges Emilia, even as by the light of his vaunted "reason" he misjudged Desdemona and Cassio as likely lovers and traitors to Othello. He may know the Emilia of a marriage to him. How should such as he divine what fellowship with Desdemona has made her?

This complacency adds even to the careless contempt with which he customarily treats Roderigo, now unexpectedly rebellious. When he sees that the trouble is serious he schemes its liquidation—and Roderigo's—smartly enough; and Cassio's death in addition will round off events very comfortably. But his luck proves to be a little out, that "devil's own luck" which has carried him round so many awkward corners—which is perhaps but another term for the quick sense of the effective moment that has marked him at his best. Roderigo blunders. He blunders. It is not irretrievable blundering, but it rattles him. And he, whose cue it is to be always so cool and detached, finds himself bustling, too, amid the bustle and confusion, and bluffing and giving orders at random. And for the very first time—although not until he has said it does he really recognize it:

> This is the night
> That either makes me, or fordoes me quite

—he is touched by fear.

When Emilia turns on him and speaks out and stands her ground he is utterly at a loss, can find nothing to do but stupidly, since uselessly, to kill her.

In the Folio's list of characters Iago is ticketed "a Villaine", as he might be in the programme of the crudest of melodramas today; and he himself rejoice in his claims to the title. Even so, and yet more explicitly, does Richard III announce in his first soliloquy that he is "determined to prove a villain", proceed accordingly, and, in his last, argue at some length the metaphysical issues of his conduct. But between the writing of the two plays Shakespeare has developed other methods. He has learned to take these theatrical types and to give them, no merely more individuality, but an inward verity as well. Out of the conventional Jew comes Shylock; Falstaff out of Prince Hal's butt and buffoon; out of the "melancholy man" Hamlet. And out of Cinthio's "wicked Ensign", and his theatrical match, and melodramatic "villaine", evolves Iago.

Points of view will remain, from which a line drawn between Iago and the villain of melodrama is so fine as to be invisible. But melodrama is not necessarily false to life; it may only unduly simplify it. And Shakespeare's problem was to retain the melodramatic simplicity with the strength which belongs to it, and to give this an inward verity too. He solves it, as we have seen, by making his Iago something of a melodramatic actor in real life. The result is a highly complex, and at moments a very puzzling, character; but in it the reconciliation between verity and melodrama is achieved. There are plenty such people in the world, who borrow, as actors do, their working material, may add bits of themselves to it, will make a superficially brilliant use of the amalgam, yet remain worthless within. But, as a rule, they lack force of character (again, as do actors, they "live to please"), and the Iago of the story must be exceptionally endowed with some sort of force. Shakespeare sees this begotten by hate, and by a hate which will have only the more force for being unreasoning and motiveless.[68] In its stupidity—there is to be no glorification of such wickedness—it can well bring him at last to his doom, but by a blinkered persistence which belongs to unreason it may first attain its ends. Iago—it belongs to the part he is playing—sees himself above all as a man of reason. He reminds us rather, behind his intellectual antics, of a hound on the trail, sensitive and alert, nose to the mud, searching and sampling, appetite and instinct combining to guide him past error after error to his quarry. His hate posseses him. It rewards him. But when it has had its will of him is left—a swaggering mountebank still. The broken, bewildered Othello asks:

> Will you, I pray, demand that demi-devil
> Why he hath thus ensnared my soul and body?

Why, indeed! The true answer, spuriously qualified, he has long ago given us—and Roderigo. Repeated amid this holocaust, would it not sound even to him so incongruous as to be all but comic? "I hate the Moor"—there has been no more to the whole elaborately wicked business than that.

But with passion and persistence and some plausibility and the narrowness of purpose that belongs to evil, what cannot stupidity achieve?

OTHELLO

We have seen how, to make the story dramatically viable, the mainspring of the play's action has to be drastically compressed. It follows that the fatal flaw in the hero's character must be one which will develop swiftly and catastrophically too. The story has provided in sexual jealousy about the only one which will.

Of vanity, envy, self-seeking and distrust, which are the seeds of jealousy in general, Othello, it is insisted from the beginning, is notably free, so free that he will not readily remark them in

68. Cinthio gives his "wicked Ensign" a motive in a one-time love for Desdemona, which, ignored, has "changed into the bitterest hate". But Shakespeare—instead of seizing on it as a human contribution to his villainy—rejects this.

others—in Iago, for instance, in whom they so richly abound. And he has never yet cared enough for a woman to be jealous of her; that also is made clear. It is a nature, then, taught by no earlier minor failings of this kind to resist a gross attack on it, should that come.

But sexual jealousy, once given rein, is a passion like no other. It is pathological, a moral lesion, a monomania. Facts and reason become its playthings. Othello does at first put up a feeble intellectual resistance, in a single soliloquy he struggles a little with himself; but, after this, every defence is swept away, and the poison rages in him unchecked. Here, then, is the sudden and swift descent to catastrophe, which the story, as Shakespeare dramatizes it, demands. A bad business, certainly, yet, to this extent, shocking rather than tragic. Indeed, did not Othello suffer so and dispense suffering, the spectacle of his wholly baseless duping and befooling would be more comic than otherwise, a mere up setting of this confidence and dignity, as enjoyable to us as to Iago; and, a ghastly fashion, it for a few moments becomes so when he is set eavesdropping upon Cassio and Bianca. Shocking, that it is, and pitiful, for all perplexed suffering is pitiful. But there is more to true tragedy than this.

The writing and rewriting of *Hamlet* must surely have shown Shakespeare the limits to the dramatic use that can be made of the purely pathological. For while little was to be done in exhibiting the character of a man consistently aping madness who would not reveal himself, even less was practicable if he were really mad and could not. With Hamlet it is the land near the borderline which proves peculiarly fruitful, since there we have him so acutely conscious of himself as to be at his readiest for that work of self-purgation by which the tragic hero finds significance in his fate.

With Othello neither the planning of the play, nor his character, nor the jealous mania which is foreign to every other trait in it, will allow for this. He cannot reason with himself about something which is in its very nature unreasonable, nor can Shakespeare set him searching for the significance of events which exist only in Iago's lies—we, the audience, should resent such futility. He is betrayed and goes ignorantly to his doom. And when, at last, Desdemona dead, he learns the truth, what can he have to say—or we!—But

O, fool, fool, fool!

The mere sight of such beauty and nobility and happiness, all wickedly destroyed, must be a harrowing one. Yet the pity and terror of it come short of serving for the purgation of our souls, since Othello's own soul stays unpurged. Hamlet dies spiritually at peace; Lear's madness has been the means to his salvation; by interpreting his life's hell to us even Macbeth stirs us to some compassion. But what alchemy can now bring the noble Moor and the savage murderer into unity again? The "cruel tears" and the kiss and the talk of justice are more intolerable than the savagery itself. Nor can remorse bridge—though too late—the gulf between the two; they were and remain beings apart. Othello wakes as from a nightmare only to kill himself, his prospect hell. And the play's last word is, significantly, not of him, but of tortures for Iago; punishment as barren as the crime. It is a tragedy without meaning, and that is the ultimate horror of it.

But Othello, when it is too late, does at least become conscious of this cleavage made in his nature. Hence his submission to Lodovico as

he that *was* Othello...

The Othello that was could never have done such a deed; an ignorant brute in him has done it. Yet it is still he, the Christian Othello, accepted, trusted, loved, who has proved viler even than "the circumcised dog" that he smote "in Aleppo once". It is the fellow to his dog in him that he now smites "thus" to end all.

If he cannot be let elucidate his calamities, Shakespeare can at least make him the very kind of man who could not. To begin with, he is "the Moor", and in this alone, a strange, removed, enigmatic figure. Before we see him we hear him only vilified as "thick-lips" and "lascivious Moor"; it is a way of adding by slight surprise to the effect he will make upon us when he does appear, so plainly nothing of the sort, but—even before we learn he is of royal blood—an aristocrat, a chief of men and the ripe soldier, sparing of words, their tone level and clear, not to be

flustered or overawed. He will have no street-brawling; that is not how he fights when he must fight. Nor will he wrangle here in public; he does not even notice Brabantio's abuse of him. To the Duke himself and the Senators he yields no more than the respect due to his

very noble and approved good masters...

They shall hear his "round unvarnished tale"; he will call one witness, Desdemona; and upon her word—nor when she comes does he even first speak to her lest he seem to bias it—will he be judged.

By touch after touch Shakespeare builds up the figure, and upon its present calm and poise the lightest is effective. Since he was a very child—since his arms had "seven years' pith"—he has known only war and adventure. And, but for love of Desdemona, he would not now put his "unhoused free condition" into "circumscription and confine". War calling, they must both obey; he leaving her then and there, she following him into danger if she may. His austerity protests that it will not be

To please the palate of my appetite...

her courage that it is even

to his honours and his valiant parts...

that she has consecrated "soul and fortunes". It is no ordinary marriage. There is nothing commonplace in either of them.

There is little tenderness in their parting:

Come, Desdemona; I have but an hour
Of love, of worldly matters and direction,
To spend with thee...

—that is all. But she accepts it so, the soldier's wife already. It is only after their separation, when he finds her safe in Cyprus, preserved from the dangers of war and shipwreck, that he realizes how much she and this new and strange thing happiness mean to him.[69] He is awed—

69. Dangers more present to the Elizabethan mind—the minds of the play's first audience—than to our own. Yet in January 1940, as I write, this is hardly so.

If it were now to die,
'Twere now to be most happy; for, I fear,
My soul hath her content so absolute,
That not another comfort like to this
Succeeds in unknown fate.

—and amused—

O, my sweet,
I prattle out of fashion, and I dote
In mine own comforts

by its hold on him. But he is as strict in discipline with himself as with others. It is his wedding night, but his parting orders to Cassio are:

to-morrow with your earliest
Let me have speech with you.

Unhappily for Cassio, he finds cause to speak with him still earlier. When the noise of the unpardonable broil has been quelled; quietly, sternly, curtly it is:

Cassio, I love thee;
But never more be officer of mine.

For in judgment he is swift and uncompromising. This is the last capital touch given to the picture of a still unscathed Othello. In retrospect we may recognize the danger that lay in a too inflexible perfection of poise; once upset, hard to region.

It is the picture of a quite exceptional man; in high repute and conscious of his worth, yet not self-conscious; of a dignity which simplicity does not jeopardize; generous in praise of those who serve him; commanding respect without fear; frank and unsuspicious and ready to reciprocate affection. Yet he has been a man apart, alone. He is not young, has fought and adventured the world over, striking root nowhere. And he is black. The Venetians, truly, not only value his soldiership, but Brabantio, he says:

loved me, oft invited me...

They seemed to be treating him in everything as one of themselves. But to have him marry Desdemona! That would be quite another question. Neither he nor she was of the eloping kind; evidently no other way looked open to them. Lay a part of Brabantio's anger to the elopement itself, of the Duke's appeasing attitude to his wish, with the Turks attacking Cyprus, not to offend his only competent general. Yet that the daughter of a Venetian Senator should

> to incur a general mock,
> Run from her guardage to the sooty bosom...

—even of the renowned Othello—is conduct unnatural enough for her bewitching

> By spells and medicines bought of mountebanks...

to be a very likely way of accounting for it. Shakespeare does not need to spend much explanatory speech on all this. Othello's exotic figure and the contrast between the two will in themselves be eloquent of it. And should we, under the spell of his nobility, be inclined to forget it—since Desdemona could!—reminder will not be lacking. For Iago's defiling eye sees only this, reads only foulness and perversity into such enfranchisement.

But Desdemona

> saw Othello's visage in his mind...

That we may see him as she did the story of his life is repeated before the Senate and to us even as she heard it. And, says the Duke,

> I think this tale would win my daughter too.

It is in her fine faith in this vision of him that she goes forward, first to a happiness justifying and fulfilling it, then to its inexplicable shattering. He finds in happiness with her a self unrealized before. It is a self created by her love for him, and will be the more dependent, therefore, upon his faith in that. It will be, besides, a dangerously defenceless self, since he is no longer a young man when it comes to life in him, and between it and the rest of his character, fully formed and set in far other moulds, there can be no easy interplay. This division between old and new in him—between seasoned soldier and enraptured bridegroom! —presages the terrible selvage to come. He does not bring to his love for Desdemona, nor wish to, the measured wisdom which experience has taught him. It is against his judgment that he yields to her pleading for Cassio with a

> let him come when he will;
> I. will deny thee nothing.

The romantic Cassio himself had acclaimed her as "our great captain's captain", of which Iago'a acid version is that "our general's wife is now the general". He is, in fact—the elder husband, the young wife!–uxorious; yet less from weakness than in tribute to this miracle she has wrought in him. Could it prove illusion—he is at the height of happiness, challenging fate, Iago at his side—"chaos is come again". But even now, and for all their love, they see life differently. Adventure behind them, she has settled down to the workaday joys of a home, in which she can be confidently, merrily, carelessly herself, so confidently, we note, that his exasperation over the handkerchief gives her only passing concern. But he still an uncharted stranger in this world, inapt, despite his quality, at its defence—which yet needs only the simple, natural instinct in a man, loving and so beloved, that all is well.[70]

Othello has a quick and powerful imagination. It is a gift which in a man of action may make either for greatness or disaster. It can be disciplined and refined into a perceptiveness, which will pierce to the heart of a problem while duller men are scratching its surfaces; it can divorce his mind from reality altogether. How is it that, even under stress, Othello does not unarguably perceive Desdemona's innocence and Iago's falsity? Instead his imagination only serves to inflame his passion. He is conscious of its unruliness.

> I swear 'tis better to be much abused
> Than but to know't a little

—since imagination will multiply "little" beyond measure; that, when passion has dislodged reason in him, is his first cry. Imagination begets monstrous notions:

---

70. Shakespeare shows us the two, upon the very edge of calamity, living together—as Cinthio tell us that his Moor and Desdemona were living—in "harmony and peace"; he contrives to insinuate thus much of this telling introduction to the story into the play.

> I had been happy, if the general camp,
> Pioneers and all, had tasted her sweet body,
> So I had nothing known...

And Iago keeps it fed with such kindred matter as the tale of Cassio's dream, with picturings increasingly physical, of her "naked with her friend a-bed", of Cassio's confessedly lying "with her, on her; what you will!"—until the explicit obscenity leaves imagination at a loss, and nature suspends the torment in the oblivion of a swoon. Later, self-torment takes the obscurer, perverser from the "horrible fancy" which sees Desdemona as a whore in a brothel, himself among her purchasers; imagination run rabid.

But, in his right mind, he can be master of his imagination too. Call Iago in "artist in real life", if a spurious one; Othello is the poet born. While the soldier he is must hold to realities, the poet in him is free in a metaphysical world in which these find a rarer meaning. The tales that won Desdemona will have been of a poet's telling—anthropophagi and "men whose heads do grow beneath their shoulders" being mere curiosities in themselves—and the more roundly told and invarnished the more befitting the matter and the man. We are still far from the Othello who hysterically charges a lost handkerchief with the very "might magic" he mocks at here.

From the beginning, when the occasion stirs him, the poet's mind shows. It shows in the delicate balance of idea and phrase, in the irony blended with beauty of

> Keep up your bright swords, for the dew will rust them.

It is a poet that seeks refuge from dishonour among imaged memories of a glory indefeasibly his, of

> the plumed troop and the big wars
> That make ambition virtue!...
> The neighing steed and the shrill trump,
> The spirit-stirring drum, the ear-piercing fife,
> The royal banner and all quality,
> Pride, pomp and cirumstance of glorious war!

then to renounce them as man renouncing life itself. This is not an exercise in rhetoric. The trumpet and drum, the fife and the banners, were themselves tokens of the metaphysical world, in which Othello found his life's meaning. The words are tokens too, which, in the melody and rhythm of the mounting phrases, he is setting to do all that worlds made musical may do to unveil that world for him again.

It is a world in which one lives alone. Iago—being what he is—has listened in amazed incomprehension. He will be ready, however, at its next unveiling, upon the block vision of

> the Pontic sea,
> Whose icy current and compulsive course
> Ne'er feels retiring ebb, but keeps due on
> To the Propontic and the Hellespont...

with a fine histrionic pretence to fellowship in it. Desdemona is given a horrifying glimpse of it as an anarchy of grotesque and infected images; flies quickening in the shambles, winking moon, the bawdy wind—a world to which he brings the miseries bred in him. He reaches towards his metaphysical world once more in the rapt calm of

> It is the cause, it is the case, my soul:
> Let me not name it to you, you chaste stars!
> It is the cause...

to enter it, his murderous passion sated, and find it void:

> Methinks it should be now a huge eclipse
> Of sun and moon, and that the affrighted globe
> Should yawn at alteration.

—no leasser figure will serve.

Othello's, we said, is a story of blindness and folly, of a man run mad. As the play is planned, evil works all but unquestioned in him until it is too late. Of battle between good and evil, his soul the battleground, even of a clarifying consciousness of the evil at work in him, there is nothing. Not until the madman's deed is done, does "he that was Othello" wake to sanity again; his tragedy, then, to have proved that from the seemingly securest heights of his "soul's content" there is no depth of savagery to which man cannot fall. Yet, in face of the irrevocable deed savage and man are one.

Shakespeare paints us a merciless picture of the awakened, the broken Othello; of the frenetically repentant creature of Emilia's scornful

Nay, lay thee down and roar...

of the man with all strength for evil or for good gone out of him, remorse mere mockery as he looks upon the dead Desdemona; of an Othello crying.

Whip me, ye devils,
From the possession of this heavenly sight!
Blow me about in winds! roast me in sulphur!
Wash me in steep-down gulfs of liquid fire!...

—sheer horror this; the howling of the damned! He speaks his own epitaph before he dies; a last echo of the noble Moor that was.

DESDEMONA, EMILIA, BIANCA

Desdemona's part in the play is a passive one. The single fateful step she takes has already been taken at the start. We have only to be told—and this we are told most explicitly—that she took it wholly of her own free will. Emilia, but for the sneaking of the handkerchief and one aimless explosion of wrath, remains passive until at last she unmasks Iago. Bianca is a cat's-paw. The economy of the action allows for no extraneous adventuring into the characters of any of the three. They respond illuminatingly to its events; and by setting them in strong contrast each to the other Shakespeare makes them, all three, the more vivid. Desdemona and Bianca never even meet. But Cassio, turning so differently from the one to greet the other so cavalierly, links the two; and what Bianca is and what Desdemona—what in the face of Iago's slanders she so transparently is *not*—springs thus into higher relief. The three provide the play with something like a pattern of womankind—motherhood and old age omitted: Desdemona's fine nature set beside Emilia's coarseness, with the little trull Bianca, who

by selling her desires
Buys herself bread and clothes...

for their ape and counterfeit.

DESDEMONA

Desdemona appears in one scene only of the three which pass in Venice and speaks just twenty-seven lines. But the action and debate centre on her, and when she has at last had her own say a very clear picture of her emerges.

What has happened in extraordinary enough in itself to rivet our attention. The tale of it is flung at us for a start in the crudest and most rancorous terms. Their rancour discounts them somewhat; still more does the sight of Othello himself, so evidently neither "gross" nor "lascivious", nor is he even found, as he might more suggestively be, in Desdemona's company. Brabantio's angry chatter about drugs, charms and witchcraft sounds overdone. But his talk of her as

> a maid so tender, fair and happy,
> So opposite to marriage that she shunned
> The wealthy curled darlings of our nation...

as

> A maiden never bold;
> Of spirit so still and quiet that her motion
> Blushed at herself...

has a likelier ring, and we expect explanation. Othello's may suffice the Duke, concerned for those Cyprus wars; but it takes Desdemona's own appearance fully to enlighten us. And the effect of it is unexpected. This "maiden never bold" is intimidated neither by her father nor "all this noble company". She does not turn to Othello for support, nor plead irresistible love for him, nor, indeed, offer any excuse whatever for her conduct. She speaks of duty, but as divided between past and future; once owed gratefully to her father, now, she challenges—there is defiance in the world!—due to her husband. Whatever else, here is no helpless maiden enticed away, whether by foul means or fair. Small wonder that, before such impassivity, Brabantio's distress freezes to a

> God be with you! I have done

—after which, while he and the Duke exchange their neat, not too engrossing, "sentences", we can observe her mutely standing there. The war's threat to part her from Othello gives her speech again; as impassive in its admission of her father's final loss of her, but lucid and fervent—her heart bared without false shame–in the plea for her rights in the love for which she has dared so greatly. Again, here is a Desdemona unknown to her father, unknown, we may suppose, to Othello too, now stirring him for the first time from his soldier's restraint to an echo of her plea. But between the explicit calm with which she can speak her determined mind and this rare favour lies in her nature a reticent and inarticulate zone, unguarded, and to prove of mortal peril to her.

Brabantio's

She has deceived her father, and may thee

—which Othello so trenchantly flings back at him, which Iago stores in his memory—is more false than true. He was deceived in her, as, with less excuse, Othello will be. She was to blame for letting him stay too long self-deceived. But there was he who should have known her best, knowing her so little as never even to suspect what ardour and resolve might lie beneath her accustomed quiet. Hard to confide in him in any case, all but impossibly hard to tell him that she loved the alien "black" Othello. How convince him but by doing as she did? It has taken the unexpected threat of separation to make her speak her heart out even now; but, speaking out, it is with no apology. Under vile accusation later on she will swear to her innocence. But if this and no more sounds better evidence of baser guilt—why, of explanations, arguments, self-justifying, of any of the means of defence commonly used by those who might be guilty though they are not, she, who could not be guilty, is incapable. Even as Othello went unprotected against the poison of mistrust of her, so she gives never a thought to protection against—how should she expect it?—his mistrust. It is she, in truth, who does not wear her heart upon her sleeve; confessing that

I am not merry; but I do beguile
The thing I am, by seeming otherwise

and thereupon, to deaden her fears for Othello's safety, even letting Cassio flirt with her a little. She is no precisian in candour. To smooth down that down that unwarranted commotion over the mislaid handkerchief she does slightly economize the facts. Moments of great joy may leave her at a loss. Upon their reuniting all her response to Othello's eloquent ecstasy is a sober

> The heavens forbid
> But that our loves and comforts should increase,
> Even as our days to grow!

She does not try to find words to express her deepest feelings; they are lodged too deep in her, they are too real. That she can plead as fluently as frankly for Cassio should be one sign at least—were any needed—that no more than her kindness is engaged. Moments of misery leave her dumbfounded too. Out of her clear sky of happiness it comes, with no more warning than the pother about the handkerchief; before all the world Othello strikes her. And she has nothing to say but

> I have not deserved this.

Then, first dismissed as a servant might be, when later she is summoned to him again, she does not reproach him, nor even refer to the incredibly terrible thing. She cannot. She is as helpless, too, to draw reasons for his anguished passion from him as he to give them. And when at last, lashing her with "strumpet" and "whore" he leaves her and the alarmed Emilia asks her how she does, her answer is

> Faith, half asleep.

She will not talk of what has passed even to Emilia. When she sends Iago to Othello to plead for her, she cannot bring herself to speak the word that has so shamed her.[71] Childish of her; but, as she says, she is "a child of chiding". Has he no pride, that she, Brabantio's daughter, who would face Duke

---

71. It may well seem that Shakespeare has here stretched a psychological point in his wish to complete the pattern of Iago's triumph; first, Othello senseless at his feet and now Desdemona kneeling there. Would she have sent him to Othello? Such unlikelihood as there may be is lessened a little by the stress laid on the fact that he is Emilia's husband, she by this her mistress' friend. But one suspects that, as with the plainly imported meeting between blind Gloucester and mad Lear, it was the effectiveness of the pattern which counted.

and Senate with composure, is on her knees before Iago? But innocence has a dignity of its own, a courage too. When, at this instant, the trumpets sound to supper, she does not need his admonition to "go in and weep not" to embolden her to do her ceremonial duty with perfect calm. Supper done, and Lodovico having taken formal leave of her, she falls back again into an obedient humility.

But, alone with Emilia, the blow, and the worse blow of

> that cunning whore of Venice
> That married with Othello

seem to have numbed her mind. One might suppose that she no longer cared even to learn of what she is accused. But it is largely sheer fatigue; and beneath the surface, where reality lies, she is as sensitively alive as ever, and to what is, for her, the essential things. She is a great lady, and has been publicly insulted—and worse. She is innocent, and has been foully slandered. She is a Venetian, and has surely but to appeal to Lodovico and Venice to protect her from this alien, this Moor—against whom, how rashly, she would not be warned. But she makes no such move, advances no such claims. She holds still by the faith in his "very quality", for which she clairvoyantly came to love him. For better or worse he is now her lord; and to her

> even his stubbornness, his checks, his frowns...
> have grace and favour in them.

Nor will proper pride, nor just resentment with all the arguments in the world for aid, change that. Better pleading will be those emblems of her chastity, her wedding sheets—to the obtuse Emilia they are just "those sheets!"—laid tonight on their bed. And when the time comes, what fitter shroud! She is not conscious, as we are, that her death is near; only that, if sorrow cannot change her, nor will time. Emilia tries to rally her with a robust

> Come, come, you talk!

She finds expression for her "wreteched fortune", not in its own bewailing, but in the melody which expressed poor

Barbara's, and in that an anodyne. And so little does she anticipate calamity that, quitting her cryptic spiritual solitude, she can idly turn her thoughts to Lodovico, play the tolerant married lady with shrugging "O, these men, these men", and, in the sequent

> Dost thus in conscience think—tell me, Emilia—
> That there be women do abuse their husbands
> In such gross kind?

be suspected by Emilia of playing—and overplaying—the innocent too.

But Emilia hardly understands her here, nor she fully perhaps herself. If she is now to live a life deformed by jealousy and suspicions, it will not suffice her simply to be sure that she does not deserve them, would not

> do such a deed for all the world.

Self-complacency is cold comfort. But some habitation of the faith she must have; so she will exchange the glory of her lost ideal for the companionable shelter of that gently obstinate delusion:

> I do not think there is any such woman.

But Desdemona's truth outshines such ingenuous streaks of self-deceptions, or the scared fib about the handkerchief, even as it transfigures the incredible lie of her dying answer to Emilia's

> O, who hath done this deed?

—the heart-rending

> Nobody; I myself. Farewell.
> Commend me to my kind lord...

—into a shaming of the mere truth. Emilia finds the word:

> O, she was heavenly true!

—not simply true to Othello, but to herself and her faith in him. This is betrayed, and she is wantonly and savagely killed. No ray of light pierces there. But they could not kill her faith—in the Othello that remained to her, for her still the true Othello, and the beauty of this.

EMILIA

Emilia is coarse clay. She is of Shakespeare's own invention, no kin to the Ensign's wife in the story. He develops her—with the economy of his maturer stagecraft—by the measure of his need for her. An attractive young woman, from whom Cassio finds it good fun to claim a kiss, Iago's pretended fears for his "night-cap" being given that much colour; such is our first impression of her. She stays mumchance enough for the moment to bear out Desdemona's bantering defence of her;

Alas, she has no speech.

But—while what Iago may say is no evidence—she will later amply corroborate his

In faith, too much!
If find it still when I have list to sleep...

by showing that she can chide very much more trenchantly than "with thinking" if she is stirred to it.

Shakespeare already has clearly in mind what he wants of her; and upon the

I am glad I have found this napkin...

and in the short exchange with Iago (their single scene alone together) he more definitely shapes her to it, and briskly, with the

This was her first remembrance for the Moor:
My wayward husband hath a hundred times
Wooed me to steal it; but she so loves the token—
For he conjured her she should ever keep it—
That she reserves it evermore about her
To kiss, and talk to. I'll have the work ta'en out,
And give't Iago. What he will do with it
Heaven knows, not I;
I nothing but to please his fantasy.

Beside the neighbouring subtleties of Iago's dealing with Othello the packed utility of this may seem technically a little crude. But Shakespeare will not interrupt that chief issue for long; and since there is little sublety about Emilia, the artlessness of the soliloquy pictures her the better:

> My wayward husband...

—her incurious, tolerant, pedestrian mind finds this the aptest term for Iago's restless exigence and uncertain temper—

> hath a hundred times
> Wooed me to steal it...

—to which point she would not go, and will not, as she answers him, admit to be going now:

> No, faith; she let it drop by negligence,
> And, to the advantage, I being here took't up.

It is a nice distinction. But she that can make it will have the less difficulty in setting down her honest Iago's share in the business to "fantasy". Better to please him too, and to find herself his "good wench" for a change from his perpetual chiding (he greets her testily; her first words to him are "Do not you chide": these jolly fellows, such good company abroad, are often less so at home); and better, by far, she must have found, not to cross him or question him it his "wit" begins to turn "the seamy side without", as it does when, misgiving seizing her, she begs the handkerchief again. "'Tis proper I obey him" is her wifely code, and the mere tone of his present

> Bet not acknown on't; I have use for it.
> Go, leave me

must warn her that she will be wise to obey him pretty promptly in this. Yet she must be conscious too that there is mischief in the matter. What licit use could he have for the handkerchief? But she chooses to shut her mind and hold her tongue.

Having thus committed her to a peccadillo which she will be loath to avow he runs the less risk of her betraying him; and, in fact, the occasion soon arising, she lies smoothly and efficiently. It is before Othello's clamour over the loss that she does so. After this it is even less easy to recant and confess; nor could she without involving Iago and incurring his anger, since she no longer has the handkerchief to restore. But Desdemona's own fib about it seems, by comparison, to lighten hers; nor, apparently, is the handkerchief the real cause of the clamour, a pretext only for such a fit of truculent ill-temper as any wife must learn to expect from any husband. Once again, then, she shuts her mind.

Not that the diabolical truth could come at present within the range of her most vigilant suspicions. She does not think very highly of the masculine nature, nor express herself very delicately about it:

> 'Tis not a year or two shows us a man:
> They are all but stomach and we all but food;
> They eat us hungerly, and when they are full
> They belch us.

But if lack of imagination leaves her blind to the heights it lets her ignore the blacker depths around her too. The Iago of the play's opening, envious and false beneath his honest surface, she will long enough have known for her husband; but of the demi-devil committed to Cassio's death and Desdemona's, and to Othello's ruin, how should she have in inkling?

While she herself, however, is hardened to jealousies and "chidings"— and of these can give as good as she gets—her lady, she soon sees, is not so thick-skinned; nor, she suspects, would Othello's jealousy, once roused by likely to end in mere bluster. Hence her "Pray heaven" that "no conception nor no jealous toy" "possess him" and her "Lady, amen!"—graver by far than Desdemona's own conscience-free

> Heaven keep that monster from Othello's mind!

And her fears are soon justified. Then it is another facet of Emilia that we see, standing stubbornly up to Othello in defence of a mistress she has learned to love, ready to stake her soul that

> if she be not honest, chaste and true,
> There's no man happy; the purest of their wives
> If foul as slander.

He dismisses her. But she has not, we find later, been above listening at the door to the terrible invective thrown on Desdemona; and her loyal indignation rises the higher at it and its meek receiving, and the higher yet upon encountering Iago's disconcertingly tepid sympathy—and some instinct seems suddenly to set her on a trail:

> I will be hanged, if some eternal villain,
> Some busy and insinuating rouge,
> Some cogging, cozening slave, to get some office,
> Have not devised this slander...

We are at one of the play's crucial moments, and it is upon Emilia—upon what she will now do, what fail to do—that the events turns. Iago's dry

> Fie, there's no such man; it is impossible

is a plain caution to her to follow that trail no further. Later, rent by remorse, she will avow that "I thought so then", and the "then" is now. She has, of course, no reason to suppose Desdemona in mortal danger, she merely sees her suffering more keenly what other wives suffer; and if Iago is drawing some still hidden crooked profit from it, his tart

> Speak within door...
> You are a fool; go to

is yet plainer warning that the less she says or knows the better for her. So she satisfies her outraged feelings with a few high-sounding words, and for the third time, and this time fatally, she obediently shuts her mind. If her conscience is uneasy it will be lightened when she remarks, upon her next sight of Othello, that "he looks gentler than he did". And then she relaxes, despite misgivings, into her habitual matter-of-fact mood, administering to her wounded, delicate Desdemona a good-night dose, not of the compassion she feels, but of a cheerful toughening conjugal doctrine of give and take, prophylactic for the future.

To the shock of the murder upon this night of murders is added the poignancy of Desdemona's death in her own arms—by so little is she too late to save her! To this succeeds stupefaction:

> O, who hath done this deed?
> Nobody; I myself...

and to that, under ban of the devoted, incredible lie, the moment's helplessness of

> She said so: I must needs report the truth.

The Othello's

> She's like a liar gone to burning hell:
> 'Twas I that killed her

sets her anguished wrath free to rage—until it is checked as by a blow at his

> Thy husband knew it all.

For a stunned while she can only repeat and repeat

> My husband!...My husband!..
> My husband say that she was false?

—each answer the tearing of a screen from before that closed mind. Yet when Iago appears he must—he, her husband!—Clear himself if he can, as surely he can. He does so, sufficiently:

> I told him what I thought, and told no more
> Than what he found himself was apt and true

—and a woman of common sense might well leave it at that. Desdemona is dead. What is her good name worth? Emilia will not.

> But did you ever tell him she was false?

He can hedge no further. Othello is listening. He faces her, this unsuspected Emilia, with a blunt "I did", and she brands him before them all as a liar.

But Desdemona's innocence so proclaimed and believed, might she not now at least "charm her tongue" and excusably let things go their way? Again she will not. There is worse hidden, and out is shall come, and she will purge herself too of her own share of the guilt—

> I thought so then: I'll kill myself for grief...

—of the guilt of the blind eye and closed mind. What this may cost her she has time to reckon while Othello lies there prostrate with remorse and Gratiano recites his mild elegy, clear warning of it in Iago's tensely vigilant silence; he has already bidden her be gone. She has only to hold her tongue as before about that tragically ridiculous handkerchief. Yet again she will not. The threatening sword is half-drawn; she might still save herself; she will not. She brings his crime home to him, confesses her ignorant share in it, and he kills her.

The coarse-grained, conscienceless, light-minded Emilia proves capable of this. She could love and Iago; she gives her life in testimony of the dead Desdemona's innocence. She passes from her merrily cynical

> Why, who would not make her husband a cuckold to make
> him a monarch? I should ventury purgatory for't

to a

> Moor, she was chaste; she loved thee, cruel Moor,
> So come my soul to bliss, as I speak true...

Othello does not heed. She prays to be lifted to her mistress' side, but they let her lie where she has fallen. Her senses failing, she can only cry pitifully

> What did thy song bode, lady?
> Hark, can't thou hear me?

Desdemona can no longer hear. The memory of a melody, of that "Willow, willow, willow..." must serve for communion between them. But Emilia has won herself a place in the play's tragic heaven.

BIANCA

The little hussy Bianca is Desdemona's very opposite, and our first sight of her is meant to make this plain. For Cassio, taking respectful leave of the one in her gentleness and dignity, turns to find himself at once accosted by the pretty, flaunting impudence of the other—who actually is to him, moreover, what Iago, abusing Othello's ear, would have Desdemona to be. And the mocking, scurrilous talk of her which Othello, eavesdropping, overhears is made to seem talk of Desdemona.

Iago, as his nature is, speaks brutally of her and to her; of her "selling her desires", addresses her, when he wants to implicate her in the midnight ambush laid for Cassio, as a "notable strumpet", and wags a moral head over such "fruits of whoring". But it is the respectable Emilia's gratuitously added

Fie, fie upon thee, strumpet!

which touches the young woman on the raw, and evokes the shrilly protesting

> I am no strumpet; but of life as honest
> As you that thus abuse me.

She is, of course, a trull, no better, and ill-behaved at that. She pursues her lover in the streets, makes scenes there, flies into tantrums, turns as jealous as her betters. The gallant Cassio, more than a little vain of her infatuation for him, treats her as such creatures must except to be treated. But she is shrewd and witty. To the gallant cant of Cassio's

Not that I love you not

she retorts with a neat

But that you do not love me.

She is plucky; she stands up to Iago's bullying. She may even love her lover in her disreputable way. For Shakespeare she is at least a human being.

BRABANTIO, CASSIO, RODERIGO BRABANTIO

Brabantio is redeemed from the convention of the hood-winked father by a few specific strokes. He swings between extremes, from his high regard for Othello to insensate abuse of him, through a chill pardon for Desdemona, in which past tenderness still echoes, to the cutting farewell:

She has deceived her father, and may thee.

He seems exceptionally credulous about

spells and medicines bought of mountebanks...

but he takes a detached view of his own nature, "glad at soul" that he has no other child, since Desdemona's escape would teach him "tyranny, to hang clogs on them". He passes from a frantic bustle of pursuit:

Raise all my kindred...
Call up my brother...
Some one way, some another...
At every house I'll call...

to quiet, solitary dignity before the Senate, as from clamour for vengeance on Othello to the magnanimous

If she confess that she was half the wooer,
Destruction on my head, if my bad blame
Light on the man!

And then and there, despite grief and defeat, he is capable of capping the Duke's encouraging platitudes with some very smooth irony. But it looks as if the shock and the strain may have broken him, and when he speaks of his "bruised heart" he means it. And later we hear that Desdemona's loss

was mortal to him, and pure grief
Shore his old thread in twain.

CASSIO

The Folio's list of characters calls Cassio *an Honourable Lieutenant*. He is seemingly a man of gentle birth, and of education; Iago mocking at his "bookish theoric". He is the unwitting implement of evil, its stalking-horse, and his place in the play's scheme is that of an average, unheroic, well-meaning man caught between tragic extremes—of wickedness and of the nobility it betrays. His faults are failings, redeemable by his own recognition of them. But here he sways, haplessly, somewhat ridiculously, between extremes within himself. He knows that he has "very poor and unhappy brains for drinking", yet he yields from good nature to the claims of good fellowship, though he says, even as he does so, "it dislikes me". He is sensitive even to self-consciousness, and, beyond that, to the point of self-display. Having listened in disciplined silence to Othello's sentence on him, in his heartfelt outburst to Iago, the

Reputation, reputation, reputation. O, I have lost my reputation! I have lost the immortal part of myself, and what remains is bestial. My reputation, Iago, my reputation!

we remark that he is listening, not unappreciatively, to the sounds of his own despair. Such misery does not strike deep, nor last long; its enjoyment is soon exhausted. Iago tactfully gives it scope, and Cassio, disburdened, not only accepts his optimistic advice without question, but will "betimes in the morning...beseech the virtuous Desdemona" to plead his cause.[72] For may not Othello's anger dissolve as easily—so this mood bids him hope—as has the bitterness of his own remorse? The man is mercurial. He is a lightweight. But there is with that something boyish about him, and appealing. Despite his despair, he thinks to bring musicians to play the customary nuptial *aubade* beneath Othello's windows; an ingenuous piece of propitiation.

He is a romantic soul. We have him, during those first moments in Cyprus, rhapsodizing over "the divine Desdemona". He is gaily gallant, finds it good fun to claim a kiss of welcome from Emilia. And Iago's "profane and liberal wit" having served its purpose while they all wait anxiously for news of Othello, he takes his turn at distracting Desdemona, more delicately and intimately, yet openly and respectfully, galling Iago with envy of his address in "such tricks", in kissing his "three fingers" and playing "the sir", having already—how thoughtlessly—patronizingly disparaged his Ancient's good breeding to her, with that

> He speaks home, madam: you may relish him more in the soldier than in the scholar.

But he has a finer sense than all this shows of Desdemona's quality. She is for him—the epithet springs spontaneously—"the virtuous Desdemona". Nor will he join in the accepted marriage pleasantries, meets Iago's ribald

> Our general...hath not yet made wanton the night with her, and she is sport for Jove

with a cold snub. And her "bounteous" compassion on him when he is in trouble raises respect to very reverence.

His attitude towards Bianca is of a piece with the rest of him. She is his mistress, she is "a customer", and he scoffs merrily

72. Note how Cassio's impulsiveness helps give the needed speed to the action.

at "the monkey's" pretence that he means to marry her. But he treats her, even as Shakespeare does, decently and humanely. He does not care to have her pursue him in the street—who would?—and, being what she is, she must put up with a blunt

> leave me for this time...
> I do attend here on the general;
> And think it no addition, nor my wish
> To have him see me womaned

nor does he scruple to round on her pretty sharply when she vexes him. But, this apart, she is his "most fair Bianca", his "sweet love". He excuses himself with courteous insincerity for a week's neglect of her, protesting that he loves her, paying her in that coin too. He is gentleman, and she, as the phrase goes, is no better than she should be. But he would never be guilty, to her face or behind her back, of the grossness of Iago's "This is the fruits of whoring".

The weakness which lets him drink when he knows he cannot carry his liquor is matched by his broken resolve to break with Bianca. He has kept it for a week; and, confiding to Iago what an infatuated nuisance she is, he protests:

> Well, I must leave her company.

Yet a moment later, after she had told him in a fit of tantrums to come and sup with her that same night or see her no more, Iago dryly demanding if he means to, he answers shruggingly:

> Faith, I intend so

the full truth beings, it would seem, that he is both secretly flattered by her scandalous infatuation for him—he makes the most of it:

> She falls me thus about my neck. ...So hangs and lolls and weeps upon me; so hales and pulls me...

—and not a little afraid of her. It is at this point in the play that he, with Othello, is brought to the lowest pitch of indignity; puppets he two of hem in Iago's hands, the one turned eavesdropper, the other fatuously vaunting his conquest of a light-o'-love.

But a worthier finish is reserved him. For his would-be murder he utters no harsher reproach than

> Dear general, I never gave you cause

and his epitaph upon Othello is fitly felt:

> For her was great of heart.

And—though here, if the story were to have a sequel, we might question Senatorial judgment—he is left to rule in Cyprus.

RODERIGO

The Folio is as exact with its "Roderigo, *a gull'd Gentleman*"; but to this stock figure also Shakespeare gives human substance. It tells another tale of moral degradation; Iago the unresisted instrument. For Roderigo begins as an honourable suitor for Desdemona's hand; and, for his service in sounding the alarm, he converts Brabantio straightway from the

> In honest plainness thou hast heard me say
> My daughter is not for thee...

to a

> good Roderigo, I'll deserve your pains.

And what could be more correct than the long, elaborate, pedantically parenthetical address to the newly wakened and distracted father at the window, with which he justifies his interference?

> I beseech you,
> If't be your pleasure and most wise consent,
> As partly I find it is...

—a mild effort at sarcasm—

> that you fair daughter,
> At this odd-even and dull watch of the night,
> Transported with no worse nor better guard
> But with a knave of common hire, a gondolier...

—as who might say today: carried off in a taxi-cab, not even a private car!—

To the gross clasps of a lascivious Moor
If this be known to you, and your allowance...

—sarcasm again!—

We then have done you bold and saucy wrongs;
But if you know not this, my manners tell me
We have your wrong rebuke..

—a neat antithesis!—

Do not believe,
That, from the sense of all civility.
I thus would play the trifle with your reverence:
Your daughter, if you have not given her leave...

—he fancies his sarcasm—

I say again, hath made a gross revolt,
Tying her duty, beauty, wit and fortunes,
In an extravagant and wheeling stranger...

—his vocabulary too!—

Of here and everywhere...

—and could listen to his own eloquence all night. We see Iago in the background, a-grin at the foolish exhibition.

Roderigo's renewed hopes soar high, then, as he sticks by the grateful Brabantio and follows him to the Senate, but only to collapse again utterly upon the surrendering of Desdemona to Othello. He stands there mute, would be left alone and ignored even by Iago, did he not at last utter a plaintive

What will I do, thinkest thou?...
I will incontinently drown myself

—the "silly gentleman" at his silliest, most pitiable, least unlikable.

He goes to the devil with his eyes open, yet blindly. His poor mind is no better than a sounding board for Iago's sophistries. Yet he takes each step downward most advisedly, and even in admitting his folly he persists in it. He is an incorrigible fool. To put money—for Iago—in his purse, to follow the wars—and Desdemona—he will sell all his land, uproot and leave himself to the mercy of events.[73] And his moral sense is as feeble and obscure as his mind is muddled. Since he cannot win Desdemona for his wife, he may get her—Iago persuades him—as a mistress, may cuckold Othello. There will be manly satisfaction in that. But when he hears that she is in love with Cassio:

> Why, 'tis not possible...I cannot believe that in her; she's full of most blessed condition.

And it is not, seemingly, that he thinks his own charms, given their chance, would make way with her, for he listens, unprotesting, to their most unflattering comparison with Cassio's. A less convinced, a more unconvincing, liberatine there could hardly be. Finally, however, patience and cash exhausted, he protests, and, in a prepared oration, following the one he launched at Brabantio's window, he calls Iago to account. He has been let in—such is the tone of it—for a pretty poor investment, financially and morally too, and must now save what he can from the wreck:

> The jewels you have had from me to deliver to Desdemona would half have corrupted a votarist: you have told me she hath received them and returned me expectations and comforts of sudden respect and acquaintance; but I find none. ...I will make myself known to Desdemona. If she will return me my jewels, I will give over my suit and repent my unlawful solicitations; if not, assure yourself I will seek satisfaction of you.

Is there, after all, any real vice in the creature? He sees himself handed back his jewels while he makes Desdemona yet another carefully prepared little speech of polite regret for every having dreamed of committing adultery with her. And his amorous advances, we may suspect, would have been hardly more formidable.

---

73. This final flourish to his scene with Iago:

> I am changed: I'll go sell all my land

had a significance for Shakespeare's audience that it cannot have for us.

But if there is no passion in him, evil or good, to stimulate, such little mind as he possesses Iago does most successfully corrupt. The denigration of Desdemona is left to sink in; the less he believes in her virtue, the readier he will be to continue his pursuit of her; his final complaint is that the jewels have had no effect. The "satisfying reasons" he has received for Cassio's death we do not hear; but an echo of them can be caught in the callous

'Tis but a man gone

with which, craven in his ambush, he draws a clumsy sword. With Iago for guide, he has travelled from the lovelorn folly of

I will incontinently drown myself

to this. Even so, he is no more of a success as a murderer than he has been as an adulterer; and his bravo's

Villain, thou diest!

is promptly changed, with Cassio's sword between his own ribs instead, into an abjectly repentant

O, villain that I am!

A last disillusion is due; his mentor's face mockingly grinning, his friend's dagger stuck in him—

O damned Iago; O inhuman dog!

Disillusion indeed! But he is so futile a fool that we spare him some pity.

The Verse

Out of an inheritance, in the main of blank verse and the ten-syllable couplet, but with the octo-syllabic and even the "old fourteener" never quite forgotten, and with a generous place left for prose, Shakespeare develops the dramatic speech of his art's maturity. He makes it an instrument which is both supple and powerful and of a wide range of effect, sensitive to the interpreting of thought charged with emotion, and allowing a sufficiently seeming spontaneity of expression without loss of coherent form. *Julius Caesar*, with its virile chorus of conspirators, Cassius' passion, Brutus' calm and Antony's adroit modulations from mood to mood, may be said to see him master of the means to it. Then comes *Hamlet*, with Hamlet himself to give it greater freedom and a new intensity.

For with *Hamlet* Shakespeare breaks bounds, to enter and make his own—and no one has followed him there—a land of rarer and harder drama altogether. The dominant figures of the great post-*Hamlet* plays live and move in a larger imaginative area. Lear scales heights as Macbeth descends to deeps without precedent. The Antony brought to bay at Actium stands a giant, a "triple pillar of the world" indeed, beside the clever fellow who outplayed Brutus and Cassius. And Shakespeare has need of more powerful and resourceful means of expression still.

Of any revolution in his stagecraft there could be little question. Though the theatre for which he has learned to work is grown richer, its mechanical and pictorial aspects remain fundamentally and unaccommodatingly the same. Nor has he ever made much of its shows and tricks, such as they are. His plays depend upon more essential things.

He might have followed Jonson's precepts and practice—who would, incidentally (some later critics to prove heartily in accord), have counselled him to leave such a subject as that of *King Lear* alone—and have entrenched himself in a strict formula, within which expression gains even an intenser power because it cannot expand. But one does not see him bartering freedom for security. It had not become him, as an aspiring "shake-scene", and a mere theatre hack, to dwell upon theory and rule. It was of rhim to turn to account any convention whatever that might suit a particular occasion. And having learned all "the tricks of the trade", he will not, in these days of his mastership, discard from his store a single one of them. The Chorus, the Presenters, the Dumb Show, a Prologue or an Epilogue—devices not to be depended on, but there may be fitness and utility in them still. A Chorus proves but an encumbrance to the swift movement of *Romeo and Juliet*, and is rejected, seemingly in midcourse; but he can turn one to good use as a courier for the heavily equipped *Henry V*, and as the best and simplest means by which to "slide o'er sixteen years" in *The Winter's Tale*. The first part of *Henry IV* asks, to this thinking, no prologue; but "Rumour, painted full of tongues" makes a useful mnemonic link with the second. Rosalind's epilogue pays overt homage to convention; its dramatic use is to reconcile the comedy itself with the concluding masque. A dumb show would go ill indeed with the intense actualities of *Hamlet*; it is quite in place in *The Murder of Ganzago*, and markedly distinguishes the play within the play from the play. And even presenters, let vanish from the early *Taming of the Shrew*, make a short and qualified reappearance—as if to acknowledge the play's sophistication—in *Cymbeline*[74] So too with his verse. He soon shook free of cramping or unmanageable metres and over-elaborate artifice, strung-out alliteration, classical tags, multiple puns and the like. But with his art at its ripest, his verse at its freest, he still does not forbid himself a neat little passage of stychomythia in *Antony and Cleopatra*, a few octo-syllabics in *Measure for Measure*; and in *King Lear*, as a fitting auxiliary to Lear's madness, we have a very medley of vernacular song, mine and antic.

From *Othello* we can pick in this category, the Clown, the Duke's "sentences" and Iago's extempore rhyming.[75] Shakespeare has fitting use for each. As to the first; the strain of the play's action is continuous and at times intense, and the identifiable characters are all caught into its rapidly flowing main stream. The strain upon an audience will, moreover, be greater if, in performance, there are no marked intervals between acts and scenes. The anonymous Clown with his conventional jokes (coarse for the minstrels, innocuous for Desdemona) is the only completely contrasted "relief" afforded us. And it is to be noted that, of his two appearances, one occurs when our attention has been closely held by Iago throughout the long scene of the night of Cassio's downfall and just before the yet longer passage, in which Othello travels the entire distance from cloudless happiness to the savage dooming of Desdemona to death (a passage in which concentration and strain will be at their closest and tensest) and the other just after this.

The Duke's sententious "sentences" make on us and in thescene the effect they fail to make more directly on Brabantio,

---

74. The episode of the apparitions and Jupiter's descent has, I know, been labelled spurious. But, in its main lines at least, it may, I think, be called Shakespeare's, and with the more likelihood, perhaps, if this aspect of it is considered.

75. It would be pedantry to add the Herald; the convention of his speech will pass unobserved upon any nonrealistic stage.

of "a grise or step" between the concluded turmoil of the elopement and the ardour for the coming departure to Cyprus and the wars. The Duke pronounces them from his chair of state as an informal and kindly judgment upon the case brought before him; the artifice of their form befits this, their smooth cadence the emollient content, while the couplets sound a full close. And Brabantio's ironically echoing reply—respectful, acquiescent, but he is as good at "sentences" as the Duke!—Provides him with a dignified and effective retreat from the action. Shakespeare wants, without any too sudden change in the steering, without upsetting its balance, to set his scene upon another course; and this is as legitimate a way as any other.

Iago's six couplets of impromptu rhyming are semi-comic relief to the strain—not on the audience, but on Desdemona while she waits for news of Othello's safety. Therefore they can be fully "dramatized"; the accomplishment, such as it is, being accounted an item in Iago's equipment, and well it becomes his intellectual swagger.

Utility is Shakespeare's sole test. He will employ any sort of device, however old and worn, if he can make it dramatically useful. The cumulative effect of the iteration of some single significant world; he has inherited this as a formula habitually carried to mechanical extremes. He never abandons it, only reduces it to the point at which it colourably reunites with our natural habit, upon which supposedly it was built, of recurring again and again under the stress of suffering, to the one thought that dominates our trouble. In *Othello* under various forms he makes frequent us of the device; directly, but within the limits of the spontaneous; oftener by inserting the iteration into the main body of speech; sometimes by using the significant word as "honest" and "honesty" are used—by the play's end what changes in tone and colour, application and implication, have not been rung upon Iago's selected epithet![76]

---

76. It is Iago, speaking to Roderigo, who first employs the word for the "honest knaves" who are loyal to their masters. It is Othello who first attaches it to him with the

So please your Grace, my Ancient;
A man he is of honesty and trust...

The epithet then sticks, with Iago himself acutely and angrily conscious of it.

The first noticeable bout of iteration is Cassio's in his lament for his lost reputation; and the sextuple repetition—though it is partly blended into his speech—gives the needed, in this case slightly comic, turn to his exaggerated grief. It can be matched and contrasted with Othello's tragic outcry when he suddenly wakes to the meaning of his terrible deed:

> If she come in, she'll sure speak to my wife;
> My wife! my wife! what wife? I have no wife

and with Emilia's whelming

> Villainy, villainy, villainy!
> I think upon't: I think: I smell't: O villainy!...
> O villiany, villainy!

Then there is the more complex, and so it will seem intentional

> Ay; you did wish that I would make her turn:
> Sir, she can turn, and turn, and yet go on,
> And turn again; and she can weep, sir, weep;
> And she's obedient, as you say, obedient,
> Very obedient...

And since it habitually serves for the underscoring of some excess of emotion we shall in consequence find the device put oftenest to Othello's own use. It shapes his very first passionate outpouring; the

> O, now for ever
> Farewell the tranquil mind! farewell content!
> Farewell the plumed troop and the bid wars
> That make ambition virtue! O, farewell!
> Farewell the neighing steed and the shrill trump...
> Farewell! Othello's occupation gone!

And, after this, instance upon instance of its employment can be found; the iterated word being either woven into a speech, when it not only heightens but controls the emotion, as with the

> It is the cause, it is the cause, my soul:...
> It is the cause...

and with

Put out the light, and then put out the light.

—the word and idea, to the thrice more repeated, binding this section of the speech together as does a recurring note a passage in music—or it may be given the simple cumulative emphasis of

O, blood, blood, blood!...
O, fool, fool, fool!...

Finally, we have iteration turned to a far-related use; a word and the idea distributed over the greater part of a scene, and recurring later, played upon with varying intonations and implications, as Iago plays upon "think" and "thoughts", "jealousy" and "honestly", until he has Othello repeating them too and letting them have their way—Iago's way—with him.

But Shakespeare's verse is the master-medium of his stagecraft; and to make it the comprehensive means of expression which it now is, and which he operates with such freedom and ease, he has absorbed into it—and will often transform until they are hardly to be recognized—not a few conventions and forms. Take the verse of any scene in the play, and try to determine its normal measures. The ten-syllable, five-beat line is still there, if not manifestly, then—and more often—embedded in the dominant rhythm. But the speaker—and it is a question of speech—who sets to work upon a fingertapping basis of rule and exception, with account to be taken of the use of extra syllables, of the curtailed or overrun line, of weak endings and the like, will soon find himself at a feeble and tangled halt. Let him rather acquire an articulate tongue, an unfailing ear for the pervasive melody and cadence of the verse, let him yield to its impetus, and —provided, of course, that he knows more or less what it is all about, and this sympathetic self-surrender will aid him there—Shakespeare can be counted on to carry him through.

Not that the verse, freely and variously though it may flow, escapes into any excessive metrical latitude, such as, in later post-Shakespearian days, will bring the weapon that it is, meant to commond attention, to breaking from simple weakness in the actor's hands. There is never the lack of a stiff short line for the forcible punctuating of any over-ambulatory passage, nor of few successive lines of strict scansion to restore, for just so long, an exemplary discipline; or the border can be crossed into a stretch of the contrasted discipline of prose. For if Shakespeare will not barter freedom for sheer strength, neither will he sacrifice strength to freedom; and a play demands some overriding unity of treatment, some force which will bind it together, if it be only to counter-balance the naturally disintegrating tendency of the individualities and diverse methods of its actors. Variety must not be let deteriorate into patchwork.

The enriched vocabulary, the bolder syntax, the unconfined rhythm, those are the more patent attributes of the maturer verse; its intrinsic virtue lies in the ready power, now developed in it, to paint and reveal character—he turns his freedom to that use. The verse of a play may be shaped and coloured as a whole by the nature of its subject and setting, as, very notably, is the verse of *Coriolanus*; or—another means to a like end—it may be in large part keyed to the interpreting of the play's central figure; and the rest within range, demands of character and the action allowed for, will be responsive. The dominant influence upon the verse of *Othello* is Othello himself. At his appearance he sets it a tone very much—and appropriately—as an officer commanding can give a tone to his regiment. The "round unvarnished tale" is exemplary: speech that moves forward to a steady rhythm; the epithetic picked and significant, yet never in sound or sense over-weighting the verse and retarding it; the imagery sparse, nor ever merely decorative, but bred always of the matter in hand and the moment's imagination. And if Cassio and Iago (on duty) and, later, Montano seem spontaneously to pattern their speech upon his, there is truth to character in that; and Desdemona, before the Senate, Othello beside her, will be, afer her own fashion, as naturally responsive.

It is, so to say, upon another plane that the Duke and Senators respond in their kind. As characters they are not sharply individualized; there is nothing in them to combat such domination. This is so too with Lodovico, appearing towards the play's end as a figure of importance to the action, but of no more specific character than is indicated by the dignity of his mission. Desdemona's

This Lodovico is a proper man

and Emilia's gayer hint. Gratiano is in the same category. But

by now a mould for the run of the verse has been formed, and the speech—no demands of character or action to the contrary—tends to flow into it. The Othello influence is neither exact or constraining. It initiates a tone and rhythm, and some measure in the use of imagery, and, on those within his immediate reach, will inevitably be strong. But it allows ample scope for individual expression; Desdemona's, in character attuned to his; Emilia's, late awakened to the matching of his anger with her own.

The opposing factor is Iago—the Iago of the soliloquies and of the unguarded scenes with Roderigo. His speech at the play's opening—its impetus and forceful rhythm and lack of all melody, regular and irregular lines chasing and ousting one another—is eloquent of this first aspect of him, of his greedy malice, the itch of his envy. In the very vowels and the dry distastefully reiterated consonants of "be-lee'd... calmed...debitor...creditor...counter-caster" sounds his contempt for Cassio:

> But he, sir, had the election;

And I...

> must be be-lee'd and calmed
> By debitor and creditor: thus counter-caster,
> He, in good time, must his lieutenant be...

His pretentious cleverness is painted thick for the start of his first lesson to Roderigo:

> Our bodies are our gardens; to the which our wills are gardeners: so that if we will plant nettles or sow lettuce, set hyssop and weed up thyme, supply it with one gender of herbs, or distract it with many, either to have it sterile with idleness or manured with industry, why, the power and corrigible authority of this lies in our wills...

—and so on. It impresses Roderigo. And from out the verbiage, the talk of "carnal stings" and "unbitted lusts", of which love, he takes it, is "a sect or scion", its satisfaction now "as luscious as locusts to be "shortly as better as coloquintida", there does at last emerge an admirably plain "Put money in they purse".

Roderigo's lessons in worldly wisdom are mostly framed to this pattern, and in prose, the best medium in which to call a spade a spade. Only once, when he is bewailing Cassio's cudgeling, does Iago hearten him with the swing and colour of verse:

> Does't not go well? Cassio hath beaten thee,
> And thou by that small hurt hast cashiered Cassio:
> Though other things grow far against the sun,
> Yet fruits that blossom first will first be ripe...

—the melody as efficacious as the argument!

Iago's soliloquies are in verse. That befits their impulsive confidence. But there is little or none of the imaginative stuff of poetry in them; and this noticeable incongruity is as befitting.

He can always, when he chooses, suit both the matter and manner of his speech to the occasion and his company; "honest Iago" is to be seen, actorlike, under any aspect demanded. And, at grips with Othello, so supplely and swiftly does he shift his address, giving and taking, advancing and yielding, now deforming Othello's thoughts, now shaping his own to their shape, that Iago the actor would seem to be, as the phrase goes, "lost in his part". But in that capacity lies his talent; and behind it there *is*, indeed, no Iago, only a poisoned and poisonous ganglion of cravings after evil.

The expressive range of the play's verse with its auxiliary prose is in its entirety a wide one. There are the utilitarian units of the messengers and the Herald who speak after their kind; there is the conventional Clown who speaks and acts after his; and the First, Second, Third and Fourth Gentlemen paint us the storm and the landfall as, it is recognized, such things may effectively be painted, this being the aim and end of their existence. Then, beneath is exotic setting and warlike trimmings, the play is, at its core, a "domestic tragedy"— and Shakespeare's only essay in this kind. So in the more familiar scenes the verse falls readily into a semblance of the to-and-fro of habitual talk. But, dominating all, is the heroic figure of Othello himself, built to an heroic scale of expression and able to animate the noblest poetic form.

The gamut must run, with no incongruous gap appearing, between the squabble over the handkerchief—

> Is't lost? In't gone? Speak, is it our o' the way?
> Heaven bless us!

Say you?
It is not lost; but what an if it were?
How!
I say it is not lost.
Fetch't, let me see it.
Why, so I can, sir, but I will not now...

—up to the highest pitch of imaginative emotion. The unity of the action makes of itself for unity of treatment, and its sustained tension will not let even the most loosely woven verse be altogether slackened. In the stress of his suffering the firm athletic temper of Othello's speech breaks; but through this it is to a natural and characteristic superlative that he lifs it in such a passage as

Like to the Pontic sea,
Whose icy current and compulsive course
Ne'er feels retiring ebb, but keeps due on
To the Propontic and the Hellespont...

Nor, in its setting and at its moment, will the sacrificial

It is the cause, it is the cause...

seem hollow magniloquence beside the simple factual horror of Desedemona's murder; not, after this, the tremendous

Methinks it should be now a huge eclipse
Of sun and moon...

nor the dazzling

Nay, had she been true,
If heaven would make me such another world
Of one entire and perfect chrysolite,
I'ld not have sold her for it

reduce Emilia by comparison to commonplace. The scene's charge of tragic emotion is enough for the fusing of whatever the range of it means of expression.

As he returns to sanity so Othello returns also to the old sober, lofty equilibrium of thought and speech. We have it in that

Here is my journey's end, here is my butt
And very sea-mark of my utmost sail...

with its memory of "the sea's worth" which could be no more to him than the worth of Desdemona's love, of the storm which spared them for the calm joy of their reuniting, of the icy current of the Pontic sea which imaged to him his implacable revenge. And in his valediction, with the remoter memories of Aleppo and the Arabian trees, the

> then must you speak
> Of one that loved not wisely but too well;
> Of one not easily jealous, but, being wrought,
> Perplexed in the extreme...

we have it brought to simplicity itself, and the beauty of that.

NOTE A

OTHELLO'S COLOUR

"Haply for I am black..."; it is Othello himself who says so. Certainly the word then and later was given wide range in such connection; it could be used to denote dark hair and complexion merely. But in this case the meaning is surely plain: he is a black man, not a white one. Roderigo's "thick-lips" on the other hand is simply abusive; and no actor of Othello is called upon to make himself repulsive to his audience—although, as to this, taste will vary both with time and clime. The dramatic point of the matter lies in Desdemona's

> I saw Othello's visage in his mind.

and all that it conveys of the quality of her love for him, its courage and clairvoyance. His looks at least must stress this, not minimize it.

NOTE B

OTHELLO'S CHRISTIANITY

Shakespeare could not, of course, make much of this if he would, since religion was a subject forbidden to the theatre; but the references to it are more than casual. It is implied in Brabantio's "Are they married, think you?" And in Iago's quickly sequent question to Othello: "Are you fast married?" Othello's appeal to the rioters is:

> For Christian shame, put by this barbarous brawl...

And in Iago's next soliloquy he speculates upon the ease with which Desdemona could

> win the Moor, were't to renounce his baptism,
> All seals and symbols of redeemed sin...

The "sacred vow" by "yond marble heaven" may or may not be intended to indicate a backsliding towards his "paynim" past—I doubt if an average audience would seize the point. But the tragic irony of his command to her to say her prayers and be reconciled to Heaven before, in her innocence, he murders her, is patent, and could have been made more so by the stronger stressing of his conversion to Christianity. And his final likening of himself to the "circumcised dog" whom he smote in Aleppo once for beating a Venetian and traducing the state, just such a one as in his own person he smites now—here the reference to his Christianity and his betrayal of its is unmistakable, even though Shakespeare would not risk making it more definite.

Barker's Prefatory Notes to the *Prefaces* (1) *Second Series*, (1930) and (2) *Fourth Series*, (1945)

(1)

Upon a minor point of method, I find one critic (otherwise most kindly) reproaching me with my use of the word playwright. It is in itself a good word, surely, and has ample sanction. But I should have pointed out, I suppose—since this he did not see—that I was carefully using it in a particular sense, for the craftsman, the play-maker as distinct from the completer dramatist, the artist. This may seem finicky, and the distinction will not, of course, be exact. But one is constantly needing to make this distinction and others like it, and qualification as constant becomes tiresome. All aesthetic discussion suffers, in its very nature, from inexact thought, doubly by the confusion and by a poverty of current terms. Both the art and the craft of the Shakespearean stages are the harder to discuss because one must so continually use words that have no agreed meaning, and often be held up by lack of any word at all that will not smack too aggravatingly of the twelve-volume Oxford Dictionary and Torquemada. Such confusion as comes from main stage, front stage and outer stage, inner stage and alcove, upper stage and balcony being used to express, not seven things but three, a reader can fairly easily resolve. But take the word 'scene', which may well be wanted on every other page, and then in every paragraph. It has more nearly a dozen meanings than one, and it actively breeds confusion. Will it be too much to say that half our modern misunderstandings of Shakespeare's stagecraft are due to the shifting (over three centuries) and varied meanings of 'scene'? *Antony and Cleopatra* with its crowd of 'scenes', which Shakespeare never named scenes at all, which if he had, would still have been quite unlike the 'scene' that the reader of to-day will have in mind, is our most distinguished victim—as I have now tried to show. But the confusion dogs us all the time. It is, however, one inevitable part of the rediscovery of Shakespeare the playwright, and evidence that a rediscovery there has to be. As to poverty of vocabulary, that trouble can be trusted to cure itself. One is chary of drastic remedies. Sir Mark Hunter (to whom I owe much more than this) gave me the excellent word 'anatopism' for a convenient complement to anachronism, which I was using too loosely. Coleridge fathered it, apparently, and de Quincey found it useful. But after dallying with it a little I felt I had better let it alone till it came back into commoner currency. Somehow, when Shakespeare's art is the topic, one does not want to have to pull up short and ask: Now what does *this* mean ?

Another kindly critic visited me with a subtler reproach. He could not quite make out what was wrong. He thought it might be that "...some of us like our Shakespeare neat, or, shall we say, prefer a direct communion with him..." I sympathise. But if a play is to be treated as a play, we cannot have it so; the actors and their acting intervene. But if these prefaces, continues my critic, are for the producer, in that they are redundant too. "For there are as many ways of producing Shakespeare capably as there have been or ever will be producers capable of producing his plays, and no other artist will be content with any other way than his own." Not quite so many, I think; and I rather distrust that artist who will not be content with any other way than his own. After all, there was once Shakespeare's. We cannot reproduce this exactly, I agree, because too much that was topical would always be lacking; nor, therefore, should we try to. But his stagecraft had its essentials, and until the producer has mastered these his own inspired way is neither here nor there. Much of Shakespeare's stagecraft—and the best of it, no doubt—is fundamental to all drama. Show it on what sort of stage you will, it cannot fail of its effect. But more than we have thought is framed to the stage for which he wrote it (why we never thought it would be is a mystery!) and, lacking the belongings of this—the essential, not the incidental and accidental belongings—it will fail of its full effect, and often of any. No one will deny, at least, that if we crush it without more consideration into the conditions of the modern theatre we stifle the life out of it.

All I have set out to do is to rediscover as much as I can of this lost stagecraft. One must, I think, make the attempt play by play. Shakespeare's stage changed a little, perhaps more than a little, during his working lifetime, and he himself enlarged its artistic resources to the limits of recognition. We have generalised far too freely upon the matter. I should have made this aim clear to my critic. But, looking back, I find I did make it clear; I am now repeating myself. However, there is no great harm in that. One remembers the Bellman's "What I tell you three times is true". He might have made it thirty.

One difficulty—and fault—I must own to. It is impossible to study Shakespeare as a craftsman only; for his craft is the lesser part of his art, and the two are inextricably woven together. I cannot do other than try to interpret each play as a whole; and, as with all art, it must be largely a personal interpretation. But if Shakespeare's duality is not to be disentangled, mine certainly is; and the artist who cannot "be content with any other way than his own" should be able to separate the useful metal from the dross. That, at least, is my hope. For these books have quite a practical aim. I want to see Shakespeare made fully effective on the English stage. This is the best sort of help I can lend.

(2)

These Prefaces are primarily intended for students of Shakespeare—my fellow students; and this is why they tend, as I continue them, to become, I fear, ever more technical and elaborate. I learn more; or, at any rate, I find there is more to learn. ...The student will, I sometimes think, gain most—if anything—first by reading them, and then forgetting them, in the renewed light of the play itself.

Among Shakespeare's greater plays—in the series, say, from *Hamlet* to *Coriolanus*—each has, I think, its own peculiar, predominant feature; the thing in it, one may surmise, which interested him most, had compelled his closest attention. At first, possibly, no more than a difficulty arising in the task he had set himself; surmounted, has become its most notable achievement. In *Hamlet* the tricks of a pretended madness are converted into the tragic realities of moral and spiritual doubt; in *Antony and Cleopatra* he must find means to project upon his token stage some effect of the wide struggles of Empire; in *Macbeth* he has to picture the destruction of a human soul. It is upon this predominant feature, this dramatic problem and its solution, that the study of the play will naturally concentrate.

Othello is dominated by the problem of the falling of this man—not only of noble nature is he, but of ability too—an unresisting victim to such a charlatan as Iago. Tricks played with a handkerchief, lies told about Cassio; these are well enough as mechanism. But the tragedy, if it is to compel our interest, must be a tragedy of character; Shakespeare, indeed, writes no others now. The problem, then, and the essential structure of the play, will be psychological, the action primarily an interior action. So it is to some extent, of course, with any play of worth; but in no other that he wrote does the immediate operation of mind upon mind count for so much, is the implicit as telling as the explicit—and sometimes more so. The central episode, particularly, in which Othello's faith in Desdemona is corrupted and overthrown, this and the technical daring of the means used to make it convincing, have no parallel. I have therefore given the fullest space to the their study, since while the scenes themselves will always be superficially effective in the acting, upon their right understanding and interpreting depends the intrinsic validity of the play.